BEYOND SUBCULTURE

Pop, youth and identity in a postcolonial world

Rupa Huq

Routledge
Taylor & Francis Group

LONDON AND NEW YORK

First published 2006
by Routledge
2 Park Square, Milton Park, Abingdon, Oxon OX14 4RN

Simultaneously published in the USA and Canada
by Routledge
270 Madison Ave, New York, NY 10016

Reprinted 2007

Routledge is an imprint of the Taylor & Francis Group, an informa business

© 2006 Rupa Huq

Typeset in Perpetua by Taylor & Francis Books
Printed and bound in Great Britain by Antony Rowe Ltd, Chippenham, Wiltshire

British Library Cataloguing in Publication Data
A catalogue record for this book is available from the British Library

Library of Congress Cataloging in Publication Data
Huq, Rupa, 1972–
Beyond subculture : pop, youth, and identity in a postcolonial world / Rupa Huq.
p. cm.
Includes bibliographical references and index.
ISBN 0–415–27814–7 (hardback : alk. paper) – ISBN 0–415–27815–5 (pbk. : alk.
paper) 1. Popular music–Social aspects. 2. Music and youth. 3. Popular
culture. I.
Title.
ML3918.P67H86 2005
306.4'8424'083509045–dc22
2005001401

ISBN10 0–415–27814–7 (hbk)
ISBN10 0-415-27815-5 (pbk)

ISBN13 978–0–415–27814–0 (hbk)
ISBN13 978–0–415–27815–7 (pbk)

FOR RAFI

CONTENTS

ACKNOWLEDGEMENTS

The completion of this book spanned some dramatic events for me – from a mugging which left me hospitalised with stab wounds at the end of 2001 to becoming mother of a baby son in Spring 2004. Various people deserve my thanks. At Routledge Aileen Irwin, Rebecca Barden, Chris Cudmore and Lesley Riddle have all been extremely patient with me. My gratitude also goes out to Andrew Blake, supervisor of the PhD which this book started life as at the Cultural Studies department at the University of East London. I would never have been able to do my doctorate without the departmental studentship I held there.

Raminder Kaur, Pontus Odmalm, George McKay, Mike Pickering and Herwig Reiter all read draft chapters and provided useful comments. Andy Bennett advised on my initial thoughts on putting in a proposal. The Leverhulme Trust provided me generous funding to undertake a Special Fellowship from 2000–2002, when this book was largely written. I'd also like to thank colleagues at the two institutions that I have worked at along the way: Georgia Irving and staff at the University of Manchester and latterly Joe Bailey at Kingston University. Above all I'd like to thank my family for being so supportive over the last three decades.

INTRODUCTION

Youth culture at the turn of the century

Defining youth culture

Both 'youth' and 'culture' are increasingly contested concepts. The compound term 'youth culture' is an evocative phrase conjuring up hedonistic images of sex, drugs and rock 'n' roll. Youth culture is also about post-war affluence (Abrams 1959) and idealism. Any inexpensive dictionary of quotations offers a multitude of entries illustrating youthful irresponsibility such as Oscar Wilde's 'youth is wasted on the young'. Common parlance concurs. 'You're only young once.' This book addresses rock 'n' roll, or rather pop music, alongside the political possibilities of youth and youth culture. These will be considered in the light of a body of work that constitutes probably the most comprehensive academic attempt at theorising youth culture: the 1970s stable of subcultural studies from Birmingham, UK. It is the central aim of the book to look seriously at youth culture and pop 'beyond subculture', taking musical scenes and their consumers and producers into its remit.

Clarke *et al.* (1976: 10) write somewhat oxymoronically: 'The term *youth culture* directs us to the *cultural* aspects of youth', while Frith (1985: 310) defines it as 'the particular pattern of beliefs, values symbols and activities that a group of young people are *seen* to share'. Even an ostensibly innocent enough seeming term like youth – the state of being young – is bound up with biology, sociology, psychological and psycho-social development (Goffman 1956; 1963), deviancy (Becker 1963; Cohen 1971; Downes 1966; Matza 1969; Matza and Sykes 1961) and education (Rowntree and Rowntree 1968; Sugarman 1973). Bourdieu (1984a: 143) has argued that 'youth' is no more than a word, as the divisions between youth and old age are arbitrary and the frontiers between them in all societies are a matter of struggle. The extent to which the concept of youth is constructed legally is indicated by the chronologies, tables and timelines relating age to legal prohibitions and rights (when people can drink, marry, etc.) in many youth-themed texts (Furnham and Gunter 1989; Furnham and Stacey 1991; Jones and Wallace 1992; Osgerby 1997; Roche and Tucker 1997). These markers have constantly shifted over time. Increased life expectancy has also lengthened the period that constitutes 'youth' in the lifecycle. The post-war advent of western youth culture has also

1

been key to increasing juvenilisation in the twentieth century as the state of being young becomes increasingly attractive to those who can no longer claim to belong to this constituency. The juxtaposition of youthful expressiveness with an ever-lengthening post-war list of protective youth-centred legislation inherent in Hebdige's (1988) dualism of youth as trouble and youth as fun highlights the contradictory way in which young people are seen as independent in their remit as cultural producers and consumers whilst simultaneously they are held in public (policy) esteem as objects requiring the exercise of restraint and control.

Defining 'culture' meanwhile presents further problems. Hebdige called it (1979: 5) 'a notoriously ambiguous concept' and Williams (1976: 76) 'one of the two or three most complicated words in the English language'. The term is often demarcated into the high culture versus mass (or popular) culture dialectic. Needless to say, youth culture is synonymous with the latter, which has been attacked by critics for amounting to Americanisation, i.e. lowbrow trash (Chambers 1985; Hebdige 1988), from the inter-war thinkers of Germany's Frankfurt school – particularly Adorno – to post-war British writers like Richard Hoggart (1958) and Raymond Williams (1993 [1958]). Kellner's (1994: 2) assertion that 'Culture in the broadest sense is a form of highly participatory activity, in which people create their societies and identities' recalls Williams's (1993 [1958]) celebrated declaration that 'culture is ordinary'. In the specific arena of youth culture, the root term 'culture' has given rise to numerous variants; most significantly 'subculture', which carries implications of the oppositional and unofficial. It is this concept – subculture – that provides the main basis for the opening chapter of this book.

About this book

Of course youth culture goes much further than simply pop music in the twenty-first century, spanning the internet, snowboarding, text messaging, football, designer fashion labels or any of the other ever-increasing non-musical cultural diversions currently on offer to youth. This book however takes youth culture, pop music and the relationship between the two in contemporary times as its subject. It is my contention that the fact that we live in globalised, diversified times necessitates a rethinking of the old received orthodoxies in terms of subcultural and popular music studies. Youth was always a site of struggle but is now a desirable state reaching into all periods of the lifecycle. Yet recent years have seen dramatic claims; for example that we are witnessing the end of history, the end of youth culture and moving towards postmodern, post-fordist, post-industrial, postcolonial and post-political times, to say nothing of a post-punk era. I will attempt to examine some of these theories alongside a series of contemporary youth music cultures. There is an inevitable inability of book-length discourse to keep up with the pace of unfolding events when dealing with such a subject. Youth culture is arguably more ephemeral and diffuse than ever before, moving far faster than academic theory ever can. Nonetheless this book attempts to trace some of these changes and rethink the relationships implicated by them.

Few academic concepts end up incorporated into wider lexicons and vocabularies but subculture is a rare example of a word that now gets bandied around in the music press and broadsheet newspapers. 'Subculture' with its mysterious underground associations is now a term in use by many people who have never studied its legacy in depth in the seminar room. At the same time the numbers of graduates exiting higher education who have taken courses on it have grown steadily and those reared on youth culture have also come of age. As media-driven subjects that most have had direct experience of, youth culture and popular music are not matters for academic enquiry alone. Common-sense opinions and journalistic commentary also abound. Youth culture is not simply a textual matter, context is equally important. Therefore *Beyond Subculture* combines twin approaches. It is presented in two sections. Part I is a theoretical overview of youth culture and popular music. These opening chapters between them chart the key transformations that have taken place in academic youth culture thinking and writing in the post-war era within the framework of changing social and political circumstances while Part II supplements this with case-study material of specific musical scenes drawing on both ethnographic material and primary and secondary sources.

The musical scenes discussed in this volume serve as illustrative examples for the changes inherent in the meaning of youth culture and popular music in an age of globalisation. I would like to think that the content represents one particular version of youth culture and popular music at the beginning of the twenty-first century. It looks at youth cultural associations of pop music: lived experiences, meanings and identifications alongside the meanings of pop music as it becomes increasingly institutionalised, co-opted, contained and controlled both commercially in its signing to major multinational record labels and legislatively.

This book makes a conscious attempt, however, to avoid the limited and unsatisfactory contextual framework of too many previous analyses of youth culture where theory has tended to be propounded at the expense of empirical evidence. The second and substantive section turns its attention to situated experiences of youth cultures. It is a central premise of the book that much previous youth culture work has been limited by the analysis of culture within homogeneous national units. The chapters look at what are often transnational phenomena. Bhangra, raï music, dance music consumption and production, hip-hop culture in the UK and France, Britpop, grunge and accompanying debates around re-releases and remixes will all be addressed. These specific youth music cultures serve as exemplars of the complexity in the current relationship between youth culture and pop music, recognising that contemporary youth culture is in many ways a socio-economic product of the post-industrial order. The growth of the creative and cultural industries – and of university courses in

Leisure Management, Sports Science and Tourism – show that work and leisure have become merged in a new sector of the economy that will be explored further in the remaining chapters.

The final chapter draws together the key threads from the preceding chapters to make some conclusions about contemporary youth culture and its relationship with pop music set within the global context. The book as a whole makes a case for thinking beyond subculture and for rethinking structurally embedded notions of youth culture and the obsession with authenticity, or 'keeping it real' at a time when musically based identities and socio-spatial relations are increasingly de-territorialised. It is argued that a more fluid and flexible set of understandings than those previously mapped out in studies of youth culture is needed in the twenty-first century to capture the rich diversity of multifaceted musical and youth cultural practices.

W(h)ither youth culture and pop music at the turn of the century?

Importantly, youth is a highly mediated social construct of constantly shifting relations and definitions. The research that resulted in this book was undertaken at a time when many cultural commentators went as far as to argue that youth culture had imploded, courtesy of an unimaginative younger cohort labelled Generation X or the 'slackers'. The late twentieth century saw claims of the end of both youth culture and childhood. Journalists who had long left behind their own gilded youth declared that modern music was bankrupt of pop's resistive role of earlier generations. Conservative critics paraded lamentations of 'the state of our young' in print – triggered by various neo-moral panics with the unholy youth cultural trinity of sex, drugs and rock 'n' roll at their core. Examples such as the *Times*'s (7 February 1996) editorial, 'The Age of Innocence is getting shorter', however, assume that the young really *are* innocent. Pearson's (1983) analysis suggests that they never were. Furthermore, today's young can be characterised as 'knowing' due to exposure to the mass media. Fornäs and Bolin (1995: 151) recall Baudrillard's (1981; 1990; 1996) concept of hyper-reality, in commenting: '[T]he mass media's constantly expanding flow of information increases people's knowledge of life. Via the media they are presented with all aspects of life long before they have a chance to experience them first hand.' Education and the media then simultaneously keep people young and prematurely age them. Pop potentially offers the possibility of escaping one's circumstances and reinventing identities but also potentially plays a role in articulating or even reinforcing young people's gender, ethnic and class identities. Crucially the concept of youth itself remains a social and cultural variable.

Pop music was always seen to exercise a border maintenance function by serving to construct the very existence of 'youth' as a distinct group. However, pop is increasingly ageing and indeed becoming part of the establishment. The runaway television hit of 2002 was MTV's series *The Osbournes*, a sitcom centred on the domestic antics of one-time heavy metal hell-raiser Ozzy Osbourne and his family. As a result of their success Sharon and Ozzy were even invited to a White House dinner. Those who have grown up with youth culture are now reaching positions of power and the power of pop is recognised by officialdom. George Bush enlisted the crowd-pleasing singer Ricky Martin in 2001 to appear at his Presidential inaugural festivities.[1] While the appearance of George Bush Senior in the 1980s alongside a pop star – particularly one of Latino origins – in this way would have been hard to imagine, in the twenty-first century it is almost expected. Bill Clinton's inauguration had earlier set a precedent by featuring Chuck Berry, Bob Dylan, Bruce Springsteen and the President himself (on saxophone) all jamming onstage together. Springsteen later appeared at a rally for failed Democrat John Kerry. When Tony Blair reached the age of 50 in 2003, British national newspapers all included photographs of the Prime Minister playing an electric guitar.[2] The attendance list for the funeral of Diana, Princess of Wales drawn up by Buckingham Palace officials notably included George Michael and Elton John among the invitees. Both the huge pop concert thrown by the palace to celebrate Queen Elizabeth II's golden jubilee in 2002 and the knighting of Mick Jagger, inducting the one-time bad boy into the establishment, serve as further examples of the institutionalisation of pop. In France the Mitterand government instituted the *Fête de la Musique*, national music day, as part of which local authorities provide large free pop concerts. In the UK the National Lottery has funded fifteen Youth Music Action Zones targeted at areas of social and economic deprivation where community youth music-making projects are run – an example of which is discussed in chapter 6.

This book then uses a number of illustrative examples to look at what binds popular music and youth culture at the start of the twenty-first century. In the following chapters the state of contemporary currents in youth culture will be examined, using a number of different case studies looking at musically focused youth cultures 'in action'. The book attempts to inter-relate cultural studies work on youth and music movements to the sociology of risk, considerations of globalisation and postcolonialism to the end of rethinking these notions 'beyond subculture'. The resulting volume does not claim to be a definitive record of youth culture but rather a series of contemporary snapshots that constitute contextualised examples of it. The musics looked at are global rhythms but I would hesitate to necessarily call them 'world music'. Linguistic, economic, political, social and cultural considerations all arise in the pages to follow; mirroring the multi-faceted nature of the subject under consideration. Alongside the 'classic' texts of subcultural studies there are now a range of secondary sources and readers on the subject. In addition to this recent years have witnessed a rise in subculture-influenced studies which offer radical critique of the concept and could be grouped together as a loose movement of 'post-subcultural studies'. This book continues in their vein of critique. If we accept that today's youth cultures are less unitary and instead more diverse and fragmented than those of earlier times, *Beyond Subculture* is something of a journey through this diversity, amongst the flotsam and jetsam of the fragments. It is hoped that the reader will enjoy the result.

Part I

THEORETICAL OVERVIEW

1

RETHINKING SUBCULTURE

A critique for the twenty-first century

[S]pectacular subcultures express forbidden forms (transgressions of sartorial and behavioural codes, law-breaking etc).

(Dick Hebdige 1979: 91–2)

A rather dull consensus of cool has begun to form about music, culture and fashion and lifestyle, and a lot of that is a result and a reflection of the decline of tribalism, as manifested in the amorphous but nevertheless fiercely identifiable subcultures which have traditionally dominated British pop culture.

('Tribal Ungathering', *NME*, 5 December 1998)

'Subculture' has in many ways come of age. The subject is a staple on many sociology undergraduate course syllabuses, commanding its own secondary texts (Frith and Goodwin 1990; Gelder and Thornton 1997; Redhead *et al.* 1997) alongside the primary source classics. The word, replete with subaltern, underground connotations, appears on the airwaves, in the circles of popular culture debate and the pages of popular magazines, even getting casual mentions in UK weekly paper the *New Musical Express*.[1] Subculture is a term that I have been aware of since at least my teenage years in the late 1980s; the word nestled in my record collection as the title of album tracks by both New Order and the Pixies. On stumbling across a copy of Dick Hebdige's seminal 1979 work *Subculture* with its arresting yellow cover depicting a spikey-haired male punk in the seemingly incongrous setting of the Cambridge University criminology library while I was a law undergraduate, I later became aware of the term as an academic concept. Certainly the notion has a long history. It was initially developed by the US 1950s Chicago school of urban gang sociology and later refashioned by the 1970s Centre for Contemporary Cultural Studies (CCCS) at the UK's Birmingham University in a 'boom' decade for the topic when a glut of British studies on subculture appeared. Yet by 1980 Stanley Cohen (1980: xxv), in the introduction to the revised edition of his earlier work *Folk Devils and Moral Panics*, wrote: 'to read the literature on subcultural delinquency is a depressing business'. The prevailing orthodoxy in the study of subcultures had fallen out of fashion.

9

Academic concepts wax and wane in terms of their influence. Although Frith and Goodwin (1990: 41) rate the 1970s as the 'zenith of subcultural theory's influence', tracing this to a 1979 review of Hebdige's *Subculture*, at the time of writing a renewed academic interest in the concept appears to be upon us, with a new generation of subculture-influenced studies which offer more than a simple restatement of received orthodoxy. Indeed the adjective 'post-subcultural' (Bennett and Harris 2003; Muggleton 1997; 2000; Muggleton and Weinzierl 2003; Pilkington 2001) and the variant 'post-Birmingham' (Thornton 1995) are repeatedly emphasised by twenty-first century neo-subculturalists. Of course criticisms of subcultural theory began from within almost as soon as the ink was dry on some of the original subcultural works. This opening chapter continues in this critical vein begun by scholars such as Stanley Cohen over two decades ago. Now that a revival of academic interest in youth cultural questions is upon us, what can we use to build on from the old Birmingham subcultural studies and what elements must we challenge?

Youth culture and the succession of often musically based scenes that Redhead (1990: 1) calls 'the subcultural chain' has been a growth industry in the post-war period. Needless to say, youth culture's academic shadow has lengthened along with it. It now commands an academic literature that is copious and diffuse and has appeared at an uneven rate. Part I of this book, an exploration of the content and context of the existing literature on youth culture, then, starts with the key concept of subculture which informs all the remaining chapters.

Romanticising resistance: Birmingham subculture studies

The prolific output of the Birmingham Centre for Contemporary Cultural Studies (CCCS) from the 1970s forms British academia's most sustained engagement with youth culture. The CCCS approach is best represented in Hall and Jefferson's (1976) *Resistance through Rituals*, a multi-authored volume which provided the blueprint for CCCS subcultural studies. Here 'authentic' subcultural identity was understood as being expressed by youth in terms of a cohesive and collective cultural resistance to the dominant order. A number of very good secondary sources now exist on the CCCS subcultural studies and their antecedents (e.g. Gelder and Thornton 1997; Epstein 1998), so I do not wish to dwell too heavily on this subject here. Rather than labriously stating in great detail what subcultural theory was, I want instead to highlight some of its deficiencies, through which central tenets of the broad doctrine will emerge as a result.

Subcultural theory attracted numerous criticisms almost from the outset – not least from some of the Birmingham authors themselves, such as Dick Hebdige and Angela McRobbie, who are part of what Wulff (1995b: 4) defines as 'an entire industry of critique [and] ... autocritique'. The main problems of subcultural theory come under three interlinked main headings – omissions, structural overdetermination and methodological problems. If we take the first

10

of these, in some ways it is easier to criticise the Birmingham School by high-lighting the categories of youth *excluded* from their analysis rather than those included. Despite the emergence of subcultural theory out of wider political and cultural movements of the 1960s and 1970s including feminism and anti-racism, women and black youth receive at best only a partial treatment in early subcultural studies outside the obvious contributions of McRobbie and Garber (1976) and the later CCCS volume (1982) *The Empire Strikes Back*. The second of these criticisms relates to subcultural studies' overly deterministic reading of youth social action, or what Kellner (1994: 37) has termed its 'fetishism of resistance'. For the CCCS youth were social actors in highly circumscribed contexts, subject to structural constraints not of their own making and largely beyond their control. This criticism is one that is strongly connected to the third which deals with methodological concerns. The heavy emphasis on (Marxist–structuralist) theory is at the expense of the empirical grounding of the Chicago school tradition. As Frith writes (1985: 349) 'subcultural theory is based on remarkably limited empirical research'. Indeed, despite including three chapters that focus on methodology (Butters 1976; Pearson and Twohig 1976; Roberts 1976), like much CCCS work (e.g. Hebdige 1979) the majority of the contents of *Resistance through Rituals* is based on media sources. Needless to say, such marginalisation of subjects such as ethnic minority youth and girls leads to distortion. I want now to discuss some of subcultural studies' omissions in greater detail.

Youth missing in action: subcultural studies' omissions

One of the most important criticisms of the Birmingham CCCS work is the lack of consideration given to females. Heidensohn (1985: 140) writes:

> girls do flit through the pages of these books and articles, but ... they are perceived and portrayed through the eyes of the 'lads' ... in almost fifty years of theoretical and ethnographic work on deviant cultures from Whyte to Willis, nothing had changed. Skinhead girls in Smethwick, Sunderland or the East End were as invisible to contemporary researchers and as liable to be dismissed as mere sex objects as they had been in Boston.

Gillis (1974) includes a chapter entitled ' "Boys will be Boys": Discovery of Adolescence 1870–1900', making this same point in relation to an earlier histor-ical period. Nava's (1984: 1) frustration that youth cultural studies 'has predominantly been about boys – usually urban white working class boys ... girls are only rendered visible where they are pertinent to the experience and percep-tion of boys', is borne out in Willis's (1977) description of male counter-school culture. Girls are the subject of sexual conquest by the 'lads' rather than presented in active agents in any way. Inuendo and machismo bravado boasts about sexual prowess are parts of their daily banter. Willis himself reports all this as a matter of fact rather than serioulsy challenging it in any way. The most he volunteers is the explanation that girls were outside the remit of the study in a footnote on methodology (Willis 1977: 159).

McRobbie and Garber's *Resistance through Rituals* contribution (1976: 212) claims that 'Female invisibility in youth subcultures then becomes a self-fulfilling prophecy, a vicious cycle ... the emphasises in the documentation of these phenomenons [sic], on the male and masculine, reinforce and amplify our conception of the subcultures as predominantly male.' In later work McRobbie (1980) finds that slotting girls into received notions of subcultures is problematic given the difficulties of defining any such thing as female subculture, i.e. a way in which working class girls can resist dominant cultural norms as a group of girls. Female skinheads and punks may, she claims, be rebelling against the mainstream culture of femininity, but within the subculture itself traditional gender divisions are still in place. Furthermore, young women seem to exist in spatial and social organisations from which subcultures in the CCCS sense cannot emerge. McRobbie and Garber (1976: 213) note 'the "culture of the bedroom" – experimenting with make-up, listening to records, reading the mags, sizing up boyfriends, chatting, jiving'. This exists not as action in the public arena but is experienced often on an individual level in private spaces (see also Frith 1978) with a more sedentary focus, which is often a necessity due to the greater restrictions placed on girls. The impact/influence of gay culture on British post-war youth culture is a further CCCS omission, highlighted by Savage (1990), who argues that gay culture underpins British subcultural style from Teddy Boy to acid house. According to Savage, the absence of gays from the subcultural picture rests on the desire of academics for an idealised 'utopia of the innocent'.

Black youth have tended to register with the social sciences under the categories of 'race' or 'migrant labour' in what Gilroy (1987) calls the 'victim/problem' discursive couplet. Despite the fact that the new commonwealth immigrants were a young population (as economic migrants often are), British blacks were another relative omission of early youth subcultural studies. Birmingham treatments of non-white groups included the work of Hebdige (1979) and Jones (1988) who looked at reggae, rasta and rudies. The CCCS's main contribution to the race came in the form of *The Empire Strikes Back* (1982), which appeared some years after the main wave of CCCS subcultural studies. Subtitled 'Race and Nation in 1970s Britain', it was a multi-authored volume with content spanning the 1981 UK urban riots and the Grunwick episode which saw Asian women taking industrial action against their employers in a dispute over working conditions. Apart from this work those studies that do exist tend either to sympathise with black youth as victims of racism or to objectify them as a source of white stylistic fetishisation/appropriation (Brake 1980; Chambers 1976; Hebdige 1979; Jones 1988). Hebdige (1979) for example argued that post-war youth cultures offered a 'phantom history' of post-war race relations in Britain; examples given included the punk/rasta intersection. Gary Clarke (1985:

88) calls this 'a coded recording of race relations' where black culture itself is rather narrowly held to be consistent with Jamaican culture. Jones (1988) also undertakes a reading of the historical relationship between black culture and white youth, but importantly he sees new ethnicities as embedded in contemporary British society, and recognises inter-racial friendship. It is likely that a new generation of black intellectuals will continue to redress the balance in this area in years to come. For example Gilroy's (1993a) reading of cultural history reconstructs a specifically 'Black Atlantic' culture which transcends nation-states and rejects the politics of separation.

Theoretical and structural considerations

More fundamental issue with the whole 'essentialist and non-contradictory' notion of subculture is taken by Gary Clarke (1981: 82–83) who writes: 'The fundamental problem with Cohenite subcultural analysis is that it takes the card-carrying members of spectacular subcultures as its starting point and then teleologically works backward to uncover the class situation and detect the specific set of contradictions which produced the corresponding set of styles.' Ethnography is used then not to elaborate or illustrate but to validate or confirm pre-ordained political positions. Cohen (1980: ix) similarly blames over-theorisation: 'The conceptual tools of Marxism, structuralism and semiotics, a left-bank pantheon of Genet, Lévi-Strauss, Barthes and Althusser have all been wheeled in to aid this hunt for the hidden code.' For example, Hebdige (1979: 18) states:

> Style in subculture is pregnant with significance. Its transformations go 'against nature' interrupting processes of 'normalisation' … our task becomes like Barthes', to discern the hidden messages inscribed in code on the glossy surfaces of style, to trace them out as 'maps of meaning' which obscurely re-present the very contradictions they are designed to resolve or conceal.

Although the CCCS's studies of 1970s youth were based in Britain, theoretically they drew heavily on continental traditions, particularly Marxism and French structuralist philosophy, emphasising the role of social structure(s) in predetermining individual trajectories. The concepts of culture, semiotics and ideology and the study of language/linguistics, anthropology and literary criticism are all spanned by this broad perspective. Among theorists drawn on by the CCCS were Saussure (1996 [1915]), who linked language and its meanings to culture (learned) rather than nature (with inherent meaning in itself); Lévi-Strauss (1955; 1964), who built on the idea of binary oppositions in his work on myths in 'primitive' society; and Barthes' (1973) work on semiology/semiotics, the science of signs. A cursory glance at *Resistance through Rituals* (particularly the first chapter and the bibliography) reveals the CCCS's fascination with structuralism, consolidated in later works. These theoretical schools were applied to 1970s British youth. Drawing on Barthes, for example, Hebdige (1979: 2–3) terms the interplay of signs and icons in youth culture 'semiotic guerrilla warfare' and links this to punk:

> outrage can be encapsulated in a single object, so the tensions between dominant and subordinate groups can be found reflected in the surfaces of subculture – in the styles made up of mundane objects which have a double meaning ... the most mundane objects – a safety pin, a pointed shoe, a motor cycle ... take on a symbolic dimension becoming a form of stigmata.

He also employs the Lévi-Straussian concept of 'style as bricolage' which mixes meanings to signify resistance to, and the subversion of, traditional norms. Some punk symbolism can be explained by other factors, e.g. the use of the Nazi symbol, the swastika, as a fashion statement, its shock value increased by the relative recentness of the Second World War at the historical moment at which its use occurred.[2] Arguably shoehorning youth into models developed for other purposes sometimes made for an uncomfortable fit.

The Gramscian (1971) notion of hegemony, i.e. the political and ideological domination of one class over others by the agreement of the dominated (rather than by their coercion), formed perhaps the most important strand in the intellectual grounding of the CCCS (Harris 1992). Clarke et al. (1976: 15) adapted Gramsci's 'dual consciousness' of the working class (an inconsistent set of values that is part-submissive, based on capitalist ideology, and part-revolutionary, determined by the experience of capitalism) to posit a '*double articulation* of youth sub-cultures' to parent culture and dominant culture. In this way, subcultures are subordinate but autonomous; there is an acceptance of one's situation but a simultaneous rejection of it through the adoption of styles that represent a refusal to accept the values of the dominant culture. Both Althusser and Gramsci are discussed in Clarke et al.'s (1976) chapter which serves as the 'mission statement' of Hall and Jefferson (1976). The Gramscian theory of hegemony foreshadows Foucault's post-structuralist reading of culture that operates through institutional structures and clusters around the concepts of history/power/knowledge. The Foucauldian concepts of knowledge, power and control of the body were influential in Hebdige's (1983; 1988) writing on youth surveillance and display.

Needless to say analytical rigidity breeds inconsistencies. Seeing working class subcultures as absolutes precludes the possibility of class mobility or any recognition of varying degrees of subcultural affiliation. Far from being unproblematic, coherent and sovereign, identity itself is constructed and multifaceted, with subcultural membership being only one aspect. In addition to this, conformist youths are conspicuous by their absence – take, for example, the over-identification of Willis with the 'lads' at the expense of the activities, opinions or voices of those less rebellious people the lads identify as the 'ear'oles' (also young, white working class males) who are described disparagingly.[3] Cohen (1980: xix) similarly expresses reservations about 'the obvious fascination with spectacular subcultures'. For Clarke (1981: 85) 'On the whole, the absolute distinction between subcultures and "straights" is increasingly difficult to maintain.'[4] Redhead's more recent critique of subculture as an object created by subculture theorists will be dealt with at greater length below.

Subculture theorists' collective obsession with class was almost exclusively limited to *working class* subjugation within structuring structures for youth, e.g. school. This axis is demonstrated in the title of Mungham and Pearson's volume *Working Class Youth Culture* (1976), another collection of essays by many of the *Resistance* authors covering much of the same ground (e.g. Murdock and McCron 1976a; Murdock and McCron 1976b), and Clarke's (1973) prototypical paper 'The Three R's – Repression, Rescue and Rehabilitation: Ideologies of Control for Working Class Youth'. In the tradition of educational sociology, Willis (1977) charted the transition from the last two years of school to entry into the labour force of non-academic working class boys in a Midlands comprehensive school. This rare example of ethnography from the Birmingham School finds that the oppositional cultural processes effected by the 'lads' ultimately, and inevitably, maintain and reproduce the social order. A similar treatment of social disadvantage and the hidden latent ideological struggle implicit in school for young working class males is provided by Corrigan (1979).

The fascination of working class youth for middle class academics existed despite the fact that a number of the branches of the post-war subcultural tree have been decidedly middle class, e.g. mod and punk, contrived by middle class students in UK art school classrooms (Frith and Horne 1987; Longhurst 1995) and 1960s student radicals.[5] Murdock and McCron (1976a: 203) declared: 'Subcultural styles can therefore be seen as coded expressions of class consciousness transposed into the specific context of youth and reflective of the complexity in which age acts as a mediation both of class experience and of class consciousness.' Writing more recently Frith (1985: 347–8) has concluded that subcultural theorists have over-romanticised working class resistance: 'There has always been a tendency for sociologists (who usually come from middle class, bookish backgrounds) to celebrate teenage deviancy, to admire the loyalties of street life.' This tendency can be seen in Hebdige's (1988: 244) self-confessional soliloquy closing *Hiding in the Light*, voicing some anxieties about his roots, in the sort of very personalised prose that both Back (1996) and Dyer (1997) have also indulged in of late, the latter two in a discussion of whiteness.

Methodology

Of course no researcher can ever ultimately be neutral, and the members of the CCCS made no pretence at being so; their very logic of inclusion (and what was excluded) betraying their agenda. With their work set in the context of multiple economic crises and social and economic polarisation in Britain (Osgerby 1997: 104), perhaps then the Birmingham School is best understood as a strictly partisan *political* project; as a last 1960s idealist flourish in its core construction of 'youth as a metaphor for social change' (Clarke *et al.* 1976: 17).

Despite the engagement of cultural studies academics in anti-racism and feminism as individuals (Barker and Beezer 1992: 2), paradoxically the political agenda of subculture theory seems to have blinded the authors to some of the less attractive features of working class youth cultures, e.g. in explanations of 'Paki-bashing' as an understandable reaction by heroic working class whites (Clarke 1976; Hebdige 1979; Pearson 1976) who seek 'a way of magically retrieving the sense of group solidarity and identity which once went along with living in a traditional working class neighbourhood' (Robbins and Cohen 1978: 137). Clarke (1976: 100) explains skinhead behaviour as a 'symbolic defence of (threatened) territory' and a 'magical attempt to recover community' by 'dispossessed inheritors', identifying 'skinhead style [as] derived from the traditional content of the working class community – the example *par excellence* of the defensively organised collective'. The aesthetic of cropped hair, braces and boots is seen as signifying their working class base. The fragmentation of traditional working class communities, as a result of slum housing clearance programmes, industrial decline, dwindling employment opportunities and corrupt central and local government, are all given as reasons for their attacks on 'scapegoated outsiders' (Clarke 1976: 102), i.e. immigrant youth. The implication is that such aggression is inevitable. Any questioning of why, for example, skinhead aggression cannot be channelled against the authorities responsible for their grievances rather than powerless immigrants is unexplored, rendering it excused as much as explained. A similar approach was taken with football hooliganism (Marsh 1978; Taylor 1971), which was interpreted as representing the working class youth's attempt to win back control of 'his' game, once again, in an attempt to retrieve a disappearing sense of community. Willis's (1977) lads are sexist, racist and homophobic, even talking about the joys of rape – but this celebration of white male heterosexual power seems to be cancelled out in his eyes by the fact that they comport themselves with dignity in the face of subordination. Cohen (1980: xxvii) astutely observes in a pre-politically correct age: 'Those same values of racism, sexism, chauvinism, compulsive masculinity and anti-intellectualism, the slightest traces of which are condemned in bourgeois culture, are treated with deferential care ... when they appear in subculture.' At the same time the idea of authenticity is one that needs rethinking in an arguably inauthentic world. In a key passage Redhead (1990: 25) remarks:

> What in practice we witnessed in the 1980s was the break-up not simply of former theoretical traditions (or master and meta narratives) about the emancipatory potential of youth in the west but the disintegration and restructuring of those formations (rock culture, youth culture)

which were produced as their objects. 'Authentic' subcultures were produced by subculturalists, not the other way round.

Mungham and Pearson (1976: 1) recognise the danger of lopsided youth identification in declaring: 'Adolescents are either condemned out of hand as ill-fitting members of a well ordered world or glorified as potential rebels and revolutionaries who will take over a world which is sick, lifeless and dull.' On 'the gap between the sociologists' abstract account of youth culture and the explanations one would be likely to get from the subcultures themselves', Frith (1985: 347) writes: 'Punks and skinheads and mods and teds are unlikely (unless they've done sociology A-level) to talk about "winning subcultural space", "resistance at the ideological level" or the "magical reclamation of community".' In making this observation he refers to the introductory chapter of *Resistance through Rituals*, a book to which he himself contributed.

The disjuncture between the researcher and the researched comes over memorably in the reactions of Willis's (1977: 194–199) lads to his first draft. There appears to be some recognition of themselves tempered with a general bafflement regarding the author's obtuse narrative. One comments: 'The parts you wrote about us, I read them, but it was, y'know, the parts what were actually describing the book like I didn't …' (Willis 1977: 194).

A period piece: understanding the CCCS in context

Subcultural theory is best described as an amalgam. Its examination of the splintering of traditional working class culture draws on established traditions including Marxism, Gramscian hegemony and Chicago School studies of urban micro-sociology grounded in US behavioural social science (Cohen 1955; Merton 1938; Whyte 1955). Elements of deviancy theory (Howard Becker's *Outsiders* (1963) and the work of Erving Goffman), Durkheim's ideas on '*anomie*', the Frankfurt School's vision of a mass society (to be discussed in the next chapter), and French structuralist political theory were also crucial theoretical influences. In this way the CCCS saw 'subcultural space' as far from unmediated.

The Birmingham theory is explicitly political: interpreting youth subculture (ritual) as a response (symbolic resistance) primarily to class oppression. Corrigan and Frith (1976: 237) write: 'Young people's experience is precisely the experience of the State's attempt (more strident than for their elders because their position is as yet less secure) to ensure their contribution to the reproduction of capitalism.' Subculture then is, for the young, a diversion from the boring powerlessness of the daily routine, with wider potential consequences for the ideology of 'everyday' social processes. Admittedly the definition of youth in question here (white, working class and male) is very narrowly focused; however, society was different in a number of ways when this definition was formulated (e.g. the British political post-war consensus on the benefits of an interventionist state was better established than in subsequent periods and the population was less ethnically diverse).

The result of these theoretical inputs was a refashioning of the concept of (youth) subculture that had been established by the empirically informed work of the Chicago school (Cohen 1955; Gordon 1947). A subcultural group is one that differentiates itself from dominant culture through its distinct attitude and lifestyle but is connected to it through wider processes. The discussions of class and ideology in youth culture found in the chapters of Hall and Jefferson (1976), taken against the backdrop of 1960s political struggles (student unrest, radical anti-war politics, etc.) that shaped many of the volume's authors, demonstrate how much hope was invested in youth as political agents of social change. Clarke *et al.* (1976: 45–7) set the tone in the opening chapter:

> Working class subcultures ... take shape on the level of the social and cultural-relations of the subordinate class. ... They *win space* for the young: cultural space in the neighbourhood and institutions ... on the street or street-corner. They serve to mark out and appropriate 'terri-tory' in the localities. They focus around the key occasions of social interaction: the weekend, the disco, the bank holiday trip, the night out in the 'centre', the 'standing-about-doing-nothing' of the weekday evening, the Saturday match ... a set of social rituals which underpin their collective identity as a 'group' instead of a mere collection of indi-viduals.

The present-centredness of the 1970s work on youth subcultures largely ignores the evidence for a much longer history of youth cultures existing long before the post-war period, such as that described by Gillis (1974) and Pearson (1983). Part of the problem then was over-theorisation at the expense of considering history. If the evidence from these earlier incarnations of subculture had been listened to more closely, perhaps some of the now glaring inconsistencies in the assumptions and values of 1970s subcultural theory could have been avoided. Looking to the future and projected demographic trends, we live in an ageing world. The 1970s work on subcultures suffered from an excessive emphasis on youth, possibly as a consequence of the post-war baby boom. Youth cultures were seen in consequence as fleeting, short-lived formations. While some aspects of contemporary youth cultures can be seen in this way, the picture is more complicated than such readings suggest. The question of what happens to those identifying with youth sub-cultures as these individuals age was not addressed by the CCCS. I will return to the idea of juvenilisation in this book but the available evidence seems to suggest that subcultural affiliations do not disappear in an uncomplicated way. Features of these identifications continue in certain ways as they become merged with other sources of identity. The ageing of pop consumers and producers provides an obvious example.

The 1980s and on: towards a post-subcultural studies

By the 1980s Hebdige (1988: 35) had declared 'In the current recession, the imaginary coherence of subculture seems about to dissolve under the pressure of material constraints.' Gloomily titled appraisals by British authors such as *Black Youth in Crisis* (Cashmore and Troyna 1982), *The Trouble With Kids Today* (Muncie 1984) and *No Future* (Cashmore 1984) appeared alongside problematising studies of youth unemployment (Junankar 1987; Roberts 1984; Wallace 1987; Waller and Barton 1986), youth training (Finn 1987; Hollands 1990) and football hooliganism (Murphy 1984; 1990; Murphy *et al.* 1988; Redhead 1987; 1993b). Moreover subculturalists reoriented themselves as a result of wider political shifts: with the collapse of state communism Marxism was jettisoned as a rationale (McRobbie 1994a: 38). Meanwhile as Denning (1991) observes in the US (fittingly under the 'Great Communicator' President Reagan), popular culture scholarship flourished, often taking postmodernism as its theoretical standpoint. The pop video for example became ripe for analysis in this way (Kaplan 1987; Fiske 1989).

We have seen how the CCCS produced a body of work with a diversity of positions which, from the outset, was being criticised from within. Partly due to the influence of the newer waves of post-structuralist and postmodern theory, in the 1980s and 1990s many of the Birmingham group critiqued their earlier work. One of the subject area's best known names, McRobbie (1991: 64–5), reconsidered her earlier work and regretted the

> disparity between my 'wheeling in' class in my report and its complete absence from the girls' talk and general discourse. … If I had to go back and consider this problem now, I would go about it in a very different fashion. I would not harbour such a monolithic notion of class, and instead I would investigate how relations of power and powerlessness permeated the girls' lives – in the context of school, authority, language, job opportunities, the community and sexuality.

Most extreme was Hebdige (1988: 8), who went as far as announcing his 'farewell to youth studies'. This disavowal parallels 'the idea of reversal' (Leenhardt 1989), the shifts in the intellectual positions of several key French postmodernist thinkers over the same period. The intellectual point of departure of the CCCS in the 1970s, based on the thought of a generation of post-war French intellectuals, makes the work of both groupings almost period pieces to be reconsidered in the light of the radically altered changing political climate of the Reagan/Bush years.

Willis's journey from *Learning to Labour* (1977) to *Common Culture* (1990: 27) sees theories of social reproduction replaced with 'a profane explosion of everyday symbolic life and activity'. This symbolic creativity feeds into a 'common culture'. Willis (1990: 1) asserts: 'Young people are all the time expressing or attempting to express something about their potential or actual *cultural significance.*' Rather like Hebdige's (1988) casting-off of youth culture,

Willis (1990: 169) pronounces 'the moment of subculture is now over', but unlike Hebdige he rejects Gramscian theory (1990: 157): 'hegemonic practices seem to be deeply uninterested in these actual processes (of fun, joy and meaning-making) and recoup "popular cultural" contents too quickly into the politics of people/power block relations'. However Willis's valorisation of the creative potential of the young in relation to popular culture leads him to exaggerate the political position of its consumers (Turner 1996: 204) and underplay the role imposed by its producers in reinforcing dominant culture values (Buckingham 1993: 206). The resulting constructions placed upon youth come across as patronising and no better than the Gramscian theory so roundly dismissed. Harris (1992: 169) writes 'Despite the solemn warnings about the need to take these skills seriously if we want to build socialism upon them, Willis has found out almost nothing about the political views of young people directly ... once again the respondents provide the innocent data and the analysts provide the politics for them.' This is a methodological criticism.

Some of the central tenets of the new wave of youth studies that developed in the 1990s distinctly resonate with earlier moments of its history. Thornton's work on rave culture uses the term 'subculture', updated for the 1990s by way of her adoption of two theoretical positions: the notion of 'subcultural capital', derived from Bourdieu's work (1979; 1984) on cultural distinction, and a (Stanley) Cohenite approach to the media. The ethnographic work of Gaines (1991) on suburban alienation, Giroux (1996; 1997) on resistance in educational settings, and Weinstein (1991) on rock are particularly significant as are the wider theories of youth and pop propounded by Grossberg (1994), Postman (1982) and Kellner (1994; 1995). Epstein (1998: 17) for example states 'While pockets of "actual" resistance occasionally appear – the 1970s punk scenes in Britain, New York and Los Angeles for example – they are quickly swallowed up into the corporate musical machine and as such can no longer be viewed as genuine resistance.' This has echoes of Abrams (1959), who first expounded the idea of subcultural incorporation by the market. To some extent this claim of neutering by commercial appropriation will be tested by all the chapters of Part II, in which different youth musical cultures are dealt with. America has also been the site of a good deal of the work on youth and ethnicity relevant to the postcolonial times we now inhabit.

While there has been something of a demise of subcultural theory, the coming of age of subcultural studies as a historical tradition or body of work can be evidenced in specialist histories that mirror the institutionalisation of cultural studies itself, with 'a national and international network ... journals, associations, degrees, publishers' lists, conferences, good things and bad things, the lot' (Johnson 1994: 357).[6] There is an ever-proliferating number of readers and histories of cultural studies available (Barker and Beezer 1992; During 1993; Gray and McGuigan 1993; Inglis 1993; Munns and Rajan 1995; Punter 1986), most of which include at least a chapter on 'subculture'. Paralleling this, the study of youth culture has seen something of a revival in recent years with a number of different studies spanning various traditions. Just as the 1980s saw some rapprochement between cultural studies and feminism, with a slew of 'feminist inspired *revanche* studies' (Chisholm 1990: 35), successive waves of cultural studies have seen the subject diversify into increasingly specialised areas. Recent years have seen the publication of youth cultural work covering psychological discourse analysis (Widdicombe and Woofit 1995) and cultural geography (Nayak 2003; Skelton and Valentine 1997). Methodologically the grounded ethnography of Willis (1977) has seen something of a re-emergence in the empirical works of Back (1996) and Gillespie (1995). The attachment of importance to the testimonies of interviewees can be seen as what Barker and Beezer (1992) see as a shift from text (pure theory) to context (ethnography) – in Willis's 'grounded aesthetics' (1990) for example.

Perhaps inevitably new youth groupings require new theoretical tools. Whether rave displays the traditional characteristics of subcultures in terms of being a tightly bonded, high visibility, fringe-delinquent working class group is questionable. Epstein (1998) identifies US-originated studies of Generation X or slackers that have emerged since the 1990s as another key phase in youth cultural studies. Slackers are the ostensibly satiated yet disenchanted and disenfranchised post-baby boom youth who are 'the children of suburbia, raised on McDonalds, shopping malls and MTV' (Epstein 1998: 18). If the 1990s were the 1960s turned upside down, unlike the hippies who could drop out with the relative security of something to drop out from, slackers grew up against a backdrop of state welfare cutbacks (or 'downsizing' in the 1990s euphemism) and they saw themselves as facing a world of diminished possibilities. According to Giroux (1997: 66), they are painted by the media as 'idle, self-absorbed and indifferent to the values of paid work as an end in itself'. Parallels exist in other countries, for example the French term 'génération bof', derived from an idiomatic expression conveying indifference. The countercultures and anarcho-punks of the late 1980s and 1990s whose spirit continues in the anti-globalisation protests of the early twentieth century are examples of non-musically centred (although sometimes musically linked), highly politicised groupings that would once have been termed 'subcultures' but are difficult to conceive of as such today. Their case is interesting because their message arguably lacks coherence as they are rather more *against* global capitalism than *for* any clearly defined set of aims and objectives. Nevertheless protestors at international world trade summits have played a role in putting concerns such as fair trade, opposition to landmines and debt relief onto the mainstream political agenda. The 'new politics' of the movement is distinctly 'post-subcultural' in approach. Inevitably academicisation of the 'new social movement theory' has taken place with foundational texts (Jordan and Lent 1998; McKay 1996; 1998) and conference and journal networks, e.g. Social Movements. There are obvious potential crossovers between subjects of interest to neo-subculturalists and social movement theorists. Martin (2002) argues for a combining of elements of the two theories towards the end of conceptualising cultural politics anew. The possibility, or even necessity, of mixed models to describe contemporary youth cultural formations is an important argument of this book too. Indeed the whole continued validity of pop as a metaphor for youth culture is one that needs examination, and will be returned to, particular as we appear to be experiencing the breaking down of bounded categories based on class, gender and ethnicity.

Rethinking subculture: a critique for the twenty-first century

The academic scrutiny of youth is no longer a new idea. Youth culture, like cultural studies at large, now commands its own canonical texts and legitimised practices. However, as we have seen, academic analyses have frequently fallen disappointingly short in their highly selective dealings with youth based on a one-dimensional, often purely textual approach. Past limitations often stem from skewing studies towards more marginal youths sensationalising the deviant deeds of the few while the essential conformity of the silent majority, those who do not want to semiologically resist through rituals, is overlooked. The contrast or supposed divide between the followers of youth subculture and the 'straights' was vastly overdramatised by 1970s work on subcultures. This generalising rhetoric is as unhelpful today as it was at the time it was first propounded and in certain ways serves only to reify the phenomena being studied, as Pickering (1997) has argued. Matters are further complicated by the fact that many of the causes and effects of youth culture are intangible, unquantifiable variables, such as 'being hard', 'looking good', and 'hanging out' (Gladwell 1997). Reacting against what has gone before is also a motor of youth subcultures, as witnessed in punk's short sharp musical shock succeeding the overblown pomposity of progressive rock, or the appearance of grunge with its lo-fi guitars and dressed-down look following rave's electronically processed music and fashion-conscious image. Some aspects of youth culture are utterly spontaneous. Others are carefully orchestrated. As first noted by Abrams (1959), youth culture is an international industry for which constant regeneration is vital, ensuring a quick turnover of all the associated consumer products such as fashion and music. There is a need to find a middle way in looking at youth cultural processes between the all-too-glib labellings of market manipulation suggested by the Frankfurt school and the resistance so beloved of Birmingham, taking account of other forms of difference, e.g. ethnic and gender distinctions.

Although the CCCS tradition is a milestone in youth culture, its importance is perhaps now beginning to look strictly historical, given its limited applicability to contemporary youth cultures due to its focus on British class relations. Mirroring the hegemonic role of English for transporting pop music, even early comparative studies were concentrated on English language cultures, such as Brake's (1995) volume on the US, the UK and Canada. Yet in explaining contemporary youth cultures, studies from elsewhere are illuminating. Northern Europe has been a particularly active site of educationally oriented, school-to-work 'youth transitions' literature, which draws on the influential German individualization thesis (Beck 1992). Scandinavian researchers have produced large-scale, often state-sponsored surveys covering taste formation and musical practices (Fornäs *et al.* 1995; Fornäs and Bolin 1995), the respected journal *Young: the Nordic Journal of Youth Research*, and work on individualization and cross-cultural youth practices (Amit-Talai and Wulff 1995). Australia too has produced various youth studies in recent years (Wyn and White 1996; Moore 1994). While British subcultural studies has drawn on French philosophy, French youth themselves have been less present; yet they provide an interesting example for their postcolonial circumstances, and are featured in chapters 4, 5 and 6 of this book. These studies all contribute to a much more complete and complex picture of youth culture than ever before. Indeed the theories generated by CCCS subcultural studies are even more irrelevant to the twenty-first century international situations of post-subcultural studies than the 1970s British youth they attempted to analyse, who were arguably already poorly served by them.

The study of youth culture, particularly in its sobering 1980s unemployment phase following the heady 1970s CCCS era has inclined towards classist readings of polarisation (Chisholm 1990). Such theories are of decreased relevance to our present times, which could arguably be characterised by greater risk (Beck 1992) or the advent of Generation X. Denning (1991) points out that it is difficult to appropriate Gramscian historicism to analyse mass culture forms including broadcasting, recorded music, McDonalds and Levis. If, however, 1970s youth studies is understood as a political project located in a particular historical moment then some of subcultural theory's more questionable aspects become more excusable. Importantly, CCCS subculturalists were never trying to provide anything but an account of British youth cultures of their time, therefore their work can be considered as understandable for what it was given the moment of its appearance but now in need of updating and revision.

The wide body of literature available on youth culture goes some way towards explaining currents in youth culture throughout the post-war era. Youth continues to fascinate both the media and academia, whatever the political complexion of governments and their attempts to control access to research funds for studying it. As Giroux (1996: 15) remarks, 'The self and social formation of diverse youth subcultures mediated by popular cultural forms such as television, advertising, pulp fiction, rock music, rap, and films remain a prominent concern of cultural studies.' The theoretical groundwork serves as an essential foundation to any study of contemporary youth culture. Without the Chicago school there would be no 1960s educational theories, without these there would be no 'radical criminology', without this no Birmingham CCCS and so on. However, any attempt to explain youth culture in the 1990s necessitates a revision of our understanding of previous cultural studies' approaches to youth cultures and critical examination of their applicability to current subcultures. The work of the Birmingham CCCS theorists are still a near-necessity in contemporary considerations of youth culture but new paths of enquiry too are necessitated by new diverse youth groupings and ever-developing youth cultural phenomena. Grand theories and linear models of youth culture are arguably increasingly redundant in the culturally pluralist, multimedia twenty-first century.

Of course 'youth culture' is not a blanket term. Neither 'youth' nor 'culture' function(s) with anything approaching unanimity. It is more accurate to think in terms of a plurality of co-existing youth cultures and avoid automatically taking class-based generational solutions to political problems as a perfunctory starting point. Such ultimately self-defeating political constraints mean that all too often 'the symbolic baggage the kids are being asked to carry is just too heavy … the interrogations are just a little forced' (Cohen 1980: xv). Rojek (1995: 101) describes 'the gladiatorial paradigm' where 'contributors seem to evaluate the power of their own arguments with the absolute destruction of the arguments of others who represent competing traditions'. Academics can be seemingly on a mission to 'prove' the salience of one theory over all others. Conventional understandings of class, age and adulthood will also need re-examining. The deficiencies of the pre-eminent CCCS youth cultural studies are no longer in question but previous theoretical approaches are nonetheless important for any examination of contemporary youth groupings and popular music. Themes such as ethnicity and gender need to be integral to future theorisations rather than simply tacked on.

The turn of the century has proved to be an interesting time to be researching youth culture and pop music. It is a juncture at which both of these entities have been normalised whilst paradoxically it is simultaneously argued that they have ceased to exist. The same applies to the term subculture itself. Many of the points made and perspectives explored in this opening chapter will be revisited in the remainder of this book, hopefully free from the intellectual strait-jacket of earlier work in the area but importantly with an awareness of youth studies' legacy, including its limitations. Cultural studies has always prided itself on its multidisciplinary, multi-perspective, polyvocal approach (Kellner 1994). In the chapters to come I propose to take a multifaceted approach to youth culture and pop music in multi-ethnic modernity. The heterogeneity of content material and theoretical positions in the following chapters is reflected in the range of source material drawn on, from academic and popular cultural sources as well as participant observation. As we have seen, however, for all its inclusive ideals, youth studies has hitherto tended only rarely to stray from a very narrow consideration of youth and culture. It is the main premise of this book to go 'beyond subculture'. The quote at the top of this chapter from *NME* refers to tribes which some have used to think about youth cultures (Bennett 2001 and Malbon 1999, after Maffesoli 1996a; 1996b). Others studying youth transitions have looked at theories around risk (Beck 1992). I want to continue then by looking at recent developments in social theory that we can use to make sense of youth culture and pop music in contemporary times in my second chapter.

2

AGE AND CULTURE

Diversifying discourses beyond subculture

> Ageing researchers who cling vicariously to their own past
> through a falsely perceived symbiosis with young people become
> thereby neither younger, nor do they remain empirically effective.
> (Chisholm 1990: 34)

> 'What will you do next?' a black youth recently asked me. 'I
> suppose you'll finish this project and then look around and think,
> "oh yes, there's the Asians, they've got a few problems. I think I'll
> go and study them." '
> (Cashmore and Troyna, 'Black Youth In Crisis', 1982: 14)

As the last chapter acknowledged, the Birmingham subculturalists occupy a
central place in the study of youth culture and almost all subsequent studies have
acknowledged their important, if flawed, contribution. However, changing times
require changed theories and chapter 2 turns to some of these. Since the 1970s
glut of CCCS subcultural studies, frequently based on 1960s fieldwork, the
world has demonstrably changed. Class and masculinity are just two areas that
are now much less well-defined for example. A further important change is the
multi-ethnic nature of much of the contemporary western world, which has
transformed many urban landscapes through commerce – Grønland, Oslo in
Norway known as 'Little Pakistan' for example. We live in much more inter-
dependent times where nations can function less and less as discrete units – a
movement often termed globalisation, to be explored further in the next
chapter in relation to music. The nation-state as an organising unit assumes less
and less importance while multinational corporations and international bodies
thrive.

Crucially we now inhabit a distinctly 'postcolonial' world. This term applies to
the post-1945 era which has seen the independence of ex-colonies of countries
such as Britain and France, whose once-presumed sovereignty over their internal
affairs and 'great dominions' is in sharp decline. In the new world order the influence of the (one-time) colonised on the ex-coloniser nations has been a key
feature of emergent post-war youth cultures of Europe. The socio-cultural effects

of this movement of decolonialisation have been profound, shaping many youth musical cultures, as we will see.

Technological advance has also ensued. The spread of communications technology and consumer durables have been contributory factors in the shifting function of the home to increasingly become a leisure space to a significantly greater degree than before. Feminists such as McRobbie highlighting the invisibility of girls in CCCS youth studies argued that much girls' leisure behaviour took place in domestic settings that rendered it invisible to the subculturalists' gaze with their Chicago School-influenced fixation on street corners and territorialised space. While in the years that have elapsed since the 1970s gender roles have become less entrenched, the domestication of leisure applies to both genders. Linked to this is the rise of media-literacy (Kellner 1994). Internet technology in particular is more interactive than the comparatively passive consumption of 'couch potato-dom' offered by similarly sedentary home-based entertainment such as radio or television in its traditional pre-digital incarnations. Indeed, with advances in traditional broadcasting to allow users more control over the output it seems that we are seeing a convergence of old and new media forms. Furthermore marked demographic change has ensued since the age of 1970s subcultures.

Redhead (1997b) has gone as far as to describe the late twentieth century as one of 'post youth (studies)'. This may be a little extreme but with increased life expectancy and falling birth rates in the west we undeniably live in an ageing world. The US phrase 'gray power' is used to describe the increased assertion of political rights by the numerically expanded over-65-year-old age group. Of course age is only one of a number of predictors of our lifeworld, alongside other factors including gender, sexuality, ethnicity and, of course, social class: a fact that applies to young and old alike. Whilst in some ways the sociology of ageing is the polar opposite of youth studies, its social, economic and cultural facets make it a topic with much in common with the study of youth.

Changes to the youth labour market rendering it more 'flexible' have for example resulted in an increased dependence of some young people on family and household structures. Manual occupations may be in decline but the service sector jobs that have replaced them cannot be accepted as necessarily spelling 'progress'. In some ways we have seen a move from the profit-centred mass production of Fordism to the profit-centred uncertainty of McDonaldisation with its low status, low wage, insecure 'McJobs'. Exaggerated claims of the improved economic conditions of the post-war west with sustained growth, full employment and higher-than-ever standards of living and salaries, overlook the precarious nature of much youth employment, which musical movements such as grunge and nu metal have been seen as reactions against (Weinstein 1995).

First past the post: postmodern tribes

The same period that has witnessed the demise of subcultural theory has seen postmodernism emerge as a powerful discourse in studies of popular culture.

McRobbie (1994a: 22) for example has enthused of postmodern pastiche: 'the ransacking and recycling of culture, the direct invocation to other texts and other images … can create a vibrant critique rather than an inward-looking, second-hand aesthetics'. In the 1980s and early 1990s in particular, postmodern thinking threatened to inherit the subcultural crown. Postmodern writers reject the all-dominating, overarching idea of a 'parent culture' that subcultural studies assumes and instead place an emphasis on culturally plural fragmentation in the face of the disintegration of structure. Cultural pluralism, the collapse of old structuring structures and the erosion of cultural boundaries are all tenets of postmodernism to be revisited in the following chapter on pop. One post-structuralist alternative post-class conception that has gained increasing recognition in recent years is the theory of postmodern tribes/neo-tribalism which I wish to discuss next. Maffesoli (1996) and Bauman (1987) argue that we are witnessing a disintegration of 'universal' models of thought. Amongst people to have used leading exponent Maffesoli in studies of youth culture and popular music in recent years are Bennett (2000) who explores the dynamic between the local and global in musical youth cultures and Malbon (1999) in his ethnographically focused study of clubbing. Neo-tribalism has been increasingly influential in recent youth studies, both as an alternative to subculture and as a concept used by theorists of new social movements.

The word 'tribe' and its adjective 'tribal' were terms long used by lay people before their adoption and adaptation by sociologists. Tribes are social groupings associated with third world societies, primitivism and savagery. The Oxford Paperback Dictionary (1988: 875) for example states its principal definition of the word as 'a racial group especially in primitive and nomadic culture) living as a community under one or more chiefs'. The second definition alludes to a collective noun. Tribes then imply the duty and hierarchy of inegalitarian, unscientific pre-enlightenment times. The British anthropologist Richard Jenkins (1997) has written a chapter entitled 'From Tribes to Ethnic Groups' where he claims that the use of the word tribe, once common currency in classical anthropology, served to reinforce a model whereby those studied were demarcated as non-civilized. He states 'By the 1960s the notion of "the tribe" was beginning to be replaced by the less embarrassingly colonial "ethnic group" ' (Jenkins 1996: 17). This observation is illuminating because it shows how people operating in different disciplinary boundaries conceive of what are sometimes the same phenomena differently. The anthropological turn away from the use of the word 'tribe' is interesting because in recent years the notion of the tribe has made something of a comeback in sociology, albeit in a newly postmodern way. Maffesoli has been increasingly popular amongst English language theorists following the translation of his (1988) Les Temps des Tribus into English as The Times of the Tribes (Maffesoli 1996a).

Maffesoli (1996a: 40) talks of 'a new (and evolving) trend … in the growth of small groups and networks' and (1996a: 46) the 'growing detachment from the abstract general public sphere'. Bauman's (1987) neo-tribes are formed as concepts rather than integrated social bodies. They are constructed with an inevitable inconclusiveness. Unlike CCCS subcultures which offered collective solutions to problems based on cohesive resistance mounted by their members, neo-tribes are much more temporarily constituted and fluid in composition. Membership of them is easily revocable and divorceable from long-term obligations. Although they may appear to be about singular identity their suppleness allows multiple identifications. However this theory lacks any real grounding. It is left to Rob Shields as author of the preface to Maffesoli's (1996a) English edition to suggest possible examples as he understands them. These include fashion victims, youth subcultures, interest groups, hobbyists, sports enthusiasts, environmental movements and consumer groups, while Rojek (1995: 151) in a similar moment of conjecture tells us 'arts festivals, soccer stands, theatre auditoriums and so on are examples of what Maffesoli has in mind'. Perhaps it is this flexibility of application that has made them so open to interpretation and attractive to writers on youth culture. Cathus (1998), who has worked at the Sorbonne at Paris with Maffesoli, has drawn on Becker's (1963) notion of outsiders in his writing on tribes. Unlike the risk society theorists, Maffesoli sees neo-tribes as collectives signalling a *decline* of individualism.

Maffesoli (1996b) has more recently elaborated on his theory of neo-tribes, which he has explained are based on collective narcissism and characterised by fluidity, fragmentation and temporary togetherness. The idea of emotion is also important to them. Maffessoli (1996b: 50) uses the English word 'feeling', which he sees as a crucial criterion for conveying the quality of interpersonal relations within tribes. This strikes a chord with the key feature of emotional response that many see as central to the reception of pop texts, e.g. Watson (1999). Guidikova and Siurala (2001) interpret Maffesoli's idea of 'feeling' and the emotional dimension as replacing more formalised bonded group ties. However we can see some similarities between the building blocks of Birmingham subculture theory and writing on neo-tribes. While modernity was a rational and individual period, postmodernity exhibits features of empathy and a loss of the collective subject. Postmodern tribes are fragile but the object of strong emotional investment. In keeping with the media-saturated backdrop of postmodern spectacle which renders people unshockable, they no longer cause outrage but become part and parcel of the urban landscape. Examples given include punks and 'kiki-followers', which express uniformity and conformity (Maffesoli 1996b: 50). This seems to suggest ultimate uniformity through supposed diversity. Again, as we will see with various other social theories to be explored in this book, neo-tribes are a response or solution to prevailing times. For example whiteness theory, as propounded by writers such as Dyer (1997) and which I will discuss in more detail in chapter 7, might be explained as a defensive mechanism to assert white identity which has grown out of a need for self-assertion in a climate of equal opportunities.

The Spanish sociologist Carles Feixa (Feixa *et al.* 2001; Feixa 2001) has used Maffesoli in his work on youth cultures in Spain and in fashioning his concept of '*tribus urbanas*' of Spain in the 1980s and 1990s. These are urban tribes that initially emerged following the death of General Franco in 1975. These youth groupings, spanning punks, mods and others, were labelled as tribes by the media. The young people involved do not always approve of being labelled in this way. Feixa for example quotes a teddy boy who retorts 'The only tribes in the world are black tribes from Africa.' Nevertheless Feixa (2001) comes up with a list of characteristics of *tribus urbanas*. They are not rooted in territorial space but instead hold more personal and vague attachments. They are temporary and minority phenomena which are unstable, occasional and discontinuous. Members do not commit entirely to the group and they have steady interactions with culture industries and institutions. Feixa *et al.* (2001: 302) highlight 'the search for a global alternative society and its subsequent isolation in building a "parallel world" ', which they see as deeply contradictory in contemporary tribes which aspire to be social movements. This tension of what the CCCS might have called 'resistance through withdrawal' recurs in the chapters of Part II, particularly in the politics subscribed to by dance music protesters in chapter 5 and in the ambivalent grunge movement which is looked at in chapter 7. In the meantime it can be stated that the postmodern tribe is in many ways an unsatisfactory classificatory system. Like postmodernism at large, its vagueness makes it difficult to 'get a handle on' and it can mean all things to everyone.

From class society to risk society: individualisation and the advent of reflexive modernity

Like the neo-tribal paradigm, the rise of individualisation and risk society theory is synonymous with the increased diversification of late twentieth century lifestyle trajectories. Nielsen (1993: 16) describes individualisation as the 'continuously expanding degree of separation of individual from their traditional ties and restrictions'. This state of affairs has accompanied a general shift in emphasis from a work-based to a more leisure-based society as part of a wider loosening of traditional structure(s) in the increasingly flexible contemporary post-Fordist society. The structure/agency debate informs the notion of individualisation. This recognition of diverse and sometimes conflicting forces of current social and youth transitions differs dramatically from the CCCS conceptualisation of social reproduction where class and gender play a determining role in dictating life trajectories. The theory's leading proponent Ulrich Beck (1992: 87) describes 'a social transformation within modernity, within which people will be set free from the social forms of industrial society'. He refers to traditional social forms, preset life-paths and rites of passage as being rendered obsolete, and puts this on a par with how the Reformation 'set free' individuals from the control of the church. In the place of the old markers of social class, family and strict gender roles it is argued that we are witnessing a 'de-traditionalisation' of society. Beck (1992: 91) declares 'as a result of shifts in the standard of living, subcultural class identities have dissipated, class distinctions based on status have lost their traditional support, processes for the diversification and individualisation of lifestyles have been set in motion'. Unlike the youth conceptualised by the CCCS who were ultimately destined – or even doomed – to reproduce their parents' life-courses, individualisation holds instead that young people are more active in making decisions that affect their lives.

It has been claimed that in a world of increased risk, traditional family, school and work ties are weakened as youth transitions get more complicated and individualised rather than collective (Furlong and Cartmel 1997). Beck (1992: 130–1) accordingly develops the concept of the 'reflexive biography'. Youth become, more than ever, empowered to write their own life history, unconstrained by birth circumstances in an age of de-standardisation. Risk society's enthusiasts are evangelical about its potential. Nielsen (1993: 18) claims that since the 1980s 'the process of individualisation – as a tendency – has left behind the last semblances of traditional ways of living and the limitations they have historically imposed on individual lives'. This suggests a climate of fundamentally altered circumstances rather than continuity with the past. Individualisation is increasingly used by theorists on the subject of school-to-work youth transitions (e.g. Furlong and Cartmel 1997; Dwyer and Wyn 2001; Heath and Kenyon 2001). Taking a rather derogatory tone, Cohen and Ainley (2000: 80) refers to it as 'flavour-of-the-month reflexive and risk sociology'. Indeed a cursory flick through the Routledge sociology catalogue for 2002 reveals a clutch of newly published books employing the use of the term in their titles from one publisher alone (Dwyer and Wyn 2001; Hope and Sparks 2000; Lupton 1999; I. Wilkinson 2001; Van Loon 2002). Many more use the ideas in their content.[1]

A number of factors are seen to contribute to the climate for individualisation, including changed labour market dynamics, education and de-skilling. A loss of traditional security is also brought about by the flexibilisation of working hours and other social structures. This is seen to bring about a 'disembedding' from prescribed norms. Importantly a collapse of the family as an institution is predicted, thus 'individuals inside and outside the family become the agents of their livelihood mediated by the market, as well as of their biological planning and organisation' (Beck 1992: 130). The individual self becomes the reproductive unit for the social in the lifeworld. For Beck (1992: 105), 'People are being removed from the constraints of gender from its quasi feudal attributes and givens, or shaken to the very depths of their souls. … The law that comes over them is "I am I".' Beck recognises however that there are multiple contradictions inherent in individualisation and that not everything can be over-ridden. Gender roles are still defined by the reproductive function of women: an inescapable biological fact. However the sexual revolution and the position of women as economically independent have changed old certainties and reconfigured established models of transition from youth to adulthood. An example can be seen in new non-nuclear forms of domestic living including shared households of independent adults with no dependants (in the traditional sense) or children, complete with their own self-selected hierarchies and internal stratification. Both Furlong and Cartmel

(1997) and Jones and Wallace (1992) talk about 'indeterminate households', the members of which do not follow traditionally ordered templates of leaving education, leaving home, marriage and children. It is not only the growth of tertiary education that has led to an upsurge in these more co-operative living arrangements – there may be economic reasons such as benefit cuts, unemployment and rising rents, and there may also be emotional motors as the household becomes a substitute or surrogate family.

We have seen how youth lifestyles are changing with the advent of individualisation. What then are the implications of the individualisation thesis for youth *culture*? Beck sees individualisation as the basis for new groupings that are less fixed and more haphazard and random than subcultures. He writes:

> increasingly everyone has to choose between different options, including as to which group or subculture one wants to be identified with. In fact one has to choose and change one's social identity as well and take the risks in doing so. In this sense individualisation means the variation and differentiation of lifestyles and forms of life, opposing the thinking behind traditional categories of large group societies – which is to say classes, estates and social stratification.
>
> (Beck 1992: 98)

This differs significantly from the resistance-to-rituals thesis for which the Gramsci–Marx axis of class relations was a key component. Indeed Beck (1992: 97) predicts the 'end of class society' by which 'social classes become emancipated' in an ongoing gradual *process* rather than a single moment. New social moments, de-traditionalised culture and 'new socio-cultural commonalities' (Beck 1992: 90) consequently emerge. Nielsen (1993: 22) talks of

> new post-traditional communities ... movements and community initiatives, collectives, changed ways of living together and living single – week-end kids and ditto parents. By virtue of their focus upon the needs of individuals, these new movements are looser and more fluid than traditional communities, but they are apparently able to function as meaningful settings for self-expression and searching for identity.

Again this sounds like it could apply to post-subcultural youth groupings. Individualisation and the risk society imply a de-standardisation of life-paths intrinsic to the period that Giddens (1990) and Lash (1994) term 'late modernity'. Risks are unevenly distributed, becoming individualised rather than stemming from wider social processes. Accordingly Lash (1994) suggests that we are in a situation where there are 'reflexivity winners' (the new middle class) along with 'reflexivity losers' (the underclass). What is 'bound to happen' becomes unbound and in its place is a dismantling of tradition. The theory dictates that former certainties disappear as people can choose from a growing number of life-course options. Latter-period Frankfurt School scholar Habermas (1981) wrote of a less tradition-bound society in rationalised lifeworlds characterised by subjectivity, self-critical reflexivity and mobilisation. Indeed many of the elements of individualisation and the risk society coincide with Habermas's earlier theory of modernisation and the public sphere. The subcultural explanation for youth cultures was firmly grounded in structuralism and grand narratives, but by the 1980s developments to the debate had moved thinking away from such mechanistic models. Lash (1994: 215) asserts 'If 1968 saw the birth of Marxism in the academy then 1989 surely saw its spluttering collapse.' Beck (1994) goes as far as to talk about a post-political 're-invention of politics'. One could see the rise of non-violent direct action, anti-globalisation movements and the declining turnout at elections in recent years as evidence of this 'new politics'. Some of these ideas will be returned to in chapter 5 when we look at global dimensions of dance music and how it has been used in what the CCCS would have termed 'resistance'.

As with subcultural theory's explanation of social relations, individualisation is a theory that is very much of specific applicability to western welfare states. This can be seen in its central idea of what Beck (1992: 128) calls 'disembedding, *removal* from historically prescribed social forms and commitments in the sense of the traditional contexts of dominance and support (the "liberating dimension")'. Giddens (1990: 21) defines disembedding as 'the "lifting out" of social relations from local contexts of interaction and their restructuring across indefinite spans of time–space'. Needless to say the structures and contexts implied are all part of western modernity as are other elements of its backdrop. Secularism, urbanisation, labour mobility, consumerism, ethnic and cultural diversity, the spread of education and the attendant increase in self-discovery and reflection are all key features of post-enlightenment societies. Individualisation's era is that of reflexive modernity, a stage on from simple modernity. Lash (1994: 115) explains '[T]he second reflexive phase of modernity has set free individuals ... from ... collective and abstract structures such as class, nation, the nuclear family and unconditional belief in the validity of science.' Academic understandings of solidly class-centred youth culture as a mass movement cohering around pop music were always suspect; as much so in the 1970s when they were formulated as today when it has become fashionable to debunk them. However, claims of individualism, like those of neo-tribalism, are also made with little empirical evidence, in the words of Cohen and Ainley (2000: 85) 'good news for armchair critics'. Furthermore, even if we were to accept individualism's cardinal premise that class has ceased to exist, many of the mechanisms that it functioned by are undeniably still in place, e.g. public schools. Youth choices are seen as progressively widening by both individualist and neo-tribal explanations, but whether such expanded horizons are on offer equally to all youth needs careful consideration.

The structure/agency debate is not a new one in sociology. Similarly we could counterpose choice (risk/individualisation) versus constraint (CCCS/ structuralism). Perhaps it is more accurate, however, to state that many of the lifestyle decisions that the young make are based on a mixture of the two. As France (2000: 325) very rightly states 'One person's choice may be another's constraint.' Living in shared adult households or living in the parental home into adulthood rather than setting up an independent household is an example. Jones and Wallace (1992) come up with a list of deficiencies of both individualisation and of what they call the social reproduction model of the CCCS before concluding that neither is ultimately satisfactory. For France (2000: 325), 'Risk and risk-taking ... has to be recognised as a negotiated process which is a product of social interactions.' If CCCS-type understandings of social reproduction were narrowly focused on street corners, theories of individualisation and the risk society seemingly offer the possibility of choice on every street corner. A middle way needs to be found between the two: a mixed model incorporating elements of both and taking account of other forms of difference. The experience of mass migration has been a defining one which has indelibly marked global geopolitics in the post-war era, particularly in the period since the 1960s. Many of western Europe's diverse multicultural populations of the present reflect colonial pasts. It is the young people who are the product of these shifts that have been important shapers of contemporary youth cultural formations.

Youth studies and ethnic questions

Despite the fact that, statistically, ethnic minority populations tend to be relatively young in terms of age profile, ethnic minority youth were relatively neglected in the CCCS subcultural studies of the 1970s, as we have seen in chapter 1. When minority youth did attract the attentions of the CCCS subculturalists, this was usually in only a partial way. The generic process of 'othering', defined by Blommaert and Verschueren (1998: 20) as 'abnormalization of the immigrant', seems to inform academic treatments of minority youth. CCCS treatments of ethnicity were largely confined to the white objectification of African Caribbean style. Hebdige's (1979) ultimately unsatisfactory 'phantom history' of race relations since the war implicitly sees white youth subcultural styles on one side or other of a symbolic acceptance or refusal of black culture. This intervention was followed by Stuart Hall et al.'s Policing the Crisis (1978), whose authors used Gramsci to discuss the moral panic attached to black youth and mugging. Highlighting the way that youth is a particularly good 'testing ground' for social theory, Reimer (1995: 128) has claimed 'it is during the restless and mobile period of youth that the need and desire to test the new and carve out individual identities is strongest'. Identity crisis, however, has been a recurrent theme in many studies of minority youth. Early studies of Asian youth for example stereotyped them as being caught 'between two cultures' (Anwar 1976; Watson 1978) in a negative over-simplification. Lawrence (1982: 132–3), in his Empire Strikes Back contribution, claimed 'theorists have mislocated the "identity crises" in the black communities ... it is because black youth know very well who they are that the heavy hand of the state has come down with such force upon them'. This shows CCCS-style Marxist political constructions placed upon ethnic minority youth very much in action. Recent years however have seen a growing number of studies examining the interplay between ethnicity and youth cultural practices and preferences.

Just as the youth-centredness of subcultural studies was criticised in chapter 1, Roxy Harris (1996: 399) has bemoaned the lack of serious attention afforded to black people at large in cultural studies, arguing that the agency of older people is overlooked at the expense of a focus on spectacular youth: 'most of the work has centred on analysis of the highly visible, overtly rebellious, reactive section of black youth ... in relation to policing, crime, youth styles, music, language and schooling'. This point mirrors criticisms of CCCS youth studies and the lack of interest in conformist youth (Clarke 1985). CCCS subcultural studies saw youth as counterpoised with 'parent culture'. Second generation minority youth in particular have such critically different experiences from their parents, so explanations of 'generation gap' are potentially of more pertinence to them than to white youth, yet there is still the sense that sociologists have often overstated such theories in relation to all young people. In a related argument, Wright (2000: 271) criticises academia for the lack of serious anthropological attention it has paid to black cultural practice and its tendency instead to leave black Britons 'relegated to the realm of sociology crystalised around issues of racism and social disadvantage, thereby disregarding the dynamism and vibrancy of Afro-Carribean life'. Harris contends that a result of the over-concentration on youth is that the actions and perspectives of the adult black population have been ignored and any agency on their part has tended to be overlooked as writers have marvelled at the spectacular subcultural styles created by their children. Certainly this argument has some applicability also to the situation of British Asian youth, whose parents are commonly assumed to be quiescent by comparison to their bhangra/Asian Underground exemplifying selves, as we will see in chapter 4.

Nevertheless, in terms of academic attention, mainstream Afro-Carribean youth have fared comparatively better than 'Asians'[2] if we consider them alongside one another, although the recent advent of the emergent area of South Asian studies has made up some lost ground. The literature tends to 'other' Asian youth. The few appearances that Asian youth do make in the classic CCCS texts tend to portray them as victims of white skinhead aggression in accounts of the white working class practice of 'Paki-bashing' (Clarke 1976; Hebdige 1979; Pearson 1976) which are entirely consistent with the 'resistance through rituals' agenda of subculture theory. As we have seen in the previous chapter, the actions of Paki-basher perpetrators, termed 'magical solutions' (Phil Cohen 1972), are seen as an almost understandable heroic working class response by threatened communities caught in the midst of economic and social change. An alleged unwillingness on the part of Asians to surrender their differences and integrate into mainstream society is also seen as a problem. Hebdige (1979: 58) declares

Less easily assimilated than the West Indians into the host community ... sharply differentiated not only by racial characteristics but by religious rituals, food taboos and a value system which encouraged deference, frugality and profit motive, the Pakistanis were singled out for the brutal attentions of skinheads, black and white alike.

It seems that the ideal then is to be absorbed by the benevolent British host, something that Asian youth are seen as incapable of. Asian youth have, like Afro-Carribeans, largely been treated in problematic terms; with most analyses concentrating on racism and race relations (Cohen and Bains 1988), at best ignoring – and at worst precluding – any possible involvement in youth culture. Rex (1982), quoted in CCCS (1983: 123), for example commented, 'Ecstatic working class youth culture appears doubly dangerous [to Asian youth]. It is corrupting the family values and damaging any prospects of instrumental success in the culture to which the immigrant has necessarily and seriously to adjust.' Underpinning these and other similar remarks are the idea of a set of 'Asian values' that are wedded to tradition and spanning religious practice, arranged marriage, female subordination and a resistance to change, i.e. integration.

However just as youth cultures are not static and unchanging, their study too has waxed and waned both in terms of the volume of output and its nature in terms of the subjects under study and theoretical approach taken. After long being at best an adjunct to 'black' youth, with the exception of mentions of 'Paki-bashing' (Clarke 1976; Hebdige 1979: 56; Pearson 1976), a number of studies of Asian youth (Anwar 1998; Back 1996; Bhatti 1999; Gillespie 1995; Hutnyk, Sharma and Sharma 1996; Maira 2002) have gone some way to redressing the balance by addressing the subject of Asian youth outside the narrow parameters of 'racism studies' and thus often striking something of a discordant note in the all-too-easy neat interlocking subcultural fit between youth and class. Interestingly, throughout 1997–8, the Sunday supplements accompanying the UK broadsheet press repeatedly claimed in quasi-sociological speak that young British Asians were moving 'from the margins to the mainstream'[3] in music (Cornershop's 1998 'Brimful of Asha', which made Tjinder Singh the first openly Asian performer to reach number one in the UK charts[4]) and comedy (the BBC series *Goodness Gracious Me*) with phrases like 'Asian invasion' and 'Hindi-pendence'. The film *East is East* (1999) also attracted similar hyperbole. Although the post-1997 Blair government's 'Cool Britannia' project which aimed to update outmoded images of the UK acknowledged British Asians, the term turned out to be short-lived. More lasting has been the changing public perception of Asians from migrants to settled population. Owusu (1999: 9) writes of this same process happening in relation to longer-established blacks and Carribeans in the 1970s: 'Unlike their parents, the second generation of black youth did not see themselves as "tempo-rary guests" of Her Majesty's government. They were not here to work and eventually return "home" to the Caribbean or Africa. Britain was their home and they were "Here to Stay!"'

Despite Sue Benson's memorable phrase 'Asians Have Culture, West Indians Have Problems' (quoted by both Alexander (2000) and B.S. Wright (2000: 286)), studies of race and racism still far outweigh academic considerations of ethnic minority cultural practices in the case of both Asians and blacks. Can we then use the word 'black' in a political sense to apply to the two? In the UK the years since the 1970s have seen the disaggregation of 'black' as a term to connote the separate categories of 'black' and 'Asian'. Gilroy (1993b: 93) regrets this as 'the sacrifice of significant political advantages', although back in *The Empire Strikes Back* he enthused that 'Youth culture has ... created an important space for dialogue between black youth from the different communities' (Gilroy 1982: 295). Baumann (1996) suggests that Asians dislike using the term black in self-appellation due to a percieved political subordination of blacks and, in a variant of hooks' argument, the conflation of dark skin and low caste. Gilroy (1993b: 94) teasingly ends his comparison of black and Asian Britain with the question 'What do we say when the political and cultural gains of the emergent black Brits go hand in hand with a further marginalization of "Asians" in particular and Muslims in particular?' The answer is not easy to arrive at. However we should also be aware of structural differences within even these categories.

Paralleling the scant existing literature on middle class youth at large, the black and Asian middle classes are greatly under-researched and yet growing in number (Robinson 1990). Peach (1996: 36) identifies a 'progressive outward diffusion' or displacement of Britain's inner city ethnic population from traditional 'black' areas such as Paddington and Brixton to suburban Brent and Croydon. In East London, new Asian-chosen leafy locations of settlement, e.g. Gants Hill, Redbridge and Ilford, are located to the east of more traditional inner city 'Asian' areas such as Tower Hamlets or Newham. Just as it is important to bear in mind that the catgory 'British Asians' does not consist simply of imported cheap industrial labour (it also includes the self-employed, from the small retailers to the big business-wallahs ennobled by Major and Blair,[5] and professionals, particularly in the NHS), Asian suburban drift is not a universal trend. Peach (1996) points to a bifurcation between British Asian communities whereby Britain's Bangladeshis and Pakistanis face an 'Irish future' as working class and council housed while the Indian population face a 'Jewish future' as owner-occupier professionals following the Jews who migrated from the East End to London suburbs such as Finchley and Golders Green (Kosamin and DeLange 1980). As with the early CCCS commentary, it is claimed that blacks are more integrated whereas Bangladeshis and Pakistanis are concentrated in ghetto style 'ethnic villages' in West Yorkshire, the West Midlands and East London. Modood *et al.* (1997) found that differences between ethnic groups are now more significant than any black–white divide, with Bangladeshis as the underachievers. Although the Irish/Jewish argument recognises differences between Asians, it is still grossly oversimplified. Within communities there is a high level of internal differentiation, e.g. the academically achieving young British Bengali (Eade and Zaman 1993) who contradicts government statistics which consistently show young Bengalis as least likely to succeed in the educational system.

New ethnicities and postcolonial times

Postcolonial studies is a key constituent part of the niche cultural studies that have flourished in recent years. Authors such as Appadurai (1990), Bhabha (1990), Gilroy (1987; 1993a; 1993b; 1993c), Hall (1988; 1991), Mercer (1994), Said (1978) and Spivak (1988) are associated with this movement. Although there are a diversity of approaches and positions within its boundaries, postcolonial theory questions the western enlightenment tradition of progress and universalism. Postcolonial theorists broadly situate cultural politics at the centre of black representation. They share a recognition of the continued effects of colonialism on contemporary political and cultural practices as well as the realisation of resulting new cultural forms. The idea of diaspora and diaspora culture is a key one here. Mercer primarily uses examples from film and pop video in his writing, and defines diaspora culture as 'the expressive codes of something immediately legible in new black hairstyles, and audible in rap, hip-hop and breakdance' (1994: 19). These cultural forms eschew any singular notions of cultural 'purity' and instead are the product of fusing, mixing and creolisation. Hip-hop culture will be returned to in chapter 6 of this book. In the meantime it is worth saying that diaspora cultures are unashamedly postcolonial and dynamic. It is the modern technologies of travel and communications that engender the possibility of diaspora communities – with the increased ease of air travel having predated the equally important emergence of satellite television and the web. These technologies give rise to complex cultural flows. The mass media for example allows diasporic communities scattered across the globe to sustain ties with their countries of origin and thereby create new lifestyles and identities. The cultural fusion and hybridity of identities envisaged by such cultures are not the product of assimilationist models of culture but the creation of new combinations.

The most sophisticated theoretical treatment that diaspora cultures have received is Gilroy's (1993a) notion of the 'Black Atlantic'. This goes some way to transcend conceptions of culture that are restricted to nation-states. The black people who inhabit African and western identities are seen to be in constant negotiation of a process of 'double consciousness'. The Black Atlantic itself is a site of complex diasporic movements which reflect African cultural flows across America, Europe and the Carribean. This builds on the notion that people can move across boundaries and as a result retain multiple affiliations. Whilst the memory of slavery is the backdrop to the Black Atlantic, Gilroy (1993c: 8) argues that it is post-war deracination and subsequent experiences of racism and anti-racism that remain more relevant to the experiences of post-war blacks, commenting 'If these populations are unified at all, it is more by the experience of migration rather than the memories of slavery and plantation society.'

Botanical metaphors are prevalent in postcolonial theory. The term 'hybridity', meaning the cross-breeding of animal or plant species, is frequently evoked alongside complexity, diversity and fluidity to describe cultural forms which exist as a result of migration. Bhabha (1990: 211) has remarked that 'the importance of hybridity is not to be able to trace movements from which the third emerges, rather hybridity ... is the "third space" which enables other positions to emerge'. Others talk of 'roots' and 'routes'. Diaspora cultures are able to remain in contact simultaneously with different points across the earth's surface, linking east and west horizontally so that one-way uprooting is no longer a reality. The concept of the 'rhizome', another postcolonial favourite, has been popularised by Deleuze and Guattari (1972; 1983). This concept derives from the botanical term for a root system with horizontal lines of connection, spreading across the ground from several points as opposed to growing downward from a single point. The idea of the rhizome challenges the idea of simple colonial relationships that one might presume of cultural hegemony. Cultural power can be seen as being exercised laterally rather than in a top-down way. Back (1996: 185) writes: 'A rhizome has no beginning or end, it is always in the middle. The usefulness of the notion of rhizome is that it provides a way of describing forms of cultural inter-being.' Elsewhere Deleuze and Guattari's concept of the body without organs has been used in rave theory (Jordan 1995; Reynolds 1998a; 1998b). Back (1996: 245) reworks the Deleuze and Guattarian rhizome into his own concept of the 'cultural intermezzo' in stating that 'the rhizomatics of contemporary youth culture are not stable and the potential for invoking racism remains within these vernacular cultures'.

Global youth, transnational culture

The coming of multiculturalism is perceived by some as an opportunity, yet for others diasporic communities present a threat, be they Asians and Afro-Carribeans in the UK, Magrebians in France, Turkish 'guest' workers in Germany or settlers from Somalia and Eastern Europe in Scandinavia. There is no clear agreement about how these migrations and the cultural transformations implicated by them should be managed. Strategies of multicultural tolerance and cultural integration are both based to some extent on ethnocentric assumptions as they construct the host and settler communities as distinct and separate. Arguably society always needs new 'others', hence the rise of islamaphobia following the end of the Cold War and the terrorist attacks of 11 September 2001. Parekh (2000: 37) remarks that in the UK context, 'assimilation has come to be seen as an impossible price to pay – blackness and Asianness are non-tradeable'. Nonetheless, although assimilationalist policies such as the French model of *intégration* have for many years not been outwardly promoted in the UK, they do appear to be making a comeback with pronouncements such as those of David Blunkett that riots in northern England by young British-born Asians in 2001 were a result of the perpetrators not being assimilated enough. Furthermore it has always been an unwritten rule that the 'success' of race relations has been measured in hegemonically constructed terms of how 'harmoniously' immigrants have integrated into mainstream host society. Both integration and the tolerance of cultural pluralism are usually practised alongside each other then, the two ethics merging into one another.

The British bhangra music looked at in chapter 4 is, it will be argued, redefining what it means to be British. The same argument can be advanced about the indigenous rap scenes existing in several non-US national contexts. Morley and Robins (1996: 122) muse 'What does it mean to be European in a continent coloured not only by the cultures of its former colonies but also by American and now Japanese cultures?' It is not new or in any way revelatory to point out that European societies have long been coloured by migration. Tea, seen as a quintessentially English drink, is patently obviously of Indian or Chinese origin. The culture of tea-drinking also existed in Asia long before it developed in Britain. However, the nature of migration has altered irrevocably in the twentieth century. Communities are no longer simply setting sail to carve out a new life unrelated to the old and permanently cutting ties to the homeland in the process. Appadurai (1990) has written of ethnoscapes, technoscapes and mediascapes as contemporary manifestations of cultural flows. These are fluid as opposed to fixed, implying constant movement and dynamism. Along with finanscapes and ideoscapes, this set of cultural dimensions describes how people, ideas and capital can circulate around the globe on a scale unseen before. Air travel, broadband media and telecommunications are obvious examples of how cultural flows are two-way processes whereby the country/culture of origin can be constantly kept in touch with. Indeed such notions of the transmission of culture are complicated as it becomes increasingly difficult to trace a 'pure' point of origin of transnational cultural forms.

Some tentative conclusions

Importantly, links can be made between all of the notions discussed in this chapter. We have seen the breakdown of the automatic presumption that youth equates automatically with rebellion and resistance to the hegemonic order. Both postmodernists and reflexive modernisers incorporate the decline of the nuclear family, community and class in their analyses. Diaspora cultures and the kind of subject positions adopted by postcolonial theorists offer a self-conscious critique of earlier migration studies in sociology which seemed to explain reductively external population movement between societies in terms of either 'push factors' or 'pull factors'. We should now focus on paradigm shifts among the second generation and beyond. There has been an upsurge of religious affirmation and identification by sections of western minority populations against a backdrop of an increasingly atheist and secular outlook adopted by the majority populations. This then presents a challenge for the management of multiculturalism in the years ahead.

Where do these newer approaches connect with the subcultural studies of the Birmingham CCCS? Some of subculture theory's deficiencies have not been adequately rectified in these diversifying discourses and alternative explanations. The neglect of women and non-white groups is a valid criticism of the CCCS's work, however much individualisation theory could also be accused of this trait. Beck's (1992: 119) notions of 'new forms of living *beyond male and female roles*' and equality of men and women are in some ways wildly optimistic, and he himself recognises the difficulty in achieving them. The specific situation of women seems to be elbowed aside by such rhetoric. Elsewhere discussion of ethnic minorities is a rare occurrence, besides Lash (1994) who makes a brief reference to diaspora culture.[6] The cultural turn has been an important development in sociology but this should not make us lose sight of demographic shifts. Jones and Wallace (1992: 152) predict that on some fronts individualisation spells polarisation and conclude, 'Overall, a more protracted and protected youth may be an emerging response to recent social, economic and legislative trends.' In simple demographic terms, the ethnic minority populations of Western European nation-states are projected to continue to rise. On some estimates, by 2011 a fifth of London's population will be drawn from ethnic minorities (Aspinall 2000), with this designation accounting for over half in some areas, based on natural expansion as a result of an ageing population along with zero migration. In addition to this, mixed marriage and a growth in the number of people seeking asylum as a result of ethnic conflict will further change the ethnic composition of societies traditionally taken to be 'whitefaced'.

Encouragingly, an incorporation of the individualist concept of 'reflexive biography' (Beck 1992: 130–1) into further youth studies should allow a better consideration of ethnic minority and female involvement in youth culture. A move away from the structures on which the social sciences traditionally focus (organisations, class, etc.), should entail a shift from the youth-favoured foci of unemployment and football, which can be held partly responsible for producing understandings of male youth culture as 'the norm'. Indeed it is feminists and black cultural theorists who have used autobiographical approaches and drawn on oral history in their work in the 'cultural turn' quest to place ethnicity and gender on a similar footing to class in identity terms. The turn of the century has seen cultural studies become less Brit-focused in outlook than it was at its outset (Cohen and Ainley 2000). We should also be aware of the degree of difference within crude categorisations and of the multiplicity of identities.[7] Diversity should be recognised in majority populations too. Giroux (1997: 200) argues for a postmodern politics of cultural difference, stating that 'national identity must be inclusive and informed by a democratic pluralization of cultural identities'. Donald has stated: 'The "national" defines the culture's unity by differentiating it from other cultures, by marking its boundaries; a fictional unity of course, because the "us" on the inside is always differentiated' (quoted in Morley and Robins 1996: 45). Whiteness, for example, is an ethnic group that many people do not think of as such, as in countries such as the UK and USA it is a majority identity. Chapter 7 will look at how whiteness is reflected and refracted in the musical styles Britpop and grunge.

The overriding theme that I want to emphasise in this chapter is the hollowness of homogeneity. Subcultural theory overemphasised the differences between subcultural groups whilst ascribing them an overly high degree of internal homogeneity. Contrary to this mythical picture, modern, plural societies are instead characterised by a high degree of heterogeneity. The so-called 'Asian' community is a case in point. It is highly internally diversified, covering a wide range of linguistic, religious, social and cultural practices, not to mention a vast geographical base, spanning East Africa as well as the Indian subcontinent rather than the somewhat misleading 'Asia' of its name. The term is then at once both narrow and wide. Stereotypes are pervasive, partly because they are quite often unconsciously evoked; however, they can diminish over time. Asian youth disturbances in the UK during 2001 might go some way towards reversing the received wisdom of Asians as forever exclusively passive victims and drawing attention to the diverse nature of this 'community'. Our rethinking should extend beyond the false binaries of child/adult to think of 'youth', beyond centre/margins, coloniser/colonised, etc. We should also attempt to look at the wider cultural influences on the multifaceted lifeworlds of young people. The neologism 'glocalisation' fuses elements of the global and local and is already being used in academic work on youth cultures (Pilkington 2001; Mitchell 2001). Class, like the existence of gender, has not simply ceased to exist. It is more accurate to recognise that class and gender will forever be mediated by geography/locality, work/education, interactions with families and other relationships, forming complex networks of social processes.

As this chapter has begun to indicate, social theory relating to youth and popular music over the last century has not developed in a particularly planned or systematic fashion. While textbooks have a tendency to compartmentalise ideas into some sort of order – usually chronological – social theory has in the main evolved in a much more irregular and arbitrary fashion than some of the secondary literature would suggest. Quite often theorists looking at youth from different perspectives can come up with completely different accounts with very little overlap, although ostensibly they are looking at the same subject.[8] This chapter has begun to sketch out the space 'beyond subculture' by filling in some of the gaps in the work of the CCCS. The next chapter turns to another aspect of youth culture neglected by the Birmingham subculturalists: pop music.

3

THEORISING YOUTH POP MUSIC:

meanings, production and consumption beyond subculture

> Rock, initially at any rate was a contemporary incitement to mind-
> less fucking and arbitrary vandalism: screw and smash music.
>> (George Melly 1970: 34)

> Every generation sends a hero up the pop charts.
>> (Paul Simon 1986)

This chapter will look at various different methodological approaches that have been taken in the study of pop thus introducing some of the broader themes running through the rest of the book. Although pop has proved to be durable and influential in contemporary society, half a century of pop history means that the past figures more prominently in pop than ever before and that youth can no longer have an exclusive claim on pop music. We will begin by considering the relationship between youth and pop in the twenty-first century and just how sustainable this is.

Theorising pop: potential problems

Both the interchangeably used terms 'pop' and 'rock' have long been seen as being umbilically linked to youth[1] and western post-war youth culture, alongside fashion and the intangible attribute of 'attitude'. The original pop–youth paradigm is well established (Grossberg 1994). The Who in 1965 concluded the now classic 'My Generation' with the immortal line 'Hope I die before I get old.' The impli-cation was that to die young and beautiful is preferable to rotting away old and decrepit in an old people's 'institution'.[2] Kurt Cobain, Tupac Shakur, Sid Vicious and Jimi Hendrix, who all lived up to this ideal, became instant youth martyr figures; the face of each launching a thousand tee-shirts displaying their birth and death dates. Pop's denial of the past is about the here and now (Bloomfield 1991; Melly 1970). As Frith (1983: 9) claimed, 'Britain's few academic theories of rock have emerged from studies of youth ... the history of British pop has always been a history of British youth styles. This reflects a general cultural point.'

How amenable is pop to academic study? As far as the CCCS went, none of the chapters of Hall and Jefferson (1976) have much to say on the subject with the brief exception of Hebdige on mod. Popular wisdom dictates that there is an inherent anti-intellectual bent in the very idea of popular culture, of which pop music is a constituent component. Chambers (1986: 13) writes that popular culture is 'flexibly tuned to the present, rejects the narrow access to the cerebral worlds of official culture'. Academic work on pop is frequently viewed with lofty contempt by educational traditionalists in keeping with accusations of 'dumbing down' in recent years across the social sciences. Shuker (1994: 76) remarks that: 'the steady stream of popular culture/media courses in the 1990s is still seen by many as a "soft option", lacking the intellectual rigour of historically legitimised areas and topics of academia'. Frith (1983: 3) has described how he had to academically legitimate his classic *Sociology of Rock* (1978) with 'hard' quantitative data, to counteract accusations of being seen as 'sloppy': 'I armed my text with footnotes and statistics: everything I said was properly documented, every assertion "proved".'

An allied argument is that pop is the stuff of emotions and thus is unsuitable as a subject of study in lecture theatres and seminar rooms (Watson 1999). The same point, however, could apply to literary studies. Indeed academic analysis of pop has often concentrated on analysing pop lyrics in the same way as the treatment of written texts (Blake 1997a: 7–13). Redhead (1995: 91) points out 'fortysomething and fiftysomething academics' attempts to utilise such rock culture for pedagogic purposes can seem so outdated in a fast-moving pop culture as to appear farcical however well-intentioned'. The following two comments from journalists voice the opinion that pop analysis destroys its 'magic'. Roy Carr, executive editor of IPC magazines, who has been offered – and has declined – various positions from US universities on the strength of his related books (Carr 1996; Carr and Tyler 1978; Carr and Dellar 1986; Carr and Farren 1994), has commented: 'You can intellectualise anything. It takes the whole joy of it and turns it into academia. The whole idea of "rock studies" is, I think, a bit of a red herring.'[3] *Times* rock columnist, Caitlin Moran has made the same point:

> Pop music shouldn't be understood. It should be mysterious. In order to understand it and place it in confines and constructs you can only lose the passion. I'd rather blindly believe. You can't stand by and dissect it. If you plant seeds in the garden you can't dig them up after two weeks to see what happened to them. They'll die. You just sit back and say 'this is ace'.[4]

Indeed, extracts from the learned journal *Popular Music* have appeared in the UK satirical magazine *Private Eye*'s 'Pseud's Corner' column, usually reserved for examples of pretentious prose found in mainstream media. Arguably the pop music of today is the classical music of tomorrow so it is entirely appropriate that the popular musical canon with a significant history behind it is now being legitimated by academic study. There has always been a time-lag between the evolving of youth musical cultures 'in action' and their objectification by the media – a process which takes even longer for academics to catch up with. The fact that both punk and dance music culture have been the subject of academic and non-academic book-length accounts celebrating their twentieth and tenth anniversaries respectively[5] demonstrates how two once supposedly ephemeral and threatening musical styles are now part of an accepted orthodoxy of 'culturally significant' musics with academic histories.

Popular music studies is often demeaningly characterised as 'journalistic'. Yet the boundaries between the categories of academia and journalism are not always clearly demarcated and fixed, as can be seen in the coinciding content of the popular anthology *The Faber Book of Pop* (Savage and Kureshi 1995) and its academic equivalent *On Record* (Frith and Goodwin 1990). Hebdige and Reynolds (from academia and journalism respectively) are featured in both. Bracewell (1997: 215) sees this convergence as the coming of age of 'a tertiary-educated sensibility that was equally related to the techniques of literary consumption and the manipulation of pop glamour'. The music writer Simon Reynolds' (1990; 1995; 1998a; 1998b) academically informed prose has extended into book-length accounts that cite rock journalists and French post-structuralists in equal measure. *The Sex Revolts* (Simon Reynolds and Joy Press 1995), for example, is a 'psychoanalysis of rebellion' in gendered rock and roll relations drawing on Deleuze and Guattari, Nietzsche, The Stranglers and dub reggae among others. A web review of the US edition of Reynolds' historical account of rave (1998b) criticises his 'pseudo-intellectual speak' arguing 'This guy obviously just read Baudrillard's "Simulacra and Simulacrum" one night while wasted and thinks that throwing around any polysyllabic nonsense qualifies one as an intellectual. (Really, we're dealing with a somewhat anti-intellectual topic here.)'[6] The inexorable spread of cultural theory is itself evident from such a statement. Frith (1996: 180) extends the argument of subculturalists playing out their fascination with what they themselves cannot be (i.e. working class, deviant youth) in their work to theorisations of pop:

> the cultural study of popular music has been, in effect, an anxiety driven search by radical intellectuals and rootless academics for a model of consumption – for the perfect consumer, the subcultural idol, the mod, the punk, the cool commodity fetishist, the organic intellectual of the high street who can stand in for them.

Here subcultural studies academics are seen as rebels *manqué* in the same way as pop journalism is unkindly seen as the vocation of the 'failed' musician.

The fact that the study of pop music is now an undergraduate subject in a number of countries is in many ways an inescapable inevitability.[7] A range of positions have been taken up by theorists of popular music culture. Swiss *et al.* (1998) usefully identify three main modes of looking at pop: (i) institutional analysis; (ii) textual analysis – spanning both musicology and lyrical content; and (iii) ethnographic analysis. Within these three basic vertical headings we can locate other horizontal cross-cutting treatments of pop focusing on areas such as policy, technology, identity and history. The content in the remaining chapters touches on aspects of each of these broad traditions.[8] In sum, I would argue that pop *is* significant enough to be taken seriously both culturally and industrially.

Musical meanings I: the Frankfurt School

'To persist with the Frankfurt School is to stay with an approach which is both narrow and outmoded', Strinati (1995: 52) has provocatively declared. Members of the Frankfurt school, who came largely from the discipline of philosophy, included Walter Benjamin, Max Horkheimer, Herbert Marcuse and Jurgen Habermas. Their influences included Marx – who was simultaneously both drawn on and critiqued – as well as Kant, Hegel and the Hungarian Marxist Georg Lukács (Sedgwick and Edgar 1999: 435). For them the rationalisation of cultural practices and preferences with the advent of mass culture had negative consequences in perpetuating consumer capitalism at the expense of the autonomy of individuals. In their opinion, under capitalism culture was ultimately reduced to the commodity form with the sole function of being traded for profit, i.e. the use-value of cultural products became subsumed with their mass production. This much maligned intellectual tradition provides some of the foundational texts in the study of popular culture, in particular the work of Theodor Adorno (1990; 1991 [1941]) on pop music as part of 'the culture industry'.

In the first half of this century Adorno wrote (1991 [1941]: 87): 'What parades as progress in the culture industry, as the incessantly new which it offers up, remains the disguise for an eternal sameness.' In other words the standardising effects of 'the culture industry' deceive people that they are presented with choice, when actually the result is growing conformity through supposed individualisation. This argument was made with reference to a range of popular cultural artefacts including Hollywood cinema and mass-produced motor cars, which served only to fool consumers that such products were different from one another when they were in fact unrelentingly standardised. Above all Adorno (1991 [1941]: 33) argued that music's industrial production killed its meaning: 'all contemporary musical life is dominated by the commodity form, with all the last pre-capitalist residues having been eliminated'. Of course with the advent of recording technologies, all types of music are now subject to this mass production and Adorno's observations are in part linked to an anti-pop snobbishness. His argument has been influential however. Clarke and Critcher (1985: 118) have for example written that the ' "freely choosing" rational consumer is a myth – choice in market societies is structured by a whole series of powerful determinants'. Industrial forces, that limit what is available in the marketplace, are given as an example alongside constraints on people's purchasing power, both economic and in terms of the leisure time available to them. It was a central contention of Adorno (1991 [1941]: 31) that 'The star principle has become totalitarian. The reactions of the listeners appear to have no relation to the playing of the music.'

Early rave DJs, shadowy figures hidden away from view, but nonetheless commanding enormous recognition and adulation, contradict this claim of over four decades earlier. We will return to dance music in chapter 5.

The Frankfurt School is often characterised by critics as élitist (Strinati 1995). Indeed Adorno (1991 [1941]: 31) drew a distinction between 'classical music' and 'light music', making his own preference for the former as the superior form abundantly clear. Adorno's (1991 [1941]: 45) snobbish disregard for the guitar and banjo as 'infantile instruments … intended for players who cannot read the notes' can be attacked. Proponents of punk saw its anti-musical virtuosity as one of its most attractive features, where enthusiasm was accorded a greater value than access to musical training. Savage (1991: 280) even includes the now infamous diagram and instructions from punk fanzine *Sideburns*, 'This is a chord, this is another, this is a third. NOW FORM A BAND', in his history of punk *England's Dreaming*. The words are accompanied by three touchingly low-tech, hand-drawn line guitar chord diagrams of the sort that Adorno so hated. Modern-day developments such as Cubase software and sampling technology are usually viewed as positive in music-making as they have de-mystifying, democratising properties potentially de-standardising music production to make it a more participatory experience. Adorno's views on music consumption deny listeners agency, seeing them as powerless to resist mass culture. Strinati (1995: 78) comments: 'Obviously audiences are by no means as powerful as the industries which produce popular culture but this is no reason to conceive of them as "cultural dopes".' Agency seems to have been a problem for the Frankfurt School, as it was for the CCCS subculturalists.

Another important criticism of Adorno's popular music theory is its generality and vagueness of scope and the fact that it is unsubstantiated by empirical evidence or even specific examples. Amalgamating all popular music into one mass is clearly unsatisfactory. Longhurst (1995) points out that people will listen to Take That and Frank Zappa differently. Even within music genres there can be a great degree of internal diversification, as we will see in Part II. In many ways Adorno talks about the culture industry as if it were part of a Fordist model of production. The economic system of Fordism (which takes its name from the manufacture of the Model T Ford motor car) entails mechanised factory production emanating from a single site. Pop, however, could be seen as being in keeping with a post-Fordist economy, as it springs from multiple sources. The basic motive of sociability that often motivates amateur musicians is shown in ethnographic studies of recent years (Finnegan 1989; Cohen 1991; Fornäs *et al.* 1995). The social actors in these studies would not characterise themselves as passive victims powerless against the flattening process of mass culture.

Some of Adorno's claims make him an easy target when writing from the standpoint of the twenty-first century. However, much of the Frankfurt School's critics' distrust of authoritarianism and the state's power to exercise social control can be explained by contextualising their historical moment of emergence in fascist Germany, which they were then forced to flee for the increasingly centralised USA (Strinati 1995: 54; Longhurst 1995: 13). Yet there are counter-examples to the centralisation of arts provision in the contemporary world. World music is something that has spread in availability at a time when the onward march of multinational ownership of the music industry has continued apace, a paradox grappled with in chapter 4.

Musical meanings II: subcultures and pop

Despite the CCCS's relative neglect of pop, subcultural theory has often been applied to youth musical movements. For example Redhead (1990: 87) wrote retrospectively: 'Punk is the best example ... [of] ... subculture, style and sound shrink wrapped for the pop culture archive. It represents not the end of the pop/rock/youth culture nexus but its most perfect product.' Wicke (1987: 87) recognises the difficulty with the in-built assumptions of homogeneity presup-posed by subcultural theorists: 'teenage subcultures with their class-specific structures and commercial mass culture, mainly produced by the media, do not form a rigid contrast to one another. They rather permeate one another, though in a highly contradictory way, and simply represent a differing application, influ-enced by class contrasts, of the *same* cultural objects, musical forms and institutions.' Contemporary musical cultures are intersecting and overlapping with one another, and are thus more diverse than normative notions of sub-cultures allow.

Hebdige (1979: 87), one of the few CCCS theorists to deal with music as a subject, wrote: 'it was fitting that the punks should present themselves as "degenerates", as signs of the highly publicised decay which perfectly repre-sented the atrophied condition of Great Britain'. The *NME* (5 December 1998), twenty years on from punk's apex, commented in terminology that betrayed its probable writing by a cultural studies graduate: 'Speed-gobbling DIY suburban folk-devils ... erupted all over the world like millions of malignant mushrooms in the wake of the 1977 punk rock explosion. Punk was probably the last yoofkult [*sic*] that genuinely did shock vicars shitless.' Every youth style since has had an air of anti-climax about it as sociologists await 'the new punk' (Grossberg 1986; McRobbie 1993: 310; Redhead 1995: 88). According to Frith (1990: 179):

> The sociological fantasy that pop musicians could be some sort of organic intellectuals was remarkably stubborn; it dominated initial left-wing responses to punk, and it was only when the material basis of the fantasy – youth as class – broke down in the late 1970s recession, that different ways of conceiving pop and politics became attractive.

Among these new interpretations of musical meaning was the attachment of post-modern social and cultural theory to pop preferences and practices.

47

Musical meanings III: postmodernism in pop

The term 'postmodernism' is not easily defined, as it is used to variously connote a number of characteristics which do not occur in any systematic or consistent fashion (Best 2002). Initially an architectural term, among its key features are the collapse of traditional social class-based formations, old high versus low culture dichotomies, and demarcations between work and leisure. For Grossberg (1994a: 212), 'Postmodernity's statements exhibit an ironic knowing distance, coupled with a sense of emotional urgency.' The ascent of consumer capitalism, a post-Fordist economy and the role of the mass media are also important elements of postmodern society. This is associated with diversification, decentralisation, inauthenticity and pastiche. Baudrillard came up with the concept of simulacra and hyper-reality where the fake appears to be realer than real. For this reason it has some overlap with Adorno's apocalyptic visions of mass culture. Rojek (1995: 160) for example writes, 'Celebrity and the star-system assume a prominent role in postmodernity.' One of postmodernism's defining features is that it is not a grand theory with a totalising explanation for the state of the world but can be applied to a diversity of practices. Even if postmodernism's definition is imprecise, without doubt one of the most fertile test-grounds for its application has been music. Indeed certain musical styles themselves have been seen as postmodern for their recycling of the past and blurring of boundaries of genre, including dance, rap and the 1980s new pop.

The *NME* (24 July 1999) has reminisced of the early 1980s as 'a time when postmodernism seemed a fizzy intellectual thrill rather than merely inescapable'. The pervasion of academic cultural theory into journalism was already evident in the 1980s in descriptions of post-punk 'new pop', examples of which included the 1982 single 'Jacques Derrida' from Scritti Politti, a band named after a three-volume Gramsci text[9] who combined Marxist politics with 1980s aspirational glamour. Writers and popular commentators such as, Paul Morley, Max Bell, and Ian Penman were able to deploy theory learnt as students to invoke a set of names well-known in contemporary cultural theory like Kristeva and Baudrillard in the columns of the *NME* and the *Face*. Simon Reynolds has done the same in the US *Village Voice*. What became known as the 'new pop' (Rimmer 1985) was in large part borne of MTV and took root whilst Gramscian Marxism became discredited and postmodernism displaced subcultural perspectives in cultural studies. Frith (1990: 183) has asserted 'New pop was a postmodern form generally – its cut-up of styles and media, its genre cross references, its use of pastiche and parody, its dressing up of mass cultural forms with high cultural claims and *vice versa*.' The term 'new pop' was of course used much more by cultural commentators than actual pop fans and died a death in the 1980s.

By the 1980s a body of literature on postmodernism in pop music had begin to accumulate, however. The advent of the ultra-consumerist worldwide-broadcast satellite channel MTV and pop videos themselves as twin arenas where marketing crossed over with art form are commonly cited (Goodwin 1993; Frith *et al.* 1993; Frith 1990: 176). Drawing on Derrida, Kaplan (1987: 148) saw in pop video 'a refusal to be co-opted into the liberalism that has brought America to its current crisis'. Referring to their cut-and-paste style she states 'the young adult's refusal to enter the realm of the symbolic could represent a healthy breaking of confining boundaries and dichotomies that were constructed originally to serve certain ends at a particular historical moment ... the vitality of rock videos shows a refusal of youth to be silenced or channelled in the old directions'. This is a qualified ambivalent statement that goes towards a position of youth populism. Unlike the rock concert, which with its fixed temporality and venue can only take place once with a set start and finish time, the pop video potentially subverts time and space negating the need for bands to spend years perfecting their musical craft on the live circuit – traditionally a key part of the apprenticeship of pop performers who, unlike classical musicians, are largely untutored auto-didacts. This development effectively short-circuits the 'gigging' process engaged in for example by the pre-fame Beatles in Hamburg or Take That in UK northern working men's clubs.

If television is potentially an enabling medium via which people across the earth's surface participate in common experiences, e.g. Live Aid, video technology takes this further with an interactive element as viewers can rewind the product to relive the moment again and again. Redhead (1990: 7) has commented: 'contemporary musical styles and forms (music video, "youth television") rewind pop history with the same mixture of longing and revulsion that contemporary street styles celebrate the various pasts of youth culture: and both do so as if there really were no tomorrow'. Music video is empowering and in keeping with popular culture as a site of resistance to capitalism. Fiske (1989: 97) for example argues that Madonna offers a means of resistance to the powerless and subordination for her fans, in his words 'a site of semiotic struggle between the forces of patriarchal control and feminine resistance, of capitalism and the subordinate, of the adult and the young'. His analysis of popular culture can be contrasted with Hoggart's decrying of the Americanisation of popular culture which becomes crudely massified.

Intertextuality, meaning that no text is not connected to others, is a connected theme particularly evident in the process of sampling, held up as a particularly postmodern pop trait for its recycling of pop's past via democratising technology. Through the sampler, fragments of music can be interwoven together with new rhythms or even with each other to create a new track. Beadle (1993: 24) explains: '[S]ampling represents the necessary search for distraction in a neurotic age. It has been described as a reaction against "the well-crafted song". It's also proved to be a way into music-making for non-musicians, like punk in the 1970s and skiffle in the 1950s.' A general climate of media saturation coupled with the legacy of musical history can be seen as reasons for this. It can be argued that increasingly media-literate young people critically read media sources and interrogate them rather than end up the cultural dupes of the sort of hypodermic syringe model as envisaged by the Frankfurt School (Kellner 1994). Chambers (1986: 12) evokes the idea of the death of the author, an ever-present postmodern concept, stating: 'we discover that we all live in a world where by choice or circumstances, we have all become experts. We confront and use signs – clothes and hairstyles, radio and tv programmes, newspapers, cinema, magazines, records, that circulating in the profane languages of habitual sights and sounds, have no obvious author.'

The new pop was only one of a number of musical alternatives on offer in the 1980s. Post-punk music fractured into different directions. Rap and electronic dance music (initially termed 'rave') are two examples that will receive a closer treatment in Part II. Frith (1990: 185) identifies the contemporaneous emergence of a counter-new pop 'New Authenticity' movement typified by artists such as Bruce Springsteen. Georgia guitar outfit REM were also often celebrated by fans of authentic rock as making 'real' music in an inauthentic post-punk age populated by a surfeit of electronic chancers. Weinstein (1995: 66) quotes the REM lyric 'It's the end of the world as we know it, and I feel fine' in writing of this vein of post-punk:

> 'The endless self-conscious shrug' is the consummation of revisiting the 1960s counter-culture's rejectionism knowing that the counter culture is dead, that one is enveloped in the simulacrum, and that the capitalist leisure culture is one's horizon. ... One has it both ways, getting to be 'authentic' while denying the possibility of authenticity.

Interestingly enough early British cultural studies from the generation of Hoggart (1958) often saw the US itself and all who sailed in her as ultra-inauthentic (Chambers 1985; Hebdige 1988). The recognition of the inauthenticity of our times, of a post-authentic era, negates the usefulness of subcultural theory. However, this in itself does not legitimate discourses of postmodernism with their attendant clichés of pastiche and the death of the author.

Pop consumption: Bourdieu and cultural capital

The late French sociologist Pierre Bourdieu is another frequently cited source on pop music for his theories of class differentiations and aesthetic taste. In *La Distinction* (1978), a text that had an English translation in the 1980s (1984b), he developed the concept of 'cultural capital', a non-economic form of capital, in the same way that Adorno and Horkheimer reinterpreted 'industry' from a purely economic notion to include the culture industries. Bourdieu based his theory on an empirical study of consumption in late 1960s France across ages, genders and different social classes, concluding that different social groupings will have different taste identifications. Thus hierarchical class relationships are reinforced and reproduced but in a more subtle way than through economic capital. His concept 'symbolic capital' is based on prestige. The idea of 'habitus', i.e. frames of reference derived from life backgrounds, education and work, is central to this. The upper classes accordingly partake in the high culture of art galleries and classical music concerts that they have been socialised into as a result of their habitus while more proletarian low culture pastimes include football and simple foods. Bourdieu (1984b: 18) has remarked that 'nothing more clearly affirms one's class, nothing classifies more infallibly than tastes in music'. This is particularly held to be the case for youth. Willis (1990: 69) for example writes 'by listening to music together and using it as a background to their lives, by expressing affiliation to a particular taste group, popular music becomes one principal means by which young people define themselves'. These remarks regarding taste are related to consumption as opposed to production.

Bourdieu's published output was nothing short of prolific, a fact exemplified in the way that he has been used by academics working in various contexts. He has for example been influential amongst educationalists, e.g. Grenfell and James (1998). Thornton (1995) has reworked cultural capital into a new concept of 'subcultural capital' which can be seen in the taste communities that develop around clubbing in the dance music scene. More important than class, 'hipness' is crucial to subcultural capital in the same way as knowledge is at the base of cultural capital. Subcultural capital is related to economic capital in a variety of occupations and income streams that have resulted from the club scene, including those involved in DJ-ing, club promotion, the record industry and music journalism. The media assumes a central importance in subcultural capital, something which Thornton argues was a critical omission in Bourdieu's work. Negus (1997; 1999) uses Bourdieu's (1984) concept of cultural inter-mediaries in his studies of the popular music industry. These are rather like the old idea of the 'gatekeeper' who controls the access to the masses of culture. Certain record company staffers interviewed, for example, cross the bound-aries between the artist and audience, mediating the meanings of and contributing to cultural products with their own 'spin', rather than detachedly playing a policing role.

Criticisms of Bourdieu's work could include its reliance on the blunt instru-ment of the questionnaire rather than taking an approach that allows the subjects' voices to be heard, and its concentration on the upper classes of France. However, the emphasis changed in some of his later work on cultural practices. The epic *La Misère du Monde* (Bourdieu 1993) focuses on society's marginalised in France, and uses qualitative interviews as its main method.

Pop production and consumption I: ethnography

The research methodology of ethnography, in which researchers engage in the first-hand study of social situations, usually by participant observation, is usually more readily associated with anthropology than with the study of popular music. Nevertheless ethnographic studies of musical phenomena have been undertaken increasingly in recent years. Such studies are primarily concerned with 'people's collective and active practice [of music] on the ground' (Finnegan 1989: 325) and are thus inextricably bound up in the local context of their study. Thus Finnegan (1989: 25) is at pains to describe the 'new town' setting of the middle England[10] town of Milton Keynes where she uncovered a number of amateur and semi-professional musicians in folk, country, pop/rock and brass bands. Cohen (1991; 1997) repeatedly invokes the specificity of Liverpool as the backdrop to her work in terms of its fabled musical heritage (Beatlemania), climate of socio-economic decline and its desire to distinguish itself from both London (the UK centre of the music industry) and its near-neighbour and longstanding rival in the north-west of England, Manchester (famed for the crossover indie-dance 'Madchester scene' of the late 1980s and early 1990s). Others focus more widely; for example Bennett (2001) takes in Newcastle in north-east England and Frankfurt, Germany in his ethnographic study.

Ethnographic studies of pop have often concerned themselves with amateur musical practices. In their examinations of local music-making, Cohen (1991) and Finnegan (1989) cited the presence of respectively 1,000 musical groups on Merseyside and 100 in the Milton Keynes area while Fornäs et al. (1995) found that 10 per cent of young Swedes were in bands. Cohen (1991: 1) describes her research as located at the 'grassroots of the music industry' which transpires to mean largely amongst post-punk all-male guitar/bass/drums/vocal groups who aspire to sign recording contracts. Here the formation of bands becomes attractive as an emotional support mechanism as well as a viable way of making a living. Cohen (1997: 31) has commented:

> It may seem a cliché, but in Liverpool involvement with rock bands is an attractive option for men, and an alternative to unemployment or monotonous, unfulfilling jobs in a city surrounded by the discourse of failure. ... Live performance can occasionally be a means of earning extra income, but the recording industry is also amongst one of the UK's most valuable export industries and its star performers amongst the richest men in Britain.

The creative and cultural industries and new post-Fordist economy, alluded to here, are of crucial importance to all of the chapters of this book. As we move towards post-industrial times, Frith (1994: 180) sees 'a situation in which the affluent are serviced by the non-affluent, the "new" workers [who] will work directly on other people's pleasure'. Again the potential of music to provide employment can be seen in this comment on the lead singer of Swedish working class band OH (Fornäs et al. 1995: 193), whose 'dreams of being a musician are bound up with efforts to turn work into leisure or to dissolve a seemingly entrenched dichotomy'. Music is seen as a sociable activity providing bonds with other youth and potentially a career path, if an unstructured one at that. In Part II of this book we will see how pop music has become a career path for musicians of different genres.

The sort of empowerment for 'players' at non-profit musical gatherings in pubs and church halls described by Finnegan is quite different to that foreseen by Fiske's (1989) reading of MTV and Madonna. Cohen's (1991) work on Liverpool sees gang rivalries between groups and the subordination of women as decorative attachments rather than integral elements of the bands (e.g., backing singers rather than musicians) in a world that is essentially one of male camaraderie. For Fornäs *et al.* (1995: 227):

> In adolescent struggles with identity, the gang fills the function of the cocoon which recreates or revives memories of early mother–child symbiosis and protects against the pressures of the system. Making rock music mediates between the maternal and the paternal, the wild and the civilised, the physical–semiotic and the linguistic–discursive.

There is an identification of affective ties in music as a way of alleviating the unproductiveness and anonymity felt by youth in modernity. Most of these groups were immediately 'in it' for personal enjoyment. For example, in Finnegan's research (1989: 268) 'player after player commented on the sense of achievement in joint public appearance "it's good to make good music", "you get a good feeling" … "the satisfaction of hearing the audience shouting for more" '. It is precisely 'feeling' that is difficult to convey in other non-ethnographic research methodologies, e.g. 'pure' textual analysis or empirical questionnaire data collection.

All of these three studies can be described as post-Birmingham or going 'beyond subculture'. Fornäs *et al.* (1995: 9) break with CCCS traditions in justifying the selection of their sample as one of ' "common", relatively "normal" young people … instead of concentrating upon specific, deviant subcultural styles'. The bands play their own material but, in a clear application of intertextuality, are influenced by earlier musical developments, particularly punk. In a work that could not be accused of neglecting theoretical considerations, the musical practices of these youth are inter-related to theories of individualisation and risk in modernity as well as the cultural philosophy of Kristeva. Finnegan (1989: 121) explicitly rejects the CCCS's 'generalised and polemical tone' for reducing everything to class divisions. She instead comes up with the notion of the 'pathway' to define the networks in which these hidden musicians function using well-trodden routes. She writes:

> Pathways … are one of the ways in which people within an urban environment organise their lives so as to manage, on one hand, the heterogeneity and multiplicity of relationships characteristic of many aspects of modern society, and, on the other, that sense of both predictable familiarity and personally controlled meaning that is part of human life.
>
> (Finnegan 1989: 323)

This can apply to employment, school and child-rearing. This has features in common with Beck's (1992) individualised concept of 'reflexive biography'.

Ethnographic studies can be easily criticised. Methodologically the position of the researcher in relation to the phenomenon researched and the imbalanced power relations between the two parties is a perennial problem. On the claimed musically distinctive quality of 'Liverpoolness' that emerges from Cohen's (1991) interviewees, Negus (1996: 185) comments that this type of adjective is 'usually musicians adopting a characteristically intuitive romantic discourse' rather than being based on much hard evidence, save for allusions to places such as Penny Lane or Strawberry Fields in song titles. Here we can see an immediate method-ological problem inherent in the qualitative open-response interview: the interviewee may simply provide the answers that are expected of them or respond in a way that ensures that they come over in a good light making the supposedly desirable goals of achieving complete 'reliability' and/or 'validity' ultimately impossible. Final outcomes are always inseparable from the author, particularly in intensive qualitative research of this nature.

Thornton (1995) provides some very rich data, most memorable being the incident described in the section entitled 'A night of research', in which she describes partaking in the dance club scene's drug of choice, ecstasy. There is a degree of self-justification in the name of professional research: 'I'm not a personal fan of drugs – I worry about my brain cells. But they're a fact of this youth culture, so I submit myself to the experiment in the name of thorough research (thereby confirming every stereotype of the subcultural sociologist)' (Thornton 1995: 89). Her confession is unfortunately never elaborated upon in terms of any emotional or chemical effects but it does nonetheless accord her study a degree of authenticity for having engaged in everyday raver practices. Indeed cultural studies has frequently neglected empirical evidence in favour of dense theory. Among the new breed of research that reverses this is Back's (1996) work on youth cultures in multicultural settings. He captures his experience of attending an Apache Indian concert in 'middle England' in what he terms as an 'urban poem' replete with highly readable 'thick description' (cf. Geertz 1985). In this way Back (1996: 225) uses his 'on the ground' experiences to develop empirically founded theory, in this example reflecting on his whiteness and how this itself is no longer is a necessary pre-requisite of Englishness. As a line of enquiry, 'whiteness studies' has flourished in recent years, largely propagated by white academics – something which we will return to in chapter 7.

Pop production and consumption II: industry

Sales charts and radio air play are alluded to by Burnett (1996: 37) in his defini-tion of pop in economic terms: '[S]ufficient purchases by the youth audience, the main consumers, define what constitute [sic] popular music at any given time.' However, even if we accept that recordings (and their sales) are now centrally positioned in contemporary pop (Laing 1990), this offers at best only a partial definition of what is constituted by the term pop music and appears as curiously clinical in its neglect of listeners' actions themselves. There are multiple ways of receiving pop's text in addition to officially logged 'record sales', including pirate and official radio, web downloads, music video, concerts, second-hand music transactions, multimedia, home-taping, CD burning and now file-swapping on the internet. Bhangra sales, to be discussed in chapter 4, are not recorded anywhere, sometimes deliberately, as specialist Asian retailers do not wish to declare their sales for tax reasons. This puts bhangra units shifted outside independent/major label dichotomies.

The central argument related to the economics of pop music, as rehearsed in countless studies, is one of subcultural incorporation where oppositional cultures become mainstream once the market steps in to capitalise on potential profit margins. The youth-as-consumer has been studied since Abrams (1959) first made this point (e.g. Nava 1991; Miles 1998). Nonetheless the economic consumption of pop music has been under-theorised relative to the study of its texts, audiences and subcultural meanings. While Adorno outlined the negative consequences of music submitting to capitalism, this critique was of a general nature and is now woefully outdated. Subsequent studies of the music business (Blake 1992; Burnett 1995; Eliot 1990; Harker 1980; Negus 1993; 1999; Sanjek and Sanjek 1991) are still greatly outweighed by research on popular music *culture*. Certainly an analysis of units shifted and balance sheets is not to the social scientist as alluring as looking at semiotic meanings and lived experiences. Traditional music industry economics dictate that musicians are contracted to record output in order to sell to consumers in a system where copyright law protects the distribution of recordings without payment to owners. However, both this model and the hegemony of the major players are under threat from changing cultures of music consumption.

The control of the musical market by multinationals is often a point of departure for music-business studies (e.g. Laing 1990; Taylor 1997). Burnett (1996: 18) identified what he called 'the big 6' as Sony, Warners, Polygram, EMI, BMG and MCA who, at the time of his study, accounted for 90 per cent of US sales and between 70 and 80 per cent of worldwide sales. Conversely a good deal of the debate on the popular music industry has been concentrated on 'indie', i.e. music on independent labels, theoretically a bulwark of musical and financial independence against the 'majors'. As Epstein (1998: 20) points out, referring to US sales figures: 'An album which sells 50,000 copies is a "flop" according to major label standards set for rock music sales, but for the independent label it is quite respectable.' Accordingly separate 'indie' charts are compiled and the term has come to transcend its ostensible function as an economic term to connote an attitude of risk-taking and anti-commercialism as well as a guitar-based musical style. There are of course moments when the 'indie' and 'major' scenes meet. When the early house-music single 'Pump Up the Volume' by MARRS reached the UK number one chart placing on the 4AD label, the Timelords (1988: 47) were moved to comment 'it was only a matter of time before something came along from within the indie scene that was neither "spotty" or "marginal" and had definite mass appeal'. Indeed the growth of the electronic dance music scene has often been on independent labels, exposing the fallacy of both terms. The band Coldplay are, at the time of writing, signed to multinational record label EMI yet their bass/guitar/drums line-up, sizeable student following and patronage by alternative music press titles such as the *NME* are classic indie traits. In addition to this a further indie/major interface exists whereby small-scale offshoots are set up by multinationals, e.g. the Island Records world music division Mango or Indolent Records, financially backed by BMG.

On the face of it the economics of the music business ought to be centrally positioned in the rapidly growing new post-industrial leisure economy where sectors and elements are inter-related and inter-dependent. The waxing and waning fortunes of the music industry were seen in the widespread press reporting of troubles at EMI in 2002–2003 on the financial pages of British broadsheet newspapers.[11] However, at the same time the music multinationals are increasingly under threat from other directions, in particular the technology of downloading music from the internet with no copyright restrictions via the MP3 file format. The technology of P2P (peer-to-peer) computing has produced websites that allow virtual meeting places for fans to exchange files and access every tune from every era for free. The music industry's seemingly limitless ability to exploit even the most subversive youth cultures, e.g. hippie and punk, for financial gain, met a new challenge with this electronic abundance of music that enabled the theft of intellectual property by digital stealth on a far greater scale than 1980s home-taping. The seriousness with which the industry took this was seen in its use of considerable lobbying power and resources to successfully prosecute the well-known Napster website, to strengthen copyright law and introduce encryption software onto CDs to stop them being copied. The economy of cyberspace is one in which information via emails, chatrooms, list-servers and MP3 soundfiles circulates freely, apart from the price of connection. This is sharply at odds with traditional music industry economics as described above. Youth are commonly identified as the key personnel behind this new form of accessing music; it is university students that have largely written the software and set up the websites that have driven this movement.[12] Indeed they have been characterised as a subversive subculture positioned in opposition to the music industry, which has effectively declared war on the internet (Alderman 2001).

Post-Fordist pop in globalisation

Along with 'postmodern' and 'subculture', globalisation is another term that has become almost normalised in recent years. Featherstone (1995: 81) defines this as:

> the sense of global compression in which the world is increasingly regarded as 'one place' and it becomes more difficult for nation states to

opt out of, or avoid, the consequences of being drawn together into a progressively tighter figuration through the increasing volume and rapidity of the flows of money, goods, people, technology and images.

Globalisation is usually associated with the interdependence of world economies and the tightening grip of multinationals on the means of production, distribution and exchange. By the 1990s 'globalisation' had added itself to the list of factors advanced as signalling a crisis in pop, largely stemming from a general sales downturn against a background of global economic recession, technological advance and leisure industry competition. Globalisation's opponents usually point to cultural homogenisation as an unwelcome consequence. Jenkins (1997: 43) argues 'it is ... painfully clear that globalization doesn't necessarily broaden the mind'. This conception of globalisation is tantamount to Americanisation or the neologism 'McDonaldisation' (Ritzer 1993). It is argued that the Fordist input–output model of standardised assembly line mass production has, since de-industrialisation and the decline of manufacturing industry, been replaced by an ethic based on the globally active US-founded burger chain McDonalds. Featherstone (1995: 8) writes 'the language of mass consumer culture is English'. Accordingly Gudmundsson (1999: 45) remarks 'Rock music bears the stamp "made in the USA" even more obviously than other forms of popular culture. The music is originally American and the language English.' This cultural hegemony is then cemented by the controlling oligopoly of the major labels. Laing (1990: 189) sees a logical extension of this in pop commercially calculated to appeal to a wide transnational public with no national or local orientations pumped out by the music industry, e.g. Abba. However globalisation need not necessarily mean the spread of mass culture characterised by first world blandness as the consumption of 'world music' from, for example, Africa or Central America by western listeners illustrates.

The global–local nexus is one that numerous theorists have agonised over. More recent reconceptualisations have talked about a movement of 'glocalisation' defined by Featherstone (1995: 9) as: 'A global strategy which does not seek to impose a standard product or image, but instead is tailored to the demands of the local market. This was a popular strategy for multinationals in other parts of the world who seek to join the rhetoric of localism.' This market-driven process demonstrates the recognition by commercial forces of the need to show outward sensitivity to local cultural needs in the face of increased local identity assertion. Local agreements with distributors mean that the multinationals operate through nationally based record companies in different nation-states (for example, Virgin France has released much home-grown French pop in recent years). Local versions of MTV are another example. The 1990s incarnation of youth station MTV Europe has been replaced with versions for France, Spain, etc., as Europe was found to be inappropriate as a cultural unit where 'one size fits all'. There is also an indigenously produced MTV India – although one could of course get into an interesting argument about what constitutes 'Indian culture' in a country of that size. Indeed even McDonalds is having to vary its product for multilingual, multifaith local markets, thus recognising difference – in the UK a vegeburger appears on the menu and in India no beef is served.

Whilst some see globalisation as perpetuating western/US domination in particular over the third world, others are enthusiastic about its possibilities as an enabling force in decentring the west and allowing marginalised communities a 'right of reply' to their positioning in the new world order, thereby potentially effacing old borders. Morley and Robins (1998: 121) write: 'Globalisation is profoundly transforming our apprehension of the world: it is provoking a new experience of orientation and disorientation, new senses of places and placeless identity.' Globalisation can then be more nuanced than a flattening one-way process of imposing products on an unsuspecting audience of cultural dupes willing to embrace this cultural homogeneity. The marketing of diversity in modernity should not be underestimated. Accordingly, in an argument to be returned to in chapter 4, Kellner (1995: 40) observes that in contemporary consumer capitalism, 'difference sells'. Thus ethnic difference becomes 'in'. Whilst globalisation can easily reproduce first world–third world power relations, the increasing power of global apparatus for the diffusion of culture also presents the possibility of illuminating cultures of far-flung corners of the globe, which become less far-flung as a result.

'C30 C60 C90 Go!' Some conclusions

This chapter has begun to look at some of the different approaches to studying pop music, to be revisited in Part II. The business dimension of pop can be seen in the vast array of spin-off products that it now gives rise to, exemplified by the launching of chainsaw Eminem dolls and a Jennifer Lopez clothing range. For Weinstein (1995: 65) the 1980s ushered in 'the era of the dispossession of "youth" from the young and the absorption of the majority of the young into the leisure culture'. The informal economy of the rave scene also saw disused warehouses deserted by industry reappropriated as symbolic spaces by youth. That pop music cannot be seen in isolation from its money-making function is demonstrated in Robbie Williams' wry comment on receiving his MTV award in 2000: 'I would like to thank MTV for five cars, the three houses and the supermodel girlfriend.'[13] Fornäs et al. (1995: 214) acknowledge the commercial function of pop but do not see this as its most important aspect:

> Rock is a mass-produced commodity, however it would be naïve to believe that being a commodity value eradicates rock's use value as an expression of the common needs of large numbers of people all over the world, or compromises its radical criticism of ruling forms of rationality and socialisation.

To some extent this claim will be tested by the chapters that follow in Part II. In the case studies to follow, the musics looked at articulate local hybridities in global contexts which require a recognition of local determination and difference as well as of wider underlying trends and the complex global flows of popular culture.

The twentieth century has seen popular music become a global commercial enterprise rather than a simple folk activity. However pop music is not only about shifting units and commercial transactions. Personal observations, e.g. of communal music making, are frequently missing from accounts of the music industry that concentrate on mass music consumption. Yet locally focused small-scale ethnographic studies with their limited applicability potentially lose sight of the bigger picture. There are obvious difficulties in trying to generalise on a wide scale from what are essentially one-town studies, particularly in an age of globalisation.

From the standpoint of the early 21st century the diversity of musical practices and increased outlets for pop fans to access and discuss pop have opened up new avenues for investigation. Many "record shops" no longer sell vinyl singles or albums although they do stock CDs, videos, DVDs and computer games. Supermarkets now sell CDs. The advent of MP3 downloads and the ubiquitousness of on-line global marketplace ebay coupled with credit card transcactions means that one hand and a few clicks of a mouse are all that are needed to purchase pop – dispensing with the need to set foot in any kind of store at all. Internet discussion forums and chatrooms are supplementing, if not totally supplanting, print fanzines of old. The mobile phone now has an unparalleled level of penetration amongst young people who can access music videos through the latest 3G models. The choice of ringtone too becomes an identity definer. The producers and consumers of twentyfirst century youth musics ulitise all of these tools as technological and cultural resources. These developments are about renewing and redefining pop rather than pop dying.

Recent years have seen repeated claims of a paralysis in pop threatening its very existence.[14] During the 1980s the pop video was perceived as a threat to youth culture's relationship with popular music and a decade later electronic dance music and its disregard for musical convention was similarly viewed. However these two factors arguably renewed pop's importance. In the twenty-first century and in the years leading up to it, debates about technology and pop have focused on the threat posed to the music industry by the computer technologies of Napster and MP3. Interestingly these are rendering music more ubiquitous, easier than ever to access as pop attains a new degree of acceptability. Sabin (1998: 1) points out that 'pop culture has gone mainstream. ... [It] is much more acceptable ... subject matter previously thought to be the domain of the alternative and music press has made its way overground.' Will the result mean a decline in the importance of pop? Probably not, as we live in an ageing world where pop now competes alongside other cultural (di)versions for youth leisure time and where, by the 1980s, as Weinstein (1995: 63) puts it, 'Rock, like youthful looks, was no longer the province of the young.' This is an inevitable result of demographic change. Drawing attention to the way in which musical tastes are highly differentiated among the category of youth, Finnegan (1989: 122) claims:

> There was certainly great enthusiasm for particular bands among young people, but 'youth culture' was not monolithic. Young people were not just differentiated by being 'young' but also subdivided by age, interests, musical preferences, family background, locality and a whole range of other factors.

Indeed there is an argument for desegregating 'youth culture' from 'pop music' based on the wide diversity of ages and social situations in contemporary pop.

There are overlaps and intersections between commonplace assumptions and the academic traditions attached to each of the first three chapters of this book. We live in an ageing world, yet paradoxically the cult of youth is almost all-pervasive in the approach to the millennium (Calcutt 1998). The omnipresence of youth paradoxically then spells its potential death. Redhead (1990: 89) wrote that 'the meta-narrative of the "liberation of youth" which deals with the most dominant of post-war mythologies in the west is now being replaced by the meta-narrative of the end of youth'. The arguments for and against pronouncing the death of youth culture pervade all of the following chapters in varying degree and will be considered in the conclusion.

Part II
CASE STUDIES

4

WORLD IN MOTION

Bhangra, post-bhangra and raï as second generation sounds in inauthentic times

> It's not as bad now, you can go to HMV and buy an Indian track that's not in the corner of a dusty world music section that nobody looks in. You want to go to that trendy dance section where all those cool, good-looking kids are hanging out.
> (Bally Sagoo, quoted in Housee and Dar 1996: 96)

> *Khaled, c'est comme Johnny, ça se discute pas.*
> (Olivier Cathus 2000)[1]

As we have seen the power of pop music as a potentially political and creative expressive art form voicing generational concerns has made it a synonym for post-war youth culture. However the study of both of these entities has often been conducted in a selective way. This chapter continues the underlying theme of internationalism in pop and youth culture in this book by turning to two styles that are often decribed perhaps rather unsatisfactorily as 'world music', although their practioners and publics include large numbers of second generation youth of minority ethnic origins. These are raï music, originally from the middle East, and the twin styles bhangra and Asian Underground which stem from migration from the Indian subcontinent to the UK. I will begin with a general discussion of world music before turning more closely to address bhangra and raï to look at the meanings of both these diasporic musics and how they can be situated within studies of popular music at large. Questions to be tackled include the place of world music in contemporary pop, whether minority musics can move from the margins to the mainstream, the musical agency of minority youth, media depictions of these musics, their marketing and the role of gatekeepers in these processes. My point of departure will be the ways in which world music is marketed.

World music and the marketing of diversity in modernity

By the twentieth century popular music had ceased to be simply a folk form and had become a commodity. As such when assessing different musical styles and the proliferating number of genres now on offer, it could be argued that if one were to take an ultra-rational post-enlightenment line, different musics have no ostensible differences in purely functional use-value terms from each other. Thus when musics are products which need to distinguish themselves from other commodities, difference becomes a key competitive advantage. Kellner (1994: 40) writes:

> Difference sells. Capitalism must constantly multiply markets, styles, fads, and artefacts to keep absorbing consumers into its practices and lifestyles. The mere valorisation of 'difference' as a mark of opposition can simply help market new styles and artefacts if the difference in question and its effects are not adequately appraised. It can also promote a form of identity politics in which each group affirms its own specificity and limits politics to the group's own interests, thus overlooking common forces of oppression. Such difference or identity politics aids 'divide and conquer' strategies which ultimately serve the interest of the powers that be.

Such imperatives operate on a number of levels which go beyond simply the story of economic transactions. Marketing diversity in this way has implications for reconfiguring traditional dynamics of cultural production in terms of production, distribution and exchange in transnational contexts as well as, by logical extension, social relations and socio-cultural change. The place of cultural intermediaries who have the power to perform 'gatekeeper' functions is also important. These sorts of products that rely on such strategies cross national boundaries and sometimes straddle sectors as well. The role of technology should not be underestimated in such cultural production processes. I want to apply Kellner's idea of selling difference in particular to music.

In some ways world music aimed at the discerning music listener is the polar opposite to the bubblegum sounds of the teen- and fan-centred girl and pop bands that many commentators and lay-people alike have criticised for their lack of resistive potential and/or musical originality as we have seen in earlier chapters. World music is frequently seen as the archetypally 'authentic' musical style of our times. The genre is usually associated with third world or non-western countries (or migrant minorities), and in this way it can be seen as a Euro-centric or western-constructed term. The idea of *marketing* however, rather than political domination, is that which is most recurrent in definitions of world music, or 'world beat' as it is known in the US. Hardy and Laing (1995: vii) for example write: 'Originally a marketing term invented to help sell African, Asian and Latin American musics to European audiences, world music also refers to styles which mix those musics with contemporary studio or performance technology.' The term dates from the 1980s. As Shuker (1998: 312) points out 'The marketing of world music, and the guides to it, usually construct the category around national identity, even though that is clearly tenuous given the diversity of styles within particular countries.' The term clearly collapses a number of musical styles under a general umbrella term, making it at best a convenient marketing and media shorthand label and at worst a fiction. Barrett (1996: 243) states: 'the fantasy [of world music] assumes that such peoples [world musicians] live in archaic stasis until they encounter western civilisation whereas there are clearly many shifts over time'. Indeed it is difficult to comment definitively about world music as it is such a broad term. On the subject of African music for example, Oliver (1990: 171) points out:

> Part of the process of gaining a wider public has been one of accultura-
> tion. Traditional African styles of music from Burkino Faso, Kenya,
> Nigeria, Senegal, Zaire or Zimbabwe may have certain elements broadly
> in common but they are also differentiated markedly from each other in
> instrumentation and performance techniques.

World music is seen as synonymous with tradition in an age of modernity.

The sort of sounds associated with the term often include: pygmy chanting; zither music; traditional throat singing; didgeridoo; sitar; and heavy percussion/ drums. Certain labels have become associated with world music and sub-genres. The best-known is probably Real World, run by Peter Gabriel and licensed through Virgin Records. In the 1990s Nation Records were responsible for releasing an output of world dance. This soon spawned ethno-trance, ethno-techno located in the soundscapes of far-off hills, forests, jungles, deserts and plains. Certainly world music's elastic boundaries encompass a wide range of styles: the 'world' racks of large UK record stores are subdivided into continents and nation-states. The resul-tant array of music to be found under this classification includes raï artists such as the Algerians Cheb Khaled and Cheb Mami, African artists Salif Keita, Youssou N'Dour and Ravi Shankar of India. However the tendency to 'other' music that does not fit into straight pop, dance, metal, etc. categories is seen by the inclusion of the post-bhangra band Joi, who are London-based and a fixture of the Asian Underground club scene using some Asian stylings married to technologically advanced electronic beats. Similarly contemporary French artists such as *chanson Française* stalwart the late Serge Gainsbourg and straightforward pop performer Etienne Daho are also 'world' artists in the UK. Certainly Gainsbourg, Daho and Joi could easily be classified as easy listening, pop and dance respectively. Considering the wider term, the definition of world music changes across coun-tries. In France, for example, French artists are filed under 'varieties Françaises' in opposition to 'varitiés internationales' (largely US and UK). There is furthermore the category of 'musiques du monde' (world music). In the UK then, world music is defined in opposition to music of the UK and US and is essentially non-English language music. In France, French song joins the list of music that world music is othered against, although the French distinguish their music against the US/UK hegemony (Warne 1997). Broughton *et al.* (1994) include both raï and bhangra in their volume on world music. In a French equivalent, Kaufman and Bertaud (2001: 125) also include raï in their definition of 'musique du monde', alongside samba, bossa nova and zouk from the French Carribean, although bhangra is not present. Zouk is another style that has not fully gained acceptance in the UK, possibly for historical and colonial reasons.

The idea of 'discovery' and staking out new frontiers has helped the growth of world music in finding western audiences. In a survey of pop in the 1980s the UK BBC world music DJ Andy Kershaw (1989) for example remarked 'Pop and rock in the west have been bloody dull [recently]. … That's why people look and continue to look to other parts of the world.' A review of the French-based Spanish-born artist Manu Chao (Forrest 2002) in a UK magazine states: 'Manu's music comes from and attracts the culturally, politically and musically open-minded.' In the same article we are told that the crowd described at one of his performances comprises 'bohemians sweating alongside students, intellectuals and travellers with dreadlocks'. Chao's discovery by the UK media was predated by his membership for years of the Virgin France-signed punk act Mano Negra. Although Chao is white this description still could suggest western fascination with the exotic, an idea not too far removed from the idea of 'othering'. A large proportion of world music content in record stores is comprised of compilations covering tracts of the globe which it would be no exaggeration to say are geographically vast: India and South-East Asia or the region of the Andes for example. Barrett (1996: 240) sees a 'touristic gaze' in the selection and packaging of these products again resting on their authentic status: 'These travel themes are sustained in the National Geographic visuals on world music CD covers … craggy, aged, "ethnic" faces; details of traditional ethnic clothing and instruments … rural landscapes.' Indeed this could be seen as being in keeping with the notion of the noble savage dating back to Rousseau (1755). By extension, western fascination with world music demonstrates a desire to return to simpler, more innocent times that have not been corrupted by western capitalism. Barrett (1996: 241) comments: 'It is not surprising that world music has flourished in recent years, given the advance of Green politics, New Age-ism, multiculturalism and other counter-measures.' World music contains the promise of a return to undoctored 'real world' sounds in an inauthentic world where people are constantly bombarded by flickering electronic imagery generated by the mass media.

Despite the inherent notions of 'primitiveness' in authenticity-laden definitions of world music, technology has been a key factor in its spread through improved recording techniques and the cut-and-paste device of electronic sampling. A well-known yet not isolated example was the release of Eric B and Rakim's 'Paid in Full', which included a sampled passage of vocals from the Israeli Ofra Haza. This sampled snatch alone, a brief moment that lasted only a matter of seconds, was enough to trigger the release of the original track 'Im Nin'Alu' as a single which became a top twenty hit in its own right some months later (UK number fifteen in April 1988, emulating the same chart position reached by Eric B and Rakim in November 1987). In 1989 studio-based electronic band The Art of Noise released the single 'Yebo', featuring the Soweto choral singer Mahlathini and his all-female backing group the Mahotella Queens, a collective specialising in mbaqanga (melodic Zulu pop music). In a remark demonstrating the way that third world nation-states in globalised modernity are located subjectively in a zone of back-wardness, Kershaw (1989) predicted: 'Their [world musicians'] records are going to be more adventurous and sophisticated as they get their hands on the tech-nology they deserve.' Technology here is seen as progress rather than as impeding some sort of holy grail of 'authenticity'. It was Massive Attack's remixes of Nusrat Fateh Ali Khan, included on blockbuster film soundtracks such as *Natural Born Killers*, and his 1995 Real World compilation with Michael Brook that raised the western profile of the late Pakistani Muslim devotional singer (Taylor 1997). A posthumous collection of remixes of his work including contributions from Talvin Singh and Asian Dub Foundation appeared on the Real World label in 1997. The sleeve of this compilation, *Star Rise*, explained: 'From the Asian Underground the new stars emerge to interpret the greatest singer of Qawwali music.' Arguably the album's production techniques owed more to computer programming skills than musicianship in the commonly accepted sense of the term and again cast doubt on authenticity, or the need for such a thing.

World music, then, is a highly contradictory style, or more accurately a 'meta-genre' in the words of Shuker (1998: 311). At one level its exportality and aptitude to adaptation and incorporation suggest a decentring of the west. However its spread has been an uneven process, arguably on western terms through multinational labels such as Real World (a subsidiary of Virgin) or other specialist UK and US imprints. This is necessary for world music to penetrate western ears, but quite often in various ways the supposedly arch-authentic performers have ended up having their voices ventriloquised through westerners. Barrett (1996: 243), for example, condemns the process whereby first world 'experts' provide CD liner notes with geography/musicology lessons for the uninitiated, claiming: 'It is a geography that fixes other cultures on spokes radi-ating out from a western hub.' World music can be seen as politically suspect for engaging in the neo-colonial practices of appropriation and domination. Van Der Lee (1998) discusses world music under the following headings: exploitation; domesticisation; dilution; exoticisation; and validation. Another example of the mediation of world music through western mechanisms, that can be inserted into this model, can be seen in the *Newsnight* item on BBC television (25 March 2002) chronicling the exploits of Blur's lead singer Damon Albarn in Mali on a musical collaboration for Oxfam in western Africa. The item portrayed muso Albarn rehearsing with African musicians who were unaware of their western counter-part's greatness back home. At one stage the narration enquired 'And what did the Malians make of their new member?', only for the question to be answered by Albarn himself, who replied along on the lines of 'they were suspicious of me at first but then I won them over'. As a pop performer, Albarn's brush with world musicians is not in itself new. One could also cite the Beatles' collaborations with Ravi Shankar or Talking Heads' use of African sounds continued in David Byrne's experimentation with South American styles as a solo performer. Another well-known example is Paul Simon's work with South African musicians at the time of the cultural boycott, which earned him large sales and disapproval in equal measure (Mitchell 1996; Taylor 1997), while Peter Gabriel has been cited above. All of these artists have been accused of cultural appropriation and the same charges could be levelled against Albarn; however, it is unlikely that the Malian musicians he played with would have been able to command the second item on *Newsnight* on their own or a large feature article in the *Guardian*, 'Gorillaz in their Midst' (25 February 2002). If these generate further interest in African music, Albarn's stated objective of awareness raising will have been achieved and by extension the other chief aim of fund-raising. One can advocate world music on the third world's terms yet this is more difficult to achieve than to champion. The representation of difference and its commodification and appropriation are amply illustrated in the case of bhangra music and Asian Underground, which I turn to next.

Second generation sounds I: bhangra and beyond

Banerji and Baumann (1990: 138) points out that 'South Asian communities in Britain have remained invisible and their music inaudible for a surprisingly long time.' In the subculture-obsessed 1970s UK youth studies, Asian youth were either seen as victims of 'Paki-bashing' (Corrigan 1979; Pearson 1976)[2] or dismissed out of hand, as in the remark 'Asians are rarely found in youth culture' (Brake 1980: 128). By the mid-1980s, however, this state of invisibility appeared to be altering, in no small part due to the emergence and media reporting of bhangra, defined as 'a dance style which originates from the region of Punjab, performed when celebrating the harvest. ... Its raw traditional sound is often supplemented with contemporary musical styles ... from the UK.'[3] Bhangra's driving rhythmic form often has at least some of the following features: hand-claps; chanted vocals; Punjabi lyrics; electric guitars; electronic keyboards providing synthesised orchestral sounds; and, most crucially, a heavy percussive beat in which the dhol (cylindrical drum) is the backbone. Past and present examples include the groups Alaap, Heera and DCS, and solo artists Malkit Singh and Punjabi MC, all British-based. Pathi (1986: 60) has described it as 'an easy blend of traditional, rural instruments and modern Western sounds'. By 1997 bhangra had been joined by a new, arguably 'post-bhangra', term: 'Asian Underground' (*Melody Maker*, 28 June 1997)[4]. This is an umbrella category that largely refered to a DJ-centred dance music scene exemplified by the London-based Anokha and Swaraj club nights, but has been applied to a diverse range of sounds spanning indie-rock (Cornershop, Echobelly), hip-hop (Kaleef, Fun-Da-Mental) or other sonic combinations (Asian Dub Foundation are reminscent of the Clash while Black Star Liner play a ska hybrid). British Asian music has reached a number of milestones in terms of its mainstream visibility. Spring 1998 saw the number one hit 'Brimful of Asha' from Cornershop. The prestigious Mercury Music Prize was won by Talvin Singh for his album *OK* in 1999.[5] Subsequent bhangra–rap hybrids have included Punjabi MC's 'Mundian Te Bach Ke' hit of 2003 that was number one in Germany for a lengthy period. However, Asian Underground in the late 1990s appeared to be on the brink of crossover acceptability, in part due to the foundations laid by the British bhangra scene that began in the 1980s. The two styles, sometimes described by the all-encompassing term 'the new Asian dance music' (Sharma *et al*. 1996), cover both a club scene and live performance instrumental/vocal acts. Diverse though these are, their unifying feature is the combining of musical traditions from western pop as well as from the subcontinent.

Bhangra has been seen in simplistic terms as identity-affirming/unifying for second generation British Asian youth. Back (1996: 219–20) calls it 'an overarching reference point cutting across cleavages of nationality (Indian, Pakistani, Bangladeshi and other), religion (Sikh, Muslim, Hindu) and caste and class'. Gillespie (1995: 45–46) sees it as 'a focal point for the public emergence of a British youth culture which transcends traditional divisions and aspires to a sense of ethnic unity ... that British Asian youth can claim as their own and be proud of'. The style press had made similar points, e.g. *ID* magazine (April 1993): 'Like all urban musics it's a soundtrack for life. ... It's the sound of bhangra, the Asian music where the language is Punjabi but the following crosses cultural and religious borders.' However this proposed inclusiveness actually falls neatly into the trap of equating 'Asians' and even 'Asianness' with bhangra; as much a falsehood as compounding all Afro-Carribeans with reggae tastes. Past imperial connotations are replicated in UK usage of the term 'Asian', which effectively reduces the largest continent to ex-British India, principally Bangladesh, Pakistan and India. As Brah (1997: 42) points out, 'there is no single "identity" that each and every Asian avows'. The term then, while homogenising people of diverse linguistic, religious and other cultural practices into one indiscriminate mass, is at once both narrow and wide. This wide conceptualisation of black can be a political term that is in some senses necessary for combating racism. Music from Malaysia, the Phillipines and Thailand are all excluded from UK conceptualisations of 'Asian' music. While bhangra has helped to bring Asian youth out of the shadows, just as Asians are not a homogeneous community there is no single Asian youth musical style. The main site for bhangra gatherings is in mainstream venues: Britain's multi-ethnic urban centres. My own observation of such events in London and Manchester suggests that bhangra gigs attract a more mixed clientele than religion- or caste-specific weddings and similar community/social functions where Asians traditionally meet; however its Punjabi roots mean that it cannot have an equally wide appeal to all Asians. Whilst not all Asians are bhangra fans the audiences at such gatherings tend to be overwhelmingly Asian, principally of Punjabi language backgrounds, being either Indian Sikhs or Pakistanis. However even these differences are not always immediately apparent given that many UK Sikhs cut their hair and that audiences are of mixed genders.

Early reporting of bhangra in the mainstream UK media tended to focus on concerts that took place in daylight hours to accomodate parental restrictions regarding Asian youth's socialising (Polhemus 1994: 111). One could easily read a subtext of Asians as unassimilable immigrants into the selection of such subject material for having to stage their own entertainment in separate spaces from the white mainstream. However while 'daytimer' accounts emphasising truancy and parental repression have been decried (Baumann 1990: 146),[6] the press has since lost interest, having refocused its interest to other youth cultural concerns. Nevertheless daytimers still continue in large urban centres of the UK. An event I attended in July 2002 in a pub in the 'black' Manchester inner city neighbourhood of Moss Side held between the hours of 12 noon and 6 pm attracted 400 revellers, yet went completely unnoticed by any of Manchester's 'official' organs for the dissemination of entertainment listings; City Life, the Guardian Guide and Metro carried no mention of it, or of any of the other bhangra events held regularly around the city that draw in youth from many neighbouring cities of the north-west. Whether this was a deliberate strategy not to attract too much undue attention or an unnecessary consideration for a series of events capable of generating audiences through its own networks, this gave it something of an 'underground' feel. Noticeably the people in attendance were of school and college age.[7] At the younger end, some males wore turbans but had not yet grown beards, others' voices had not broken. Alcohol was on sale and neither sex seemed to be restricted in partaking of it, or of smoking. At a city-centre evening event held on the same night from 10 pm to 2 am, a much smaller number (perhaps in the region of 100), drawn from a slightly older age range, turned out. Musics on offer included garage and hip-hop alongside bhangra. Again males wore designer clothes and females dressed largely in black and in trousers. This conventional youth dress code differs from the traditional dress worn by bhangra-goers observed in 1980s commentary.[8] There is a convergence then of mainstream youth cultural fashion in bhangra gatherings. Elsewhere however divides persist. Apart from the continued media invisibility of bhangra, a further example can be seen in the alternative networks of distribution, production and exchange of bhangra albums in specialist Asian retail shops where their sales make no impact on the compiling of mainstream 'official' charts, first commented on by Baumann (1990) at the time when the music's means of recording was the cassette format. Whilst I do not wish to propagate the now discredited 'between two cultures' (Anwar 1976; Watson 1977) line of stereotyping Asian youth, certainly we can make a case for bhangra culture inhabiting a separate space from mainstream pop and youth culture. The situation is however much more complex than a simple wilful separatism practised by Asian youth.

Even accepting the peculiarly UK definition of Asian, can the groups and artists of Asian Underground even be seen as Asian? Significantly, following personnel changes, both Cornershop in their chart-achieving line-up and Black Star Liner at the time of their Mercury Music Prize nomination each included only one Asian member, despite categorisations of them as 'Asian' bands. Are the respective Asian members representatively so? It is argued that much multicultural art is subject to 'the burden of representation' (Mercer 1994: 233–58;

Gilroy 1987; Huq 1996). Asian artists are seen as spokespeople for their 'community' and 'generation'. By Autumn 1998 an anti-Talvin Singh backlash was well underway in the Asian press while he picked up mainstream media plaudits. The heightened expectation invested in the new Asian dance music can make 'cultural significance' a cross to bear, subjecting artists to an unparalleled degree of scrutiny. Tjinder Singh, lead singer with Cornershop, has claimed 'Other bands are just there. We've had to justify ourselves a lot more than anybody else.'[9] The (black) journalist Kodwo Eshun illustrates the argument well with his 1993 commentary on Apache Indian in music magazine *The Wire*: 'Because he's more interesting in theory than in hearing, people don't realise how dull he really is' (quoted in Mitchell 1996: 65). This mass media legitimising role is in some ways more acute among specialist (UK Asian) press titles, e.g. *Eastern Eye* or *Asian Times*. The burden of representation hinges on two opposing arguments: it can either be seen as a duty of minority performers to use their privileged space to communicate issues pertinent to their community, or alternatively it is an irrelevance to limit an artist's work to their ethnicity and thereby ghettoise them.

The following two remarks demonstrate a desire by Asian performers to break out of this cycle:

> First we're not expected to make music at all, then people expect to hear sitars and tablas. We're still using those sounds but we're trying to invert it into a much more militant, aggressive context. Asian music is an exotic attachment, world music, etc. but we make the music we hear every day. It provides us with a medium to talk to people, to get social and political ideas across, to get the attention of youth.
>
> (Dr Das of ADF)[10]

> He said to me, 'why didn't you play tabla on it?' I said 'Pardon?' He said 'you know, *Asian* sounds'. ... Just because I'm Asian it doesn't mean I have to walk about with a tin of mango chutney all the time.
>
> (Inder, lead rapper with Detrimental, describing doing a remix for Kiss FM)[11]

There should be more roles available to Asian cultural practioners than simply appearing as ethnic court jesters for white audiences or adding exotic trimmings to white cultural products, both variations of the 'exoticism' function of world music as outlined by Van Der Lee (1998), but this inevitably requires time.

Second generation sounds II: do the raï thing[12]

The same post-1980s period that has seen the flourishing of bhangra has witnessed the rise of raï, a music which can similarly now be found in the world music racks of record stores worldwide and that can be traced back to a similar colonial precedent. Raï was spawned from the former French colony of Algeria. Accordingly it first reached a wider western audience in France, where many of its leading lights are now based. The occurrence of the Festival de Raï de Bobigny in north Paris began raï's French visibility. By 1992 it reached prominence further afield when the movement's best-known exponent Cheb Khaled scored a huge worldwide hit with the track 'Didi', the first Arab language entrant ever to the French top 50 charts. There are key common properties shared by raï and bhangra; notably their resonance with minority youth. In France, raï's main fanbase are beur youth – a slang term of self-appelation, referring to french-born youth with origins in the north Arab region of the Maghreb comprising Morocco, Tunisia and, above all, Algeria. This audience then provides a parallel with the broad UK category of 'Asian' youth with which bhangra is associated. However, there are also key differences. Although the root term is a Punjabi word, bhangra music and, to an even greater extent, Asian Underground, can be seen largely to have evolved outside the Indian subcontinent that they are associated with. By contrast raï is a musical style which was not only created, but also had a long period of gestation, in its country of origin Algeria, although it has since spread in popularity, notably in France since the mid- to late 1980s where, like bhangra, it has displayed a healthy aptitude to combine with other musical stylings. A number of secondary sources on raï music exist in France (Daoudi 2000; Daoudi and Milani 1996; Mazouzi 1990; Tennaille 2002). Documentation in English is rarer, although its academic acknowledgement is growing (Lipsitz 1994; Mitchell 1996; Schade-Poulsen 1995; Warne 1997). Colonial ties bind bhangra (and Asian Underground) to Britain and raï music to France. Ostensibly both are 'world' musics. Although big name raï performers such as Khaled have played London concerts largely to packed venues of French expatriates since the 1990s, raï has taken longer to penetrate the mainstream English-speaking public beyond the followers of 'world music'. The appearance of raï stalwart Cheb Mami providing extra vocals on Sting's 'Desert Rose' hit single of 2000[13] prompted the UK release of Mami's album *Meli Meli*, with the CD case sporting a sizeable sticker advertising this connection. However, although the English-speaking world had been largely resistant to the spread of raï until that point, it was certainly no overnight phenomenon.

The beginnings of raï can be traced to Algeria in the 1940s when the country was part of the French empire. Broughton *et al.* (1994: 110) describe raï as 'Algerian "rebel" music – originally an accoustic folk style from Oran … [but] now a very hi-tech sound, with electric guitars and synthesisers … characterised by its lyrics of dissent from conservative Islamic values.' Here immediately we can see parallels with bhangra, which had its origins in a folk-dance style. Bhangra too, like raï, is often based on repetitive rhythms as opposed to melody. As folk forms, both of these musics were orginally based on oral repositories and impro-visation rather than amplified and recorded sound. The harnessing of technology in raï has been key to its cultural practice and development. Schade-Poulsen (1995) notes the following reasons for the rise of raï in post-independence

Algeria: the doubling of the number of inhabitants; urbanisation and the growth of cities; and the growth in number of youth to consume mass-produced cultural goods in their leisure time. The reason identified for its crossover beyond Algeria is often given as the medium of the compact cassette. During the 1980s 2.5 million cassettes were sold for every vinyl album in Alegria (Daoudi 2000: 48). Again this 'cassette culture' is a direct parallel with the initial means of circulation of bhangra. Again multinationals moved in later to sign various raï acts to their rosters in the 1990s, from which point the scene became visible to the *grande publique* of France and beyond.

The youth aspect of raï culture can be seen in the naming of its major practitioners with the prefix 'Cheb', connoting young (the male form). The best-known examples are Cheb Mami and Cheb Khaled, although the latter has dropped this term from his name – presumably as he no longer considers himself to be young. The music has also taken on oppositional undertones in resisting both Algerian Islamic fundamentalism and French racism. The reggae of Bob Marley has been seen as one political raï template (Morgan 1994: 129). Khaled has declared:

> Fundamentalists don't want our concerts to happen. They come and break things up. They say raï is street music and that it's debauched. But that's not true. I don't sing pornography. I sing about love and social life. We just say what we think, just like singers all over the world.
>
> (quoted in Lipsitz 1994: 125)

The music's use in anti-racist protesting in France could be seen in the inclusion of raï DJs on the bill when the local authority of Strasbourg mounted a free open-air concert in protest against the congress held in the town by the FN (Front National, the extreme right-wing political party headed by Jean Marie Le Pen in 1997). Cheb Mami has lived in France since undertaking his military service for Algeria in the late 1980s, although this detail is often overlooked in marketing him as a product.[14] The assasination of raï singer Cheb Hasni in Algeria is believed to have been a factor in Khaled's subsequent re-location to Paris. Musically Schade-Poulsen (1995: 110) draws a distinction between raï from Algeria and the more polished mass-market versions of it aimed at a worldwide audience. Khaled's new-found success, which has been principally in France, is almost dismissed with a footnote branding it 'with a star system and a musical product which have little to do with Algerian raï'. Of course such a comment only tells part of the story because there are fundamental continuities between the two in this chapter.

The original raï sound includes woodwind, percussion and stringed instuments played with bows. Traditional raï instruments include lutes, flutes, zithers, oboes, tambourines and bagpipes. In unamplified form, these instruments made it suitable for playing in initimate venues at family occasions such as weddings and circumcision gatherings. The basic formula has however been supplemented with technological advances. Although the importing of western elements into raï could be interpreted as indicating a 'watering down' of the raï prescription, there are antecedents to this that date back a long way. Significantly, until Algerian independence in 1962, raï's birthplace Oran contained French, Jewish, Spanish and Arab quarters and was the region of Algeria most heavily populated by expatriate French people. Daoudi (2000: 9) describes the co-existence of neo-Alsacian and Breton village halls and churches on the landscape alongside Arab areas with ever-looming mosques and minarets. This highly specific localised environment played a crucial role in raï's inception. Although it is tempting to see colonial relations as a one-way destruction of indigenous customs and practices, the influences of the colonisers upon the colonised and vice versa can be more subtle than this. Dauodi (2000: 23) sees orchestral accompaniment as being the most essential feature of the modernisation of Algerian music. Amongst French singers that were popular amongst the youth of pre-independence Algeria who contributed to this development are Edith Piaf, Maurice Chevalier and even the Spaniard Julio Iglesias, who has sung in French. Cheb Khaled has repeatedly cited perennial French rocker Johnny Halliday, now something of a French institution, as a key influence.

Discussion: music and messages of raï and bhangra compared

Divorced from its youth music context, the root meaning of the word raï is 'opinion' (Morgan 1994; Schade-Poulsen 1995). Its lyrics can be seen as opinionated, just as those of bhangra have at times been (Dudrah 2002). However the danger of an over-concentration on lyric analysis is exemplified in the way that quite frequently in live performance raï lyrics are changed according to audiences and circumstances. It is only since the music has existed in recorded form in fact that meanings are becoming easier to pin down. Barrett (1996) asserts that the left-liberal politics often assumed to be inherent in world music are often misplaced with the misunderstanding of foreign language lyrics sometimes being a contributory factor. Schade-Poulsen's (1995) translation of raï lyrics to some extent illustrates this. He draws a distinction between 'dirty raï' and 'clean raï'. Most of the lyrics in the first category are not about heroically fighting oppressive regimes in a strongly political sense but more in keeping with youth cultural hedonism in their celebration of women and drinking. One could see this head-on confrontation of the taboos of sex and alcohol as being more overtly political in Muslim nations than they are in the west, but the sort of lyrics about female conquests could also be seen as highly politically incorrect for their objectification of women. Schade-Poulsen (1995) goes through the translation into English of a number of 'dirty raï' and 'clean raï' stanzas; however he admits the limitations of lyric analysis, based on all listeners getting the same understanding out of lyrics, which they will not necessarily do. Since raï has come to be produced in France, its form often incorporates French phrases, or numbers sung entirely in the French language. Cheb Mami's *Meli Meli* album for example included the pivotal track 'Azwaw' in both Arabic and French versions. The French version entitled

'Au Pays des Merveillies' (At the Country of Marvels) had been a hit single in France in 1998. Also present were bilingual tracks, e.g. 'Parisien du Nord' featuring the rappers K.mel and Imhotep of the group IAM. Translations in the accompanying lyric booklet of all of its fourteen songs in both English and French suggested a concerted effort at crossover. Such initiatives again contribute to breaking down 'world music' style barriers for the western listener and goes some way to demystifying raï.

Although British-born Asian youth speak English as their first, and increasingly their only language, the lyrical content of bhangra recordings is still frequently in Punjabi, although it is the rhythm which has more significance as bhangra is primarily a dance music style. The source material covers a range of themes from the romanticism of Bollywood to the daily realities of urban Britain (Dudrah 2002; Kalra 2000) substantiating the early internet claim: 'Lyrical content of Bhangra songs relates to celebration, or love, or patriotism or current social issues.'[15] In Asian Underground, being mainly dance music, tracks are often instrumental in nature using samples or live passages of Indian instrumentation. Where lyrics are present, these are often largely in English, reflecting the predominantly English language base of its creators, perhaps punctuated with a smattering of Indian language, e.g. as seen in Cornershop's use of Punjabi on certain tracks and the occasional Bengali phrases used by Asian Dub Foundation (ADF) and Joi. The new Asian dance music has been celebrated for its political content; however the cases to demonstrate this are chosen in a selective way, usually with ADF or Fun-Da-Mental[16] as examples (e.g. Hutnyk 2000; Sharma *et al.*, 1996). ADF grew out of a London community music project, have also played numerous anti-racist benefits and notably championed the case of a young Asian waiter jailed for self-defence following a racist attack, via the single 'Free Satpal Ram'. DJ John Pandit, the band's self-styled 'political strategist' initially in ADF's career maintained a day job as a youth worker for a Civil Rights Advice and Support group in Tower Hamlets, East London. He told me that political music was thus a logical progression:

> We find it difficult to be just entertainment. A lot of groups will have a radical sound and attach themselves to these campaigns because it's flavour of the month ... [but] we've been through this, seen it all, Ani [Dr Das] from his educational point as a tutor and me being involved in anti-racist work for 10 years now.[17]

Many of today's second generation artists conversely often consciously refrain from overt politics. Despite encountering a band provocatively named 'Fuck Authority', Finnegan's (1989: 127) study concurred with the apolotical line, as seen in the following quote: 'The common image of identifying rock music with protest – more especially with "youth" and/or "working class protest" was ... not generally borne out by this study.' The British Indian Talvin Singh sees himself essentially as a drummer: 'I don't really want to be political all the time. I don't fit into that and I don't want to. I wanna enjoy things which I like whether they have an Asian value or not.' Visiting India aged eleven to be shunned by his Indian peers for being 'too British' and his English classmates on return for being 'too Indian' has marked him more than any postcolonial political vengeance: 'These cultural crises really stay in your blood but instead on being sour about it, I bring that into some beautiful energy rather than going "you fucked us up. I'm gonna fuck you up." Fuck *who* up? Are these people any part of that? Let's move our shit on.'[18] The Asian jazz-fusionist Nitin Sawhney has rejected any such resistive responsibility in his work, declaring: 'I hate everything about politics. To me politics was [*sic*] about white, middle-aged men. I don't wanna preach to people. I don't think I've got the right to preach anymore than anyone else.'[19] In his work however he has performed subtle politics, for example in articulating the migratory experience of his parents' generation on his album *Broken Skin*. Likewise, it has been shown that heterosexual masculinity in varying degrees has been the over-riding feature of Algerian raï lyrics rather than political sloganeering (Schade-Poulsen 1995). Interestingly the 1980s militant beur group Carte de Séjour (Temporary Resident's Permit), while signed to Universal Music's French subsiduary Barclay, had a hit in 1986 with an embryonic pop-raï crossover cover version of the classic *chanson Française* ode to its country 'La Douce France' (Gentle France). Although the lyrics remained totally unchanged from Charles Trenet's original, which had celebrated the singer's idyllic schooldays and happy French childhood from the bottom of his heart, the song's general register and intonation of lyrical delivery imported a new twist onto the song whereby the lyrics became interrogating rather than stating fact, with an undercurrent of sarcasm. Again this highlights the inadequacies of reading music solely as a written text and isolating it from its context or ignoring the musical form.

As in bhangra, two-way cultural flows and intersections abound in raï's development. The music has progressed, undergoing adaptation whereby it has been suffixed and prefixed with a wide range of other musical styles to give plural raï or 'le raï pluriel' (Daoudi 2000), whose forms include reggae-raï, ragga-raï, disco-raï, pop-raï, funk-raï and raï-rock. This departure from notions of cultural purity is inevitable. It not only demonstrates graphically the healthy musical promiscuity that has always coloured raï but also the way that musics once considered outside the western pop tradition have now become part of it in the wide range of musics that raï has become associated with. For Schade-Poulsen (1995: 88) these reconfigured forms have 'modernised an older repertoire and put it on the level of universal pop music while keeping its Algerian character'. The undeniably derivative musical products of this encounter are also increasingly being inflected by a contemporary French character, encapsulated by the phrase 'le raï beur' (Daoudi 2000: 69). Cheb Khaled and Cheb Mami were, at the time of their emergence, hailed as significant for the fact that they were born in post-independence Algeria. The beur generation are French-born to Maghreban parents. This makes their experiences of colonialism even more remote. Along with their parents, their immediate concerns have been their negotiation into

French society, rather than the de-colonisation of north Africa. The telegenic Faudel for example was born in suburban Paris in 1978. His best-selling pop-raï single of 1996, 'Tellement n'brik' (I Love You So Much), was bilingual with verses alternating between French and Arabic. Romantic love then persists as a lyrical theme but the nature of social commentary also evolves. Cheb Abdou for example is openly gay – markedly different from the earlier misogyny of raï lyricism. Zebda from Toulouse, a mixed-race collective whose musical mix straddles rap and raï, scored a number one hit in 1998 with 'Tomber La Chemise' (Drop the Shirt). The accompanying album *Essence Ordinaire* mixed musical styles, humour and realism, for example reflecting on racism in contemporary France on the track 'Je Crois Que Ça Va Pas Être Possible' (I Don't Believe It'll Be Possible), where the lyrics deal with the rejection encountered by the narrator in seeking employment and housing. Although the band sing in French, other aspects of their cultural product reflect the beur origins of members, including some of the raï-derived rhythms used and the band's name in itself.[20]

Also demonstrating a rupture with world music's insistence on 'authenticity', the musicology of bhangra and Asian Underground breaks with tradition in overcoming the difficulty that 'pure' Indian music has of being 'uneasy listening' to the western ear. A list drawn up of the wide spectrum of sounds from the Indian subcontient could potentially include the devotional sounds of ghazals, ragas and quawali and Bollywood soundtracks featuring ultra-inauthentic playback singers, so-called as their recorded voices are 'played back' to the actions of actors who mime singing during musical numbers in films. Indian scales, the flexibility of melody lines and vocal techniques using microtonal differentiation as an expressive force and timings based on unequal bar patterns all differ from standard features of western musicality. However, just like the set of styles that have been termed 'after raï' (Daoudi 2000), bhangra has given rise to a number of hybrid categories that include its fusion with ragga music in 'bhangramuffin'[21] or 'raggas-tani' (*ID*, April 1993; *The Times*, 25 January 1993; McRobbie 1994a: 183) and 'bhangle', a bhangra–jungle hybrid described by Cynthia Rose on the internet.[22] At the time of writing there is a current vogue for two-step garage and r'n'b bhangra mixes whose exponents include Punjabi MC. These are consistent with shifts in the division of labour in recording technology, ushering in reduced studio time and sampling (Beadle 1993) and also demonstrate bhangra's commendable adaptability. The sleevenotes to Bally Sagoo's classic Hindi film-theme remix album *Bollywood Flashback* (1995) proclaimed it to be 'the most modern Hindi album ever'. Arguably it was Norman Cook's skilfully speeded-up remix of Cornershop's 'Brimful of Asha' that propelled it to number one, *not* the tune itself which had failed to impact on the charts in its original dirge-like form some months earlier. The primacy of remix over original calls into question the very notion of 'authenticity' that has been accepted as axiomatic in pop, not least of all in the area of 'ethnic' music. However bhangra and Asian Underground can act as an enabling medium through which young Asian and non-Asians may be able to discover 'authentic', i.e. earlier, Indian music, e.g. the film tracks remixed by

Sagoo or the singers venerated in the lyrics of 'Brimful of Asha', named after septuagenarian playback diva Asha Bhoshle and also mentioning Mohd Rafi, Lata Mangeshekar and French 1960s pop star Jacques Dutronc.[23] Concerts combining classical Indian musicians with second generation mix-merchants have also resulted in some interesting mixed audiences spanning the Asian 'parent' and youth generations as well as white indie and world music fans – e.g. Fun-Da-Mental's tour with devotional Quawali singer Aziz Mian and Talvin Singh's Royal Albert Hall appearances with Ustaad Sultan Khan.

Bhangra is problematic in terms of its location. Is it world music, British, Asian or indeed black music? The centrality of black music on white culture has itself been much discussed (Chambers 1976; Gilroy 1993a; 1993b; 1993c; Hebdige 1979; Jones 1988). Both post-bhangra and bhangra music draw on black influences among other varied styles. For Gilroy (1993a: 35) it is the spontaneity of African-derived black music that makes it 'something of a magnet for other social groups', e.g. the call and response of rap. This is also a tradition in Asian music, however; as it is in almost any culture with an organised religion. Oliver (1990: 7) questions categorising Asian music as 'black', a term that many Asians reject (Baumann 1996; Brah 1997; Modood 1992). Indeed the term itself is loaded with essentialist concepts of musical authenticity and political meaning. Unlike 'black' music which has always had an allure for whites, as we will see in chapter 7, aside from the brief Ravi Shankar-led 1960s moment of rock's quest for orientalised spirituality, Asians have largely been ignored in pop.[24] However, at the Manchester daytimer of July 2002, as well as the bhangra room there was another room on a different physical level of the building where ragga, hip-hop and hard-core garage were played. Perhaps due to the venue's normal role as a place where reggae sound-systems play and the black DJs in the second room, the audience included a smattering of black youths. Gilroy writes (1993a: 203): 'In reinventing their own ethnicity, some of Britain's Asian settlers have also borrowed the sound system culture of the Carribean and the soul or hip-hop styles of black America … as part of their invention of a new mode of cultural production and with an identity to match.' This statement however begs far too many questions: 'borrowing' is quite simply how cultures change; the rhythms of bhangra and Asian Underground are also adapted from existing Asian musics. Indeed a black student that I spoke to in the bhangra room told me that he was in attendance 'because my [Asian] mates dragged me down. This music's new to me but I love it though.' The comment would appear to suggest the inverse of Gilroy's argument, demonstrating that two-way cultural flows permeate bhangra. Stretching theories of 'black' music to the British South Asian community proves largely unsatisfactory, e.g. Gilroy's (1993a) diasporic concept of the 'black Atlantic' which transcends nation-states and hinges on slavery, leaving Asians somewhat cast adrift.

Raï culture has given rise to an entire micro-industry which it is at the centre of. Raï films include the banlieue[25] fable *Raï* (1995), the Marseilles-set *1, 2, 3 Soleils* (1993) for which Cheb Khaled's accompanying soundtrack won a French

Victoire de la Musique award, and *100% Arabica* (1997), a comedy in which both Khaled and Cheb Mami appeared as actors. Much in the same way as *East is East* received distribution in major cinemas, *100% Arabica* played on a large number of screens and was marketed as a mainstream comedy as opposed to an art-house film. The film could be accused of suffering from burden-of-representation-type constraints in trying possibly to portray too much in a single film. The inclusion of racism, fundamentalism, urban deprivation and raï could potentially appear as cliché-ridden, but it represents an important stage in the acceptance of raï music and beur youth. Second generation British Asian music also does not exist in a vacuum. Other cultural forms from the same circumstances of production co-exist with it: second generation cinema, writing, theatre and comedy too have risen to prominence in recent years.[26] These are importantly, unlike the well-known Bombay 'Bollywood' film industry, in the English language with perhaps a smattering of words in South Asian tongues, fittingly as the output of a British-born generation with English as their first, and increasingly only, language. Leeds bhangra outfit the KKKings, whose name evokes both Guru Nanak's prescribed 5 Ks of Sikh conduct and the Ku Klux Klan, released a bhangrafied bastardized hybrid of Cliff Richard's 'Summer Holiday' and the Sex Pistols' 'Holidays in the Sun' with the single 'Holidays in the United KKKingdom', focusing on the refrain 'Holidays in Asia'. The 1992 albums *Never Mind the Dolaks* and *Bomb the Tumbi* from bhangra acts Satrang and Safri Boys played on the Sex Pistols' *Never Mind the Bollocks* album title and on the name of chart dance-outfit 'Bomb the Bass' respectively by substituting the names of two Indian music instruments.[27] This reflects a 'playful' (and hence potentially postmodern) side of second generation Asian pop in subverting convention and tweaking received othordoxies.

The development of both raï in France and bhangra and its successive forms in the UK in the way that they have gone from being from minority-consumed cassette cultures to major label going concerns are both illustrative of the way in which the music industry attempts to appropriate what it sees will make profits. With Khaled among Barclay's biggest grossing acts, Cheb Mami on Virgin and Faudel signed to Mercury, can we see that earlier fears of a decline in raï have been disproved? Schade-Poulsen (1995: 84) declared: 'Today … the raï boom has peaked.' Morgan (1994: 32–33) mused that 'the idea of investing large amounts of cash in the career of an Algerian singer was viewed as a huge risk by many' and that 'Latent racism impedes the French major labels from developing raï artists on French soil.' Were such prognoses overly pessimistic? The answer is yes and no. Certain 'name' raï artists have achieved a transition from minority to mainstream, particularly those who have been able to follow through 'adapt or die'-type ulti-matums (Morgan 1994). In 1998, representing a bridge between the generations, Khaled, former Carte de Séjour singer Rachid Taha and Faudel joined forces on stage at the Bercy Arena in Paris for the celebrated *1, 2, 3 Soleils* concert and album, ostensibly a visible landmark in raï's rising international popularity. However, aside from these 'bankable' names, the picture is more complicated. Banerji and Baumann (1990) made similarly negative predictions about the future of live bhangra but well-attended gatherings continue. In terms of recorded acts, bhangra and Asian Underground provide ample examples of major record label acts that have subsequently had their contracts terminated due to poor sales, demonstrating the way that the industry can take away what it gives. John Pandit of ADF told me: 'The music industry is so important for British capitalism that they need to compartmentalise everything. They have their own markets like the gay market, the pink pound. Now there's the rupee pound, a new Asian audience. It's the history of western imperialism: "let's talk about exotic Asians".'[28] Making a similar point, an article in *ID* (April 1993) claimed of bhangra: 'Of late, it has begun to seep into the mainstream pop world, where it's a new wrinkle to a business forever seeking something different, devouring "exotic genres" like a starving dog in a butcher's shop.' These two remarks evoke Kellner's (1994) 'difference sells' idea, however we should qualify it with the recognition that in rational capitalist economics there is no room for loss-makers. By 2002 ADF were no longer on London records, Talvin Singh had been released from Island and Bally Sagoo was long gone from Sony, as was the once-much celebrated Apache Indian from Island. All had been victims of recent culls to clear unprofitable acts once their novelty value had dissipated. Throughout the same period the independent label Wiija had stuck by Cornershop, conversely nuturing their talent from its indie-rock beginnings through to a number one UK single and beyond.

How far are colonial relationships replicated in world music? For Warne (1997: 135) it is a white liberal preoccupation: ' "World music" then becomes a projection screen for the anxieties and neuroses of ethnic majority Westerners dealing with the guilt of a colonial past.' World music could be seen as keeping third world inhabitants in their place. Although sociological literature has tended to see ethnicity, in its earlier guise of 'race' as a form of stratification with an equivalent function to that of class (e.g. Bilton *et al.* 1987 who include it with 'forms of subordination'), CCCS-style class readings of social reproduction are complicated by recent immigration as this almost effaces second generation British Asian class consciousness to the point of their parents' arrival in Britain 'as post ex-colonial subjects ... circumscribed by colonial precedents' (Brah 1997: 21). In world music peoples from formerly colonised nations have shown that they can work together in truly multi-ethnic partnerships beyond the obvious coloniser/colonised divides. Archetypal raï exponent Cheb Mami appeared on the 2001 album of archetypal post-bhangra artist Nitin Sawhney. The British Egyptian singer Natacha Atlas, formerly of 1990s Nation Records mixed-race dance collective Transglobal Underground, has since going solo recorded three albums of largely Arabic language middle-eastern tinged music that has found her widespread success in France, particularly among raï fans, while she remains far more of a minority act in her native UK. Her 2001 album *Ayeshteni* included two French language tracks; a raï-styled cover of Jacques Brel's 'Ne Me Quitte Pas' (Don't Leave) and 'Le Soleil d'Egypte' (Egypt Sun), written for Atlas by Zebda.[29] Cheb Khaled became a huge star in India after 'Didi' received a bhangra remix. Khaled's *Kenza* album included 'El Harb Wine' (Where to Flee?), a

Hindi–Arab duet with Talvin Singh's female vocalist Amar. These transnational flows open up the possibility of new cultural alliances forged by the formerly colonised.

The role of gatekeepers as tastemakers has been important in exposing minority musics to mainstream audiences. Minority gatekeepers however operate on a different level to those of the mass media. The Asian youth lifestyle magazine *Snoop* covers subjects including music and Hindi film reviews. According to its editor, Shabbs:

> The time has come to stop pandering to the white mainstream. We do not have to like Nitin Sawhney [trendy Jazz fusionist] just because Jools Holland [BBC television presenter and powerbroker] likes him. British Asians today are proud to be both [British and Asian] and if any of us want to listen to Malkit Singh [traditional bhangra artist], we will do so without losing any of our cool.[30]

When I interviewed Talvin Singh, he claimed to have done over 300 interviews in the preceding month during which he was 'stitched up' (misrepresented) the most by Asian youth magazines *Second Generation* and *Snoop*, by whom he felt betrayed, 'specially as they give you all that "Asian brothers" bullshit'.[31] Specialist gatekeepers can then be more demanding of the acts that they regulate access to, rather than uncritically welcoming minority music as a more mainstream, liberal-leaning, world music-supporting newspaper such as the *Guardian* might do. Shabbs of *Snoop* has argued for the importance of the minority press in illuminating radical minority performers over and above 'known' examples:

> it is a sad reflection on us that so many of these artists came to our attention as a result of a window created by mainstream media responsibilities. We should have opened the doors ourselves given that in the fields of theatre, music and comedy – there have previously been many superior acts than *Goodness Gracious Me* [popular BBC 2 all-Asian comedy show] and Talvin Singh, [who have been] ignored because the white media hadn't given them their seal of approval.[32]

Once these cultural products attain a degree of success whereby the role taken by a minority gatekeeper such as *Snoop vis-à-vis* an artist such as Singh will turn more into one of monitoring, rather than attempting to 'break' an artist through to a wider public.

Is the role of the gatekeeper from inside the musical establishment then simply to give the minority artist a 'leg up' or what Van Der Lee (1998) describes as 'exploitation' and 'validation'? A number of big-name collaborations have assisted raï in crossing over in France, in the same way that other international musical styles previously entered national consciousness after being championed by more mainstream performers. Reggae in France was first used in the late 1970s by the popular *chanson Française* singer-songwriters Bernard Lavalliers and Serge

Gainsbourg, the latter having worked with producers Sly and Robbie. This in turn helped pave the way for Francophone reggae made in France from artists such as Princess Erika and former tennis-player Yannick Noah. An example of a reggae–raï crossover hit is the 1996 duet 'Fugitif' performed by the Algerian-born Cheb Mami with the Caribbean Tonton David. Far from just being a way of Mami getting in on David's coat-tails, this could have also had the effect of exposing Mami's audience to reggae.[33] Khaled has undertaken numerous mutually beneficial celebrity pairings of this nature.[34] His Barclay career has seen him use western producers including Don Was of 1990s US band Was Not Was on the 1992 album *Khaled* and progressive rock mainstay Steve Hillage, who has also produced Rachid Taha, on *Kenza*. Khaled's French language 1996 hit Aïcha was written by mainstream middle-of-the-road French singer-songwriter Jean Jacques Goldman. The symbolic value of the partnership of Khaled, an Arab, with Goldman, of Jewish extraction, was not lost on the media and the track won a Victoire de la Musique award. *Kenza* continued the Goldman connection ('C'est la Nuit' included in both French and Arabic versions) and also saw Israeli chanteuse Noa join Khaled for a cover of John Lennon's 'Imagine'. These associations then work on dual levels. In this way Cheb Mami's recording with Sting can be understood as Mami acting as a gatekeeper himself rather than simply adding a bit of exotic colour to the latest release of an ageing rocker. Encouragingly the sociology of the 'new ethnicities' (Back 1996; Back and Solomos 1997; Brah 1997: 169; Cohen 1996; Hall 1991) recognises ethnic minorities as dynamic rather than quiescent.[35] It is hoped that future youth culture research can reverse the status of ethnic minorities from 'othered' outsiders peripheral to mainstream society and reposition them as interwoven into its fabric.

How lasting will the legacy of these musics be? Shabbs, editor of *Snoop*, commented on the hyperbole surrounding Asian Underground: 'The Brits fascinated by our alleged hip-onslaught do so as voyeur. If this [attention] is giving our confidence a boost, it is a good thing – as long as we do not fall apart the moment that interest is deemed "passé".'[36] The age-old media appetite for feeding off new trends towards the ultimate end of 'build 'em up, knock 'em down' was to a degree already inferable by 1998 from the tone of the mainstream London listings magazine *Time Out*'s 'Clubbing' column which was suggesting that 'Asian underground' was a 1997 phenomenon whose time had passed.[37] There does appear to have been a recognition of bhangra and Asian Underground from the UK pop establishment, as seen in the nomination lists of the Brit awards and Mercury Music prize in recent years, but the shortlisting, which seems to include one 'Asian' act annually, can be critiqued as tokenistic. Even following Talvin Singh's Mercury prize win of 1998 he has remained a niche artist.

After a decade of development outside Algeria there is meanwhile evidence that raï is on its way to becoming a 'French institution' in the same way as quintessentially French rock 'n' roller Johnny Halliday. The quote at the top of the chapter from Cathus surrounding the release of the album *Kenza* makes the point that Khaled has achieved the same level of public adulation. Nonetheless while an integrationist such as Khaled, who has lived in France since 1996, is acceptable to the French, this does not mean that there will necessarily be a blanket acceptance of raï to follow. Warne (1997: 145) points out: 'It would be naïve to assume an unreserved acceptance within the French mainstream for a culture often viewed as suspect due to its Islamic connections.' This is in spite of the fact that raï was perceived as *anti*-Islamic when it began in Algeria where Khaled and others received death threats for performing it. Following the terrorist attacks of 11 September 2001 Cheb Khaled's US tour planned for later that month was cancelled. Concerts were re-scheduled for the beginning of 2002 when they took place without major incident. Nevertheless while raï initially came to France because singers could allegedly express themselves more freely on French soil than in Algeria, it appears that there is something of a glass ceiling in operation. There is space for a limited number of performers at the top but mobility for those at the bottom is more difficult. Raï has also had certain awards bestowed upon it, perhaps most significantly the 'Victoire de l'artiste-interprète de l'année' (artist of the year) by Khaled in 1995 as voted by an industry panel of 3,000 individuals that make up SACEM (Société des Auteurs Compositeurs Français).

Situating bhangra and raï music

Frith (1996: 269) writes: 'Music is the cultural form best able to cross borders – sounds carry across fences and walls and oceans, across classes, races and nations.' These properties make it an ideal medium of articulation for the migratory experience. However the young creators of contemporary Asian Underground, bhangra and raï music in Europe are second generation minority youth. There needs to be a rethinking of such people no longer as migrants but as a settled population. In another comment relating to the socio-spatial properties of pop, that has been quoted on more than one occasion (Bennett 1998; 2001; Negus 1996, Stokes (1994: 3) states: 'Among the countless ways in which we "relocate" ourselves, music undoubtedly has a vital role to play. The musical event, from collective dances to the act of putting a CD into a machine, evokes and organises collective memories and present experiences of place with an intensity, power and simplicity unmatched by any other social activity.' Accordingly Schade-Poulsen (1995: 88) declares that 'The consumers are offered the possibility, when dancing to a raï cassette of being taken into the atmosphere of a live performance.' Admittedly music can transport us elsewhere in place and time in the same way that a photograph can act as a memory-jogger, however not all people react to musical texts in the same way. For listeners oblivious to the Algerian origins of raï listening to its recorded version, the time and place might mean their summer holidays, in France, or even elsewhere on the European mainland, where 'Didi' was played nightly in the local bar. For people listening to bhangra the time may be when they were revising for their exams or working in a factory or skipping school to go to a daytimer.

Certainly it is tempting to interpret world music as bringing listeners to primitive third world landscapes, or to see second generation sounds as enabling the listener to escape their time, place and circumstances thus relocating and liberating youthful participants away from their parental moorings. Schade-Poulsen (1995: 107) has also alluded to raï as servicing a 'need for youth to create a sphere for their concerns, independent of the parent generation'. Shuker (1998: 26) makes a similar point: 'For young Asians, bhangra is part of an assertion of cultural identity distinct from that of the establishment and their parents.' Yet bhangra is popular with the parents of Asians. Furthermore electronic dance music, rap or grunge as well as raï all in some ways aim to mark out a distinctiveness from the parental generation. Perhaps the 'second generation' aspect here is of relative irrelevance to the rebellion. Indeed tracks such as Cornershop's 'Brimful of Asha', a paean to septugenarian playback diva Asha Bhoshle, express continuities with parental generation music.[38] Received notions of pop rooted in a culture of generational conflict, central to the idea of subcultural authenticity, are clearly misplaced. Straightforward correlations between youth and pop are, as we have seen, becoming increasingly difficult to sustain. Identities themselves are ever more fluid in post/late/high modernity (Fornas et al. 1995; Beck 1992). Musical identity is a complex construct that is multi-dimensional. Future conceptualisations of youth culture should break out of the limitations of the analysis within bounded, implicitly homogenous national units when music such as bhangra, Asian Underground and raï clearly demonstrate that in today's society of multi-ethnic modernity musics are often de-territorialised and reterritorialised from fixed socio-spatial settings.

As they are both the offspring of mixed parentage, now made in Europe as much as in the East, both raï and bhangra do not fit easily into this music-business-meets-anthropology category of 'world music' discourse that it has often been slotted into (e.g. Burton and Awan 1994). It is difficult to straightforwardly apply this term to second generation sounds for its inbuilt assumptions of 'authenticity' and 'indigenous peoples'. Fock (1999: 75) more usefully refers to bhangra and raï as 'radically modernised folk music'. They are also importantly both part and parcel of global contemporary postcolonial youth culture (Lipsitz 1994). Schwarz (1996: 190) writes:

> Arguably, the culture of insular England was formed as much by its overseas possessions as by the island territory and in its own — often resoundingly reactionary — way white English ethnicity is, despite all protestations to the contrary, a hybrid, the expansion of England in many different locales, which have fed back and transformed the metropolis.

As Britain's Asian communities experience a suburbanisation (Peach 1996), the borders of this metropolis themselves are being reoriented away from the traditional 'inner city' ghettos of ethnic youth. The musics discussed use elements of the global and the local. They are often played (live or in recorded form) in small-scale neighbourhood gatherings, e.g. in particular suburbs, but the ethnicised soundscapes they inhabit have wider resonance. Bhangra's influence stretches beyond the United Kingdom to Canada and the USA – other areas of Asian settlement – not to mention back to India itself. A similar pattern can be seen with raï which in its westernised versions is popular in the Maghreb and beyond. Khaled apparently caused near-riots in his concerts of 2000 in Tunisia and in Algeria where he played for the first time since his self-imposed exile in 1986, although the concert at Algiers attracted controvsey for being effectively limited only to a very middle-class audience of punters who could afford the entry.[39] Cheb Mami's appearance in front of 100,000 in Algiers in 1999 also had a similar 'homecoming' significance. In the early 1990s Apache Indian too has played large-scale gatherings in Delhi and Bombay (Mitchell 1996) and in doing so, according to his 1995 press release from Island Records, 'fulfilled his lifetime dream and returned to his native India, his first visit since he was seven years old.'[40] This shows the complex two-way cultural flows between the west and 'countries of origin'.

The examples I have outlined point to a rejection of the insistence on authenticity that has long been interwoven in world music. One could easily descend into clichéd postmodern prose here about the inauthentic or anti-authentic world we inhabit and how this renders clinging to ideas of authenticity obsolete; however, such an argument is supported by evidence. World music is a term fraught with complications. It is a designation that second generation practioners are often uncomfortable with as can be seen from the quote from Bally Sagoo, at the start of this chapter, where he claims that he wants to be accepted more as a 'trendy' dance artist and compete with non-world artists on his own terms. This can also been seen in his 1995 Sony press release which described him as 'the Asian equivalent of Jam and Lewis or Jazzie B', evoking the names of well-known dance producers. Disregarding the technologically advanced form of Sagoo's work, even the most emblematic forms of 'world music' cannot be held up with any conviction as culturally pure forms. Migrations of all kinds have a deep-seated history in, and resultant cultural effect on, the products of virtually all of the genres that have come to be be recognised as 'world music', be this the transition from rural to urban settings with the background of French de-colonisation in post-independence Algerian raï or the more obviously transnational second generation sounds of contemporary made-in-Europe bhangra, Asian Underground and beur-raï. Indeed musics can re-position themselves over time and thus cease to be regarded as 'exotic' or 'world' genres. Other musical styles have passed into received orthodoxy, for example even the most basic inexpensive electronic keyboard bought in a toy store will include pre-programmed rhythms such as 'rhumba' and 'samba' alongside 'waltz', 'fast rock' and 'slow rock'. It may only be a matter of time before 'bhangra' and 'jungle' join them.

Van Der Lee (1998: 45–6) comes up with a seven-point typology of world music with categories in descending order of authenticity. First is (i) ritual rural music (ii) high art (classical) music from overseas, followed by (iii) folklore music and then (iv) folk music with European influences. The last three categories are illustrative of cultural mixing. They are (v) the Western assimilation of Eastern music traits, then (vi) the Western assimilation of non- western traits and finally (vii) 'neo-world' music or 'mish-mash' fusion; the least authentic of all. On this scale bhangra and raï began somewhere located between points (iii) and (iv). They have passed through (v) to (vi). Exactly where the Indian experimentation of mainstream pop performers such as Boy George and Madonna is located could arguably be in either (vi) or (vii). As a guide recordings in (vii) are explained to be 'almost exclusively western products' (Van Der Lee 1998: 46). However such a qualifier does not necessarily simplify matters. Current experimental crossovers, such as Asian Underground tracks which are often constructed from software packages such as Cubase might be described as belonging to the (vii) category on production techniques alone, but if they are performed by Asian performers can this stop them from sliding down the authenticity scale? Cornershop's deftly executed Punjabi language version of the Beatles' 'Norwegian Wood' on their third album of 1997 appeared contemporaneously with the 1960s-styled UK guitar movement Britpop (discussed in chapter 7). Lead singer Tjinder Singh commented: 'The reason we did a cover of that song was because so many British bands are just ripping off The Beatles one hundred per cent at the moment – we wanted to put our twist on it by translating the vocal into Punjabi' (Thompson 1998: 178). This spans Van Der Lee's categories (v) and (vi). This re-working demonstrates a new inflection into any straight one-way notions of 'appropria-tion' as the track was the first ever to chart that included the Indian instrument the sitar. Certainly in the 1990s the fact that despite their outward appearances, the Asian-fronted groups Cornershop, Echobelly and the Voodoo Queens all played indie rock rather than the bhangra one might automatically expect of Asian youth meant that all three attracted almost exclusively white audiences, although the burden of representation dictated that in interview they were repeatedly questioned on their 'Asianness'. Perhaps the only thing that can unreservedly be equated with authenticity then is the impossibility of achieving it.

World music is associated with backwardness and ignores the way that non-western cultures have progressed. The crossover of the music created by British-born Asians (back) to an Indian subcontinent often best known to them through holidays raises questions of how authentically 'Asian' the new Asian dance music is. Technology is also seen as inauthentic. Crispian Mills of the group Kula Shaker, who have been criticised as white musicians playing Indian music, has spoken out against Asian Underground music for being inauthentic, claiming 'It's like a different universe. There's a big difference between Asians in Asia and Asians in Britian.' I do not wish to get embroiled in the 'Kula Shaker debate' here as the band will be returned to in chapter 7 on 'White Noise'. Mills however seems to propagate an aspic-preserved version of India in the claim: 'What's cool about Indian cities is that, even though there are millions of cars and the pollution is chronic, they still have hordes of cows wandering down the streets. There's a sense of balance we don't have in the west.'[41] This is consistent with the idea of world music and the third world as comparatively uncorrupted by western ways (Barrett 1996). In contrast Talvin Singh enthuses of an often overlooked dynamism of the modern subcontinent: 'People have this idea of Bombay being a place with loads of poor people. It's a crazy city. I find Bombay closer to New York than London … every other person is a video maker. Rave music is so big among Asian kids now.'[42] Even the technologically advanced Asian Underground has entrenched links with previous 'world' styles, most obviously bhangra. Back in 1997 it became common for Asian Underground practitioners to disassociate themselves from bhangra as can be seen in the comment of DJ Sanjeev from Asian Underground sound system Earthtribe: 'To us bhangra felt like a wedding scene. Fifty year old men getting onstage looking like Christmas trees … it was never us.'[43] Nonetheless, later styles of Asian-produced pop mixing eastern and western styles could almost certainly never have existed without bhangra, which laid many important foundations for their development. Moreover some one-time major label bhangra artists who were signed up by multinationals in the mid-1990s in the erroneous hope that they would be cash-cows have now come full circle. Apache Indian, who has received a disprorortionate level of academic interest to his chart career (see e.g. Back 1996; Gilroy 1993a; Lipsitz 1994; Mitchell 1996; Polhemus 1994; Taylor 1997), is now running his own bhangra label, as is Bally Sagoo. The sleevenotes of Sagoo's *Bollywood Flashback* (1995) album dedicated it 'To all the staff at Colombia records … for giving myself the opportunity to prove myself to the western market.' By 1998 his first post-Sony release (for Birmingham independent bhangra label Oriental Star) stated: '*Star Crazy* is dedicated to all his fans especially the hard-core bhangra addicts who supported him throughout his mainstream releases.'[44] The implication was a sense of release at having been let go from the clutches of a major, although Sagoo's remarks might be simply 'sour grapes' or even spin.

Conclusion: bhangra and raï music as second generation sounds beyond subculture

It would be facile to read both bhangra and raï as twin results of increased confidence on the part of second generation minority youth where their parents had been quiescent. However by implying a lack of confidence in the first generation, such claims deny earlier waves of cultural and political activity by minorities in Britain and France. Examples exist in, for example, the strikers at the Grunwick film processing plant led by exploited Asian women workers or anti-fascist action by the Southall Youth Movement in the UK in the 1970s and the 1983 'marche des beurs' – a large-scale march demanding political rights for a generation. Multiple paradigm shifts can be witnessed in the existence of second generation and third generation minority youth in Britain and France. Cultural identification is complex, constructed according to multiple determinants (Rutherford 1990). Ethnicity is only one of these. The manifestation of religious identities sometimes downplayed by the parent generation spells a continuity or even reassertion of 'traditional' identity for South Asian and beur youth. A simultaneous lessening knowledge of Asian languages and a weakening of the extended family (Modood *et al.* 1994) with tertiary education away from home signals a fragmentation. A multiplicity of identities and affiliations informs the cultural bearings of the second and third generation, quite unlike the idealised past of 'home' of the first. Modood (1994) rates bindi-wearing amongst Hindu women at 35 per cent, with twice as many in the over-35-year-old bracket. However a stark statistic such as this received a new twist in 1997/8 when the bindi briefly became a fashion item marketed at mainstream youth with chainstores such UK fashion chain Top Shop stocking them (cf. the profane impact of semiology as argued by Hebdige 1979). The 'coming of age' of the first generation of beurs that expressed political activism on a large scale can be seen in the appointment of the first beur to the French Cabinet in 2002 following the accession to power of Prime Minister Jean-Pierre Raffarin. Tokia Saïfi, who was made minister of sustainable development, reminisced about attending the 'marche des beurs' in 1983 in a round of media interviews surrounding her appointment – which was also significant for the fact that she is a woman in a largely male cabinet line-up.

Impacts and influences between the coloniser and colonised have always been about two-way movement. This can be seen in the tracing of 1908 as the year of the first Arab café in Paris (Daoudi 2000: 72). Van Der Lee (1998: 48) also points out that historically, most empires have absorbed cultural traits from colonised territories resulting in a re-shaping of imperial culture. In consequence, 'A new mainstream has in turn been re-diffused through the area of influence.' Raï and bhangra complicate and even to some extent contradict claims of American-driven cultural imperialism in music (Burnett 1996; Tunstall 1977; Shuker 1998: 79–82) by contributing towards a de-centring of western influence in popular music. Rather like the term 'beur', Kaur and Kalra (1996: 219) have even gone as far as the coin the neologism 'BrAsian' to describe British Asian identities defined as 'the complex subject positions of migrants and their offspring settled in Britain with links both imagined and material to South Asia'. New times can then demand new lexicons.

There has been a growth of interest in traditional musics in western Europe – not only the styles termed 'world' but also folk genres, e.g. the popularity of Breton music in France on albums such as the best-selling album *Panic Celtique* by Manau, a white band from the island of Corsica, fighting for self-determination from mainland France, who play a rap hybrid. Again this bears out Kellner's (1994: 40) 'difference sells' maxim. Concurrently the last two decades have seen raï and bhangra music's spread accelerate. Both have grown from cassette culture status to become styles signed with major label multinational corporations. World music is a problematic descriptor with distinct echoes of colonial relationships in 'othering' and exoticising non-western mainstream pop music. However these twenty-first century second generation musical proponents are counterbalancing these old notions. It is Birmingham in the UK that is now widely recognised as the home of bhangra music rather than the Punjab (Back 1996; Dudrah 2002; Gabriel 1998), although there are strong bonds and continuities between the two.[45] Elsewhere too we are witnessing a mainstreaming of 'world' styles. Lipsitz

(1994: 122) declares that 'Paris is an African as well as a European city.' Indeed along with Khaled and Cheb Mami other world music stars now domiciled in France include the Gipsy Kings, Manu Chao, Mano Dibango, Youssou N'Dour and Salif Keita. In other words they are no longer in distant, dark corners of the globe but based on first world western soil. This should negate then the sort of 'safe othering' that world music often implies where inhabitants of the third world are deemed acceptable and even heroic whilst they are at arm's length.

Morley and Robins (1996: 108) rightly remark that 'Globalisation as it dissolves the barriers of distance makes the encounter of colonial centre and colonised periphery immediate and intense.' Indeed, even if it hasn't happened yet, there is no reason why Khaled, or any of the other individuals on the list of 'domesticised' world artists above, should not eventually become a recipient of the French Légion d'Honneur. After all Johnny Hallyday (born Jean-Phillipe Smit) who was decorated with the award in 1997 was himself born in Belgium. In the UK Talvin Singh was invited to play at the Labour Party Conference of 1998 when the Blair government was still taken with the idea of 'Cool Britannia' (Huq 1998a). Although this notion has not weathered well, perhaps the monolithic UK block term 'Asian community' is becoming increasingly invalid in the light of a recognition of difference that this entails. Van Der Lee (1998) predicts a redundancy of 'world music' itself as third world musicians increasingly compete on equal terms with those of the first world. As hinted above, authenticity too should be a prime candidate in our conceptual scrapheap in considering musical cultures – an idea returned to in subsequent chapters. In conclusion then, the diverse loose groupings of musical styles encompassed in raï and bhangra between them constitute a key part of contemporary postcolonial, diasporic, current youth culture. We will encounter more examples in the following chapter which turns to dance music cultures.

5

DECONSTRUCTING DIFFERENCE
IN DANCE MUSIC

Subculture and club culture at the turn of the century

> The trouble with rave is that it has no articulated ideology, no sense of purpose and after a long night's raving, the brains of a deckchair.
>
> (Adam Sweeting, *The Guardian*, 7 November 1992)

> God is a DJ
>
> (Faithless)

Dance music as a meta-genre has demonstrated an impressive staying power and now is the subject of a number of histories spanning the academic, quasi-academic and popular spheres. In my use of this term for the purposes of this chapter, I am not simply referring to (any) music for dancing to; after all such a definition might implicate forms such as the foxtrot. The following chapter deals with DJ-centred club-context sounds that are derived from various roots including 1970s disco and 1980s electronica, using technology such as sampling and scratching. The public act of bodily expression, dancing, is central to such styles but is not a necessary requirement for being considered under this umbrella term: ambient music, for example, which often forms the soundtrack to the chill-out room for winding down at club events, in Toop's (1995: 52) words is an 'oxymoron … dance music for sitting still'. As the youth cult that first came to public attention for its drug of choice ecstasy, dance music has inevitably enough come of age and split into a number of new directions as what was once considered a niche market in itself has diversified into a multitude of sub-genre specialisations, undergoing something of an institutionalisation along the way. It is important then to be aware of the complexity of the overlapping plural scenes of contemporary dance music culture, which is far from being a singular entity. This chapter looks at various aspects of dance music and attempts to fill some of the gaps that there are in existing accounts by looking widely at 'difference' in dance music across its interlocking scenes, with particular reference to how it can be reconciled with the notions of subculture as discussed in the first chapter.

Returning to the themes first broached in chapter 1, it would be easy enough to see rave and dance music as another installment in the unfolding history of UK subcultures. However a number of rave chroniclers have been at pains to distance themselves from the Birmingham CCCS, e.g. Thornton (1995) and Redhead (1993a: 23). Whether contemporary dance music cultures display the traditional characteristics of subcultures in being a tightly bonded, high visibility, fringe-delinquent working class group, or can even be conceived of as a 'youth culture', is a complicated issue. Many of the words that have been applied to the burgeoning literature on post-subcultures can be applied to dance music: it is variously global, diasporic, multifaceted and hybrid. The many styles which constitute contemporary club culture are characterised by a high degree of internal differentiation and heterogeneity. Tomlinson (1998: 199) has written 'Rave is largely, if not exclusively a youth phenomenon, and youth is a vital component of the rave culture in general.' However, be this as it may, by the beginning of the new millennium there was a generation of dance music fans who had been participating in club culture for a decade: a market segment termed 'middle youth'. As a result the continued validity of pop as a metaphor of youth culture is one that needs examination in an age when youth lifestyles are reaching up into this category and compressing downwards into the pre-teen years. I want then to explore whether the unfolding of dance culture represents a fundamental break with past youth cultural history or is instead, as others have suggested, 'a new version of an old story'. Rave's advent signalled at once continuity and rupture with the past. Antecedents that contemporary dance culture has been traced back to in both spirit and sound include hippie, punk, hip-hop and disco. Geographically Mediterranean holiday resort dancefloors, north European metropolitan recording studios and Goa beach landscapes can all be seen as active sites of dance culture. Contradictions in clubbing will be examined, such as the 1990s free party scene and its paradoxical techno-pagan mix. The regulation of dance music cultures will also be turned to as this can be seen as the repression of difference.

Futurism and nostalgia

Summer 2002 – I am supplying the musical entertainment as DJ in a central London private member's club at a joint thirtieth birthday party for two friends. I have brought some current tunes with me but it's the old stuff that seems to be the best received or, more accurately, the old numbers that have been made known to a new public through remixes and sampling. I segue the Sugababes number one hit 'Freak Like Me' into Tubeway Army's 'Are Friends Electric'. Featuring an eerie syncopated female vocal, the former largely derives from the latter and has rendered Gary Numan's taut keyboard riff-driven 1978 single playable without sounding dated. Euro DJ Armand Van Helden's hit 'Always Crashing the Same Car' has done the same for Numan's 1979 hit 'Cars'. I have been instructed to play a set of late 1980s/early 1990s 'Madchester' hits reflecting the age of the birthday pair. Many of the tunes I play are ones which I'm listening to anew after several years. Tracks by the Happy Mondays and Stone Roses get a particularly good reception. After I start running out of Manchester tunes, which I can see are losing the younger contingent from the dancefloor, I switch to some more recent material. Listening to these tracks through my headphones and amplified through the PA system I am struck by how many of the tunes seem to have an aura of *déjà vu* in them. Bassment Jaxx' 'Where's Your Head At?' and Daft Punk recall early 1980s analogue synthesisers and the Human League circa 'Being Boiled' without any direct sampling. 'Survivor', meanwhile, by Destiny's Child sounds like an update of Gloria Gaynor's perennial favourite 'I Will Survive'. The selection of Kylie Minogue's remixed 'Can't Get Blue Monday Out of My Head', which overlays the Australian girl singer with New Order, works well. As an amateur surveying the dancefloor from my vantage point behind the mixer, two turntables and CD deck, it is genuinely flattering when people come up to me to compliment me on my choices. I am experiencing at first hand DJ culture which in the words of Brown (1997: 96) is 'democratic with a capitalist inflection; the music is pure product, consumer-tested on the dance floor with an in-built obsolescence factor'. My involvement of playing records alone with some limited mixing might look like quite a surface level one, but it is a learning experience. I have the technology before me to go further and create new music. It seems fitting then to take a step back and look at how futurism and nostalgia have been closely intertwined in the production and reception of dance music since the beginnings of 'rave culture'.

Whilst the enabling technologies of digital music making are radical in electronic dance music, imbuing it with futuristic promise, like various musical styles before it the genre has contested roots with a multitude of potential antecedents. Bara (1998: 69) includes a techno timeline which begins in 1897 with the invention of the Telharmonium, described as a far-removed ancestor of the synthesiser that weighed 200 tonnes and measured 18 metres in length. The traditional point of departure for considerations of rave, as it was initially known, is usually 1988, the year of what became known as 'the second summer of love' with its obvious reference to 1960s hippiedom. Punk parallels also surfaced in rave's construction in relation to previous youth culture. The style assumed an 'outsider' status positing it away from the mainstream and making a virtue of anti-musical virtuosity seen in its description in the *New Statesman* (13 October 1989) as 'Britain's most sustained underground since punk.' US disco and hip-hop provide further links (Fikentscher 2000; Hesmondhalgh 1997; Tomlinson 1998) to the soundtrack known as house which began in 1980s Chicago. A common emergent characterisation of the scene was as inauthentic pop lacking depth. 'Acid House: How Dare they Call It Music?' demanded the *Sun* (7 October 1988). The *Observer* (18 November 1990) saw the advent of rave as signalling a 'revival minus the revolution' replete with 'uncomfortable realism, an air of despair ... optimism is just not on the agenda in the new sixties'. It was almost as if the right disapproved of dance music's disregard for traditional musical structure while the left decried it for its lack of message. Anxieties about the alleged lack of purpose or point in rave recall earlier debates in the history of recorded popular music.[1]

Although admittedly Adorno was writing in a different time about a different type of music, Reynolds and Oldfield (1990: 174) bring to mind his well-known 'forcibly retarded' state of musical consumption in stating of late 1980s dance music 'Above all, this music is shallow, an array of surfaces and forces that engage the listener through fascination (what was that sound?!): there's no depth, no human truth or social concern to be divined'. They conclude 'And this is a blank generation if you ever saw one, sucked into house's void and left adrift, prettily vacant ... happy as a nodding dog' (Reynolds and Oldfield 1990: 179). Perhaps the ultimate manifestation of this is seen in the importance attached to the BPM (beats per minute) rating of tracks. This index is crucial to the creation of dance remixes. The drum and bass producer and classically trained musician MJ Cole has described the process thus: 'It's like a musical jigsaw puzzle. You might have a 130 bpm track and you want to get it up to two thirds of the speed of the vocal track. You can get quite technical'.[2] It has been claimed that the optimum BPM is that which emulates the beating of the human heart as heard from the womb, although in jungle a slow bassline complements a faster top rhythm making the drum and bass variant 'gabber' for example appear 'speedy' to most ears. Beadle (1993: 138) claims: 'real musical knowledge is an advantage but not always necessary, providing you're not profoundly deaf'. Even if you *are*, the music is felt through pulsations on the dance floor as much as it is heard. In the same way as the rap styles to be discussed in the next chapter, just as it redefines traditional roles in music production dance music's reception redefines the production of musical knowledge in the same way. With its demystification of music-making requiring minimal formal training, contemporary dance music complicates the consumer/ producer divide.

Dance music traits of sampling and sequencing contrast sharply with insistence on the principle of authenticity and all that this entails. Langlois (1992: 237) has highlighted the blatant artificiality of dance music: 'There is no pretence that the record represents a live performance. To the audience this is of no consequence ... it is sensation rather than false integrity they are after.' The live performance, melody, harmony and the human voice have been sacred in other late twentieth century western musical forms. Dance music eschews the traditional band line-up for the DJ. As one early account of house explained 'DJs don't just play records on this scene. They create a wider seamless beat context into which individual records fit. As controller of the perfectly plotted beat, the DJs usurp singers, songwriters and so on as the main creative impetus of the music' (Owen 1986). The technological base of the music – evidenced in the name of the style 'techno' – is one of its most noteworthy features and entirely fitting for a generation who have grown up with computers. If the 1980s saw a long-running battle of the guitar versus the synthesiser (Johnstone 1999), by the 1990s the turntable was incontestably accepted as an instrument, a development that began in the late 1970s with both early disco and rap music. Remix culture and the software to do this such as the Cubase and Logic programs take this further. By the twenty-first century this sampling equipment is being supplemented with other technical sophistry including the hardware to mix sonic software such as CDs and down-loaded MP3 soundfiles. A review in the *NME* (16 June 2001) of the album 'PS You Love Me', itself a parody of the Beatles' 'PS I Love You', by US laptop musical exponent Kid 606 describes him as not as DJ but as 'Californian PowerBook jockey'.

The long-established popular music studies line of lyric analysis is of strictly limited relevance to much dance music due to its largely instrumental form. Instead deconstructing dance music down to its very root, its principal function is the pleasure of the dance. Willis (1990: 65) makes the same point describing house music as 'an uptempo and highly syncopated dance music with lots of over-dubbed cross-rhythms, sampled voices and effects ... the words [aren't] of any real significance ... the "feel" behind the music [is] of more importance'. Ward (1993) claims that within rational industrial/post-industrial societies dance will be peripheral to the main forms of activity and social relationships and therefore those for whom dance does play an important role are definitely marginal and almost always suspect, a point also made by McRobbie (1984). Electronic dance music, devoid of any 'authenticity'-laden musical properties (e.g. untreated vocals, live instruments), is arguably nothing more than a vehicle for dancing. Taking Frith's (1996: 125) live performance distinction between 'serious music', which is virtuous, cerebral and judged a success if it elicits still appreciation, and frivolous 'fun music' designed for moving the body to, dance music definitely belongs in the latter category. The interactive element can be seen in the way people will whoop and cheer at appropriate moments at club events. The natural accompaniment to a music that dispenses with the need to know anything (formal) about music is 'a dance which required "no expertise whatsoever",' (Redhead 1990: 6). The *NME* explains of acid house's initial popularity (25 April 1998): 'People who'd never dreamed of dancing before were now doing so with a frenetic intensity, arms aloft, as if locked in religious experience.' Again here we see demystification: in this case in a dance with no steps.

From a UK perspective futurism and nostalgia were both apparent in early twentieth century dance music styles and events. Garage was widely heralded in the popular media as the sound of young urban Britain for the early twentieth century, ubiquitously blaring out of cars, from pirate radio stations, BBC Radio 1 and in shops. The sound was modern yet the word 'garage' is not new in musical terminology; neither is r'n'b, sometimes used to describe the same music – short for rhythm and blues. Importantly, terms are elastic and both are shifting signifiers. In the early 1960s mod guitar merchants The Who advertised themselves with the tag 'maximum r'n'b'. By the late 1960s garage was taken to connote the scratchy guitar power-chords of groups such as punk precursors the Stooges. By the 1980s both of these terms were being applied to electronic dance music. US garage was pioneered by DJs such as Frankie Knuckles. Depending on what generation you belong to then 'garage' as a musical descriptor can mean quite different things, from US 1960s proto-punk raw guitar rock to the smoother post-millennial sounds of two-step rhythms as practiced by garage pin-ups such as Craig David and

Daniel Bedingfield. Talking of contemporary dance styles again the boundary markers are not strictly defined: one man's garage may be another's handbag. Twenty-first century garage music was widely celebrated as being symbolic of the UK's multicultural metropolitan melting pot; however its rise occurred contemporaneously with other dance events with different prescriptions. An example exists in the nostalgia-based schooldisco.com nights held in many British city centres, playing mostly 1980s and 1990s pop to audiences dressed in school uniforms. Like my experience of DJ-ing at the thirtieth birthday, these events reflect the tastes of a generation of 'middle youth', now harking back to their schoolday soundtracks of Wham! and Duran Duran.[3] This category have grown up immersed in electronic gadgets from video-games and MTV via CD-ROMs and DVDs through to mobile phones. Indeed mobiles themselves are a clear site of identity formation and of nostalgia and futurism, manifested in their musical customisation in ringtone choice (electronic dance music is particularly suited to this) and the installation of computer games such as retro favourites PacMan and Space Invaders. There is no reason why 21st century young people may not attend school disco nights as well as more strict 'dance clubs'.

Commercial cross-overs and geographies of dance

Of course dance music is a constituent part of the wider leisure industry and is now a multi-million dollar/pound/Euro business. Music cultures are inseparable from the business dimension that they operate in, as has been stated earlier. Traditional models of youth culture dictate that movements begin with a moment of subcultural purity amongst the elite before incorporation into the mainstream follows (Hebdige 1979). Underground thus inevitably becomes overground. At the most obvious level this can be seen in the major label signings of dance acts by multinationals in bidding wars. Steve Allen of WEA's dance label Eternal has been quoted by Sweeting (2000) as claiming: 'With something like garage music, which is happening at the moment, there's always the fear of missing out. It was like Britpop or drum'n'bass acts – every company had to have one ... they're terrified of missing something that everybody else has got.' Cross-overs in dance music have been multifarious. There has long been an interface between television advertising and pop music (Blake 1997b). This was taken to an extreme when all the tracks from the 1999 album 'Play' by US dance act Moby were featured in various lucrative advertising campaigns around the world including those of France Telecom, Volkswagen and Nissan. This subliminal advertising of the album re-propelled it to number 1 in the UK album charts a year after its initial release. By 2002 sales figures of 10 million copies worldwide had far outstripped the record company's original target of 150,000 sales.[4] Yet, as Hesmondhalgh (1997: 175) points out, 'Dance music has always had a profound ambivalence about being popular, about being a mass form.' The *NME* (22 April 2000) stated of UK garage:

It's a uniquely British genre cross-pollination that manages to combine the darkly urban thrill of illicit, pirate radio station broadcasts and sound-system culture with the syncopated buzz of a heat-seeking pop moment. It's an urban fusion that, in a similar way to jungle five years before, has evolved completely independent of the music industry.

Indeed parallels could be drawn between the genre-specific jungle/drum and bass alternative networks of production, distribution and exchange which exist alongside the more public face of dance music in early commentary on bhangra (Banerji and Baumann and 1990) as a parallel music invisible to the mainstream charts, as discussed in the previous chapter. Thornton (1995) is among those who counterpoises the concepts of 'mainstream' and 'underground' as opposites. Characteristics associated with the mainstream are of following commercial formulae aimed at shifting units with minimum risk-taking. Conversely the underground is seen as a site of innovatory experimentation. The tension between the two is highlighted in the comment of Tony Portelli, managing director of independent garage label 4 Liberty (quoted by Sweeting 2000):

> Ninety per cent of the time the major labels will get it wrong. They'll pay 150 grand [£150,000] for a single that sounds like it's from our scene, but then they'll spend as much as that marketing it to make it a hit because they have to chase the money. When it gets to number one, you've got the whole country singing along to a record that's awful, and it's seen as coming out of the UK garage scene. That's what we're worried about.

Inevitably there has been some co-option and mainstream incorporation of once-underground acts. There has also been a concerted attempt to cross-over garage to the US, which has met with success and can be seen in the adpotion of the two-step beat by American artists such as Justin Timberlake, Jennifer Lopez and Britney Spears.[5] UK acts such as the garage group So Solid Crew have retained an underground image while enjoying commercial success and major record distribution. Conversely, despite the efforts of the Mercury Music prize, Roni Size and Talvin Singh (recipients of the award in 1997 and 1999 respectively) remain niche artists.

The democratising and enabling potential of new technology in reducing the costs of music production has resulted in more than the rise of the 'bedroom DJ' (Langlois 1992) who plays principally for their own pleasure. There is also an argument to be made for an alternative career structure in the new post-industrial economy of dance culture – a segment of the burgeoning wider leisure sector that provides a viable means of paying the rent for many employed in it. When asked about doing remixes, for example, the producer Matt Cole raised economic and artistic issues: 'They're quite tempting – financially. You have various considerations: time, do you only remix credible records? But money as well. Remixes can be quite cold. Get the track, send the DAT off, get the money.'[6] Here a tension is identified between the taste value judgement of retaining credibility and the financial motive, i.e. between the cultural capital and economic capital that might flow from taking on the work. The ideal is to reconcile both but dance culture does contain instances where the two elements are not in directly equal proportion. Fatboy Slim famously remixed Cornershop's 'Brimful of Asha' for no money as a pet project without being asked. The remixed version made number one in the UK charts.

McRobbie (1999: 134–5) has commented of these new working conditions:

> The old jobs, which for many meant a lifetime of unrewarding labour, have gone for ever and there has been instilled into a younger generation, at some deep level, a determination for work to mean something more than a hard slog ... to turn youth culture into a job creation scheme has become one possible thing to do.

Of course 'gone for ever' is something of an overstatement as elements of the old trades live on. In addition to those directly making music, dance culture encompasses various support elements including events promotion, the design of flyers, lighting, visuals, etc., that all require skilled craftspersons, if not quite heavy industrial labour. Digital media, e.g. desktop publishing, has changed traditional working practices in many areas facilitating the circulation of these cultural goods. Indeed those involved are a generation who have grown up with computers in educational, work and leisure spheres. Many careers in this new economy are based on self-employment as opposed to established career paths such as those that Willis's (1977) lads were expected to pursue by default. In this way these new forms of employment are cause and effect of contemporary risk society (Beck 1992) as they are characterised by insecurity; however evidence shows that the flexibility and job satisfaction traded off are seen as a worthwhile counterbalancing to this instability (Banks *et al.* 2000). The base of skills required by DJ-ing alone was highlighted in a television documentary aired by the UK's Channel 4 in 2001, depicting a female classical cellist taking up the challenge to perform a live DJ set in a top London club after just 4 weeks training. The implication behind the acquisition of the expertise required to mix records in time and simultaneously please the crowds present was 'it's not as easy as it looks'.[7]

The geographical centre of gravity in dance music, like the genres that the term encompasses, can be said to be forever shifting. A number of its subgenres and derivations incorporate the names of places across the globe where the styles have flourished: Chicago house, Balearic beats, Belgian newbeat, Detroit techno, Italian house, Frankfurt techno, Goa trance, etc. Fikentscher (2000) uses New York as the setting for his study of underground dance music arguing that the city has a special place in dance culture for its heterogeneity in terms of ethnic and sexual groups. In the UK a wave of crossover pop-dance music acts in the late 1980s and early 1990s led to the re-imaging of the northern British city of Manchester from the province of indie miserablism that had spawned Joy Division and the Smiths to dance city, rechristened 'Madchester' for its flippant values (Champion 1990; Haslam 1999; Redhead 1997a: 91–4; Russell 1993). By the mid-1990s Bristol (Johnson 1996) was touted as the key city of British dance with the advent of trip hop that used dance beats at its core. Regional diversity and postcolonial inflections have been a healthy feature of the UK dance music scene. Bracewell (1997: 233) has written:

> The dance scene had little to do with Englishness, and everything to do with multiculturalism and the portability, via technology, of a unifying attitude to different regional centres – be that Bristol, Leeds, Birmingham or Brighton – as defined by their local nights and DJs.

Importantly though Englishness itself is redefined by rave and its offshoots which include entities such as the 'New Asian Dance Music' (Sharma *et al.* 1996). Certain cities too became key points of UK rave cartography for the reputations of clubs based there. An early pre-superclub example was the legendary Hacienda in Manchester (Savage 1992). London's Ministry of Sound fast gained the status of 'superclub' as, in addition to the venue itself, it boasted widely available merchandise such as a monthly dance magazine, range of clothing and range of memory-jogging star DJ-compiled CD mix albums – all branded with the MOS logo. Sheffield's Gatecrasher, Liverpool's Cream and Birmingham's God's Kitchen have also emerged as clubbing landmarks. Furthermore, in much the same way as legal clubs brought about something of a regeneration of many British city centres (Lovatt 1996; O'Connor and Wynne 1996), the unlicensed free party has spread its influence beyond the centre to the margins, rippling out a different type of urban regeneration based on the culture industries in inner cities and peripheral industrial estate zones (Hemment 1998: 210).

Dance music is rooted in the 1980s US sound of house, a term itself emanating from a pioneering US club. By the 1990s however, large-scale dance music festivals were being held across the globe. Colombié (2001: 77) includes a map of events played by the Parisian DJ collective Sound Conspiracy and their associates in 1998–9, which includes most of mainland Europe (e.g. Italy, Germany, Portugal, Austria), countries in the former Eastern bloc (including Poland, Hungary and Romania) as well as Argentina, Brazil, South Africa, Egypt and Australia. The fabled location of Goa in India also features on the map as a destination played by the sound system. Indeed Goa, long frequented by western hedonists for its protoypical rave 'full moon parties' dating back to the 1960s, is the only place name to appear in the glossary of terms that Fontaine and Fontana (1996: 104) include in their volume on rave. Carrington and Wilson (2001) talk about the 'post-rave tourist'. For them this is a natural development for a generation for whom air-travel has been normalised. Indeed travel supplement writing in recent years has concurred.[8] Mediterranean holiday resorts have been particularly active sites for global club culture, as captured in the line 'Ibiza, Majorca and Benidorm too, I've searched all these places but I've never found you' on New Order's 1989 single 'Fine Time'. The Spanish island of Ibiza in particular is now synonymous with holiday clubbing at venues such as the club Pacha. The location was always an inexpensive one for British holidaymakers with numerous cut-price carriers offering flights. By the 1990s it was a regular fixture on the calendar of DJs and clubbers alike. Clubbers have been calling the tune in the youth travel market, impacting wider trends in tourism. The UK tour operator Club 18–30, which has long run reasonably priced Mediterranean package holidays for young single Brits, found itself radically re-drawing its strategy to incorporate clubbing events into its product, hosting its own nights and selling tickets to larger promoters' events.

Questions about sustainable development and the environmental impact on local communities are begged by the temporary seasonal influx of ravers into post-rave tourist sites. The Ibiza circuit essentially consists of big name DJs flown in for the summer season from the UK and elsewhere. This suggests an importing of a product from outside rather than an active engagement with indigenous culture. Certain places have attempted to rein in rave activities. The police in Goa are on record condemning ravers for their disregard for nature and predilection for drugs. In 2001 a 'zero tolerance' clampdown on drugs was pronounced by authorities in Cyprus resort Ayia Napa, which allegedly resulted in an upsurge in tourist traffic to Ibiza, including from the US and southern hemisphere.[9] Yet post-rave tourism is potentially one way in which the negative homogenising influences that many fear are a natural consequence of globalisation can be counter-balanced. Carrington and Wilson (2001: 2.1) optimistically describe two-way influences between DJs and the global settings in which they play their wares: 'DJs and promoters travel to foreign countries, are exposed to fresh varieties of music and nightclubs, and ultimately integrate ideas gleaned from these experiences into their domestic dance music cultures.' Examples of internationalism in dance music styles abound. Indeed the de-centred importance of lyrics and general non-linguistic form of dance music have ushered in a new wave of Euro disco encompassing the much trumpeted *nouvelle vague* of French dance music, including such acts as Cassius, Air and Daft Punk (Huq 1999b). Other memorable dance albums of recent years include the Spanish flavoured *La Revancha Del Tango* (Revenge of the Tango) from French DJ duo Gotan Project, which marries castanets and accordions to modern dancefloor sensibilities. The Asian Underground club scene is commonly characterised as a UK one, produced by a British-born generation of Indian subcontinent parentage subject to multiple musical influences (Huq 2003). Importantly however, such influences can circulate without listeners having to set foot elsewhere. With the proliferation of cable and satellite technology sounds can travel without the need for people to do so.

The suppression of difference: regulating the global dancefloor

Early rave was seen as ideologically vacuous. Previous predilections for youth culture sloganeering idealism, such as the hippy mantra 'Be reasonable, demand the impossible' or punk's war cry 'anarchy in the UK', were replaced by short, sometimes monosyllabic, utterances, like 'sorted' and 'safe' – often connected to ecstasy taking. Garratt (1998: 258) remarks 'At a time when the political ideology was all about the individual, E culture offered a glorious communal experience, an illusion of unity that was exhilarating.' Controversy surrounded the late 1980s contemporary dance music predecessor 'acid house' for its very name alone. Before long it became clear that it was the amphetamine-based substance MDMA, commonly known as ecstasy or E, *not* LSD, that was the drug of choice for rave and the musical styles descended from it. Indeed negative ecstasy casualty-type stories have long made newspaper headlines in the UK – a noteworthy example being that of Leah Betts. Subsequent similar cases have continued to attract press fascination.[10] There is evidence to suggest that ecstasy seemed to intensify certain features of the music. Pini (1997: 154) writes: 'being "ecstatic" has in many ways replaced previous youth-cultural "styles of being": being "political", being "angry", being "hard" and even (certainly at the very beginning of rave in London) being "fashionable" '. Other commentators are more explicit about the drug itself and its direct effect on dance culture (Collin 1997; Reynolds 1998a; 1998b). It was also only a matter of time before 'being angry' surfaced in rave culture, but this was only when rave itself was under threat from the law.

Despite the *Independent*'s (3 March 1990) early observation that 'Acid House, whose emblem is a vapid, anonymous smile, is the simplest and gentlest of the Eighties' youth manifestations ... non aggressive (except in terms of decibels)', rave and dance music have had multiple brushes with the law in various countries. Major legal restrictions on holding events have twice been enacted; by the Entertainments (Increased Penalties) Act 1990 – commonly known as the 'Bright Bill' after its sponsor Graham Bright MP – and the Criminal Justice and Public Order Act 1994, abbreviated to CJA, which started life as the Criminal Justice Bill (CJB). The different respective kinds of raver targeted by the Bright Bill and the CJA are key in explaining the differing grassroots responses. In 1990 the object of official fear was the stereotypical ecstasy guzzler that tabloid scare stories had created. The resulting 'Freedom to Party' campaign enlisted Thatcherite commercial rave promoters to its cause with Conservative party links who argued that rave regulation was an anathema to the prevailing enterprise culture (Osgerby 1997). In 1994 the legislation had free parties and more specifically the 'crusty', a highly mythologised technopagan/raver/squatter/traveller stereotype (Press 1995)[11] in its sights. The use of the word 'free' was interpreted by proponents as both denoting 'no entrance charge' and commensurate with liberty itself, e.g. 'The nature of a free festival is just that: freedom. You can do what you like, it doesn't matter how bizarre, as long as it doesn't impinge upon other people. No moralism. No prohibitions' (Stone 1996: 185). The rise of free parties can be linked with economic recession (Collin 1997) or even a general refusal to participate in commercial capitalist dance culture as seen in the movement's own internal moral code proffered by free-party news-sheet *SchNEWS* (3 November 1995) 'Free parties is [*sic*] about saying no to crap clubs with rip-off prices with numbskull bouncers.' Simultaneously as tabloid tales of crusty debauchery situated this neo-folk devil at the centre of a new moral panic, perhaps somewhat inevitably 'crusty' underwent something of an acceptance by mass culture. Lowe and Shaw (1993: 161) interviewee Jeremy highlights the contradiction therein: 'People called us crusties and that label's stuck and become a sort of fashion thing which is ridiculous really because it was the opposite of that. ... It was anti-fashion, anti-image. It was supposed to be a viable alternative way of life.'

The CJB included a state definition of rave sounds as 'music wholly or predominantly characterised by the emission of a succession of repetitive beats'. This provision was widely ridiculed for its illogical premise – virtually all western music is essentially organised sound dependent on repetition.[12] The politics of CJB opposition was linked to longer established traditions of anarcho-punk, squatting and new age traveller culture[13] and elements of environmentalism, e.g. anti-road development protests (Gilbert 1997; Huq 1998a; McKay 1996; Press 1995). The resulting movement can be seen in some ways to be post-subcultural and postmodern, prefiguring the anti-globalisation movement of later years, referred to in chapter 1. The central philosophy of non-violent direct action (NVDA) eschewed structures such as parliament and instead engaged in 'actions', for example the occupation of the back garden of the then-Home Secretary Michael Howard for an impromptu rave. NVDA has echoes of Beck's (1992: 29) notion of a reinvention of politics based on local interest group issues. Other noteworthy features of CJB politics coincide with Beck's 'sub politics' which are defined as reflexive and rule-altering, unlike traditional politics in which politicians are accepted as knowing what is best. Class as a rationale for the protests was notably absent in the 'new politics' agenda of the anti-CJB campaign. Civil liberties instead were emphasised by the loose alliance of organised and *ad hoc* groups fighting for the cause in the slogan 'Defending diversity, defending dissent.' Just as the CCCS subcultural theorists can be accused of letting their interest in class politics affect their accounts disproportionally to perspectives of the actual participants themselves, the resistance campaign mounted in defence of rave was seized on by many on the UK old left, e.g. magazines such as *New Statesman* and *Red Pepper*, as evidence that 1990s youth had not been apoliticised by Thatcherism. The CJB's specific impact on the dance movement has been one of rave's most widely detailed aspects in academic accounts (Gilbert 1997; Hutnyk 1996; Huq 1999a; McKay 1996; 1998), although again the illegal warehouse and squat party events that it was focused on only constitute a small section of contemporary dance culture.

The UK's legal approach of repression playing on drug fears in relation to dance events is not an isolated example. In addition to the rave tourism examples above, New South Wales in Australia published a code of practice for dance parties which was predicted would potentially result in 'The Death of Diversity' (Chan 1997). France too was the scene of a flourishing free party scene from the 1990s (Colombié 2001; Perron 2001). Punitive rave regulation, in the form of controversial curbs proposed by right-wing parliamentarian Thierry Mariani as an amendment to a government home affairs bill, split the then-socialist cabinet and galvanised a resistance campaign mounted in opposition. Again the age-old sense of adults legislating against something that they don't understand, i.e. youth having more or less harmless fun, was a common motor as it was with both the Bright Bill and CJB campaigns. The amendment was eventually passed in October 2001 stipulating that dance event organisers secure prior permission from the relevant local authorities before the holding of gatherings. Left-wing daily *Libération* (3 August 2001) pronounced 1993–2001 as the 'era of rave' which had effectively been terminated by the legislation. The first effects were felt in January 2002 when a sentence of three months imprisonment and a fine of 510 Euros was meted out to two organisers of a rave that had attracted 4,000 people the previous January in Reims. Further provisions included the seizing of equipment. Representatives of the free party movement had been invited to consultations on the legislation's drafting but the talks were boycotted by them, leaving them attended by legal dance club promoters alone.[14] In looking at the application of the UK CJA it is important to remember that there was much more to the Act than simply rave regulation provisions. In retrospect it appears that some of the more heinous sections concerning stop and search have ended up being enforced more than rave powers, e.g. in detaining asylum seekers.

As has been commented of attempts to put curbs on the internet and police cyberspace, exercising control over illegal dance gatherings to some extent is almost trying to regulate the unregulatable. The US philosopher Hakim Bey (1991) has been picked up by various theorists of dance culture for his concept of the TAZ (temporary autonomous zone), which is seen as analogous to rave. Fontaine and Fontana (1996: 95–6) for example stress the escapism and anarchic self-determinism inherent in rave and warn that it is what makes it so alluringly ripe for attempts at legislative control.[15] In keeping with the postmodern premise of accelerated culture (Rojek 1995: 157) time and space are reconfigured in the illegal free party scene. To dance like there's no tomorrow is made literal as the days dissolve into one another. The temporal parameters of perhaps 10 pm to 2 am at a legal club (bettering the traditional rock concert) are stretched to potentially infinite duration at an illegal event as there is no curfew when the licence ends. The illegal event is essentially a non-linear event, with no fixed place (secured venue) or (finish) time (Gilbert 1997; Scheher 1995; Stanley 1997; 52) both are dependent on the DJs' willingness to carry on playing (supply), the crowd size the next morning (demand) and police intervention. The illegal rave will often take place in the open air or on squatted premises. The creative use of derelict dwellings or warehouses in the fractured spaces of industrial decline with initiative and imagination (Richard and Kruger 1998: 163) to encompass the visual and aural stimuli of the rave often uses an electricity supply diverted from elsewhere, a typical attribute of squatter culture.

Dance music as subculture

The post-war youth studies paradigm of youth culture as subculture and of the inevitability of subcultural incorporation to the mainstream is now well known and has been addressed in chapter 1 of this book. The CCCS work on subculture in particular is a useful reference point in looking at club culture. CCCS orthodoxy was about youth resisting through ritualistic behaviour in opposition to the dominant order, however such readings of youth culture as a symbolic working class response to lowly status are inappropriate to describe contemporary dance music cultures. Club culture, like acid house and rave before it, has always been more about having a good time than shaking the establishment to its very foundations or challenging the dominant order. Its dalliance with politics around the CJB enthused left-liberal commentators from academia and media alike as conjuring up images of a new version of the old subcultural idea of youth as agents of radical social change but this was ultimately short-lived and only applied to a minority of those involved in dance culture. Perhaps the chief failing of subcultural theory in its failure to explain electronic dance music and club culture is its obsession with authenticity, which is difficult to reconcile with a blatantly inauthentic musical form. Redhead's (1990: 25) assertion that 'authentic subcultures were produced by subculturalists not the other way round', quoted in chapter 1, is of key relevance here. Perhaps the only way to describe multifaceted youth cultures such as club culture is with multi-dimensional models. Society is perhaps changing faster than any terms we wish to slap on youth cultures can, be it subcultures or the currently vogueish neo-tribes.

Another criticism of subcultural theory is that it ascribes lifetime commitment, whereas participants are always drifting off into other scenes. Sarah Thornton has come up with the idea of club cultures. These

> are taste cultures. Club crowds generally congregate on the basis of their shared taste in music … taking part in club cultures builds in turn further affiliations. … Clubs and raves therefore house ad-hoc communities, with fluid boundaries which may come together and dissolve within a single Summer or endure for a few years.
>
> (Thornton 1995: 3)

The fact that there was an r'n'b/garage room in the Manchester bhangra daytimer that I attended in July 2002 shows that there are obvious crossovers between the musical scenes described in this volume and that none of the categories under discussion are separate and discrete from one another. Youth cultural affiliations probably always were too ephemeral to be the basis of secure identities. The teddy boys, skinheads, mods, etc. described by the CCCS have also not been suspended in time. This is because all forms of culture are dynamic and are in some ways about process rather than being fixed entities. This fact underscores dance culture at every level. It can be seen in the way that terms emerge and recede at a dizzying rate. Hesmondhalgh (1997: 168) wrote: 'The terms ... "rave" and "acid house", now sound as out-of-date as the phrase "beat combo" must have done to the early '70s hippies.' Terms also translate differently in international contexts. At the time of writing 'rave' is still very much a current phrase in France. Ecstasy is abbreviated to E in the UK and Australia but X in the US and 'ecsta' in France.

The line of youth cultures described by the CCCS were in large part *spectacular* subcultures who attached great value to visual style, e.g. the mods, teds, punks, etc. The dance music scene has often been contrastingly characterised as faceless – Melechi (1993: 37) calls it 'a scene without stars and spectacle, gaze and identification'. White label 12" vinyl singles have been seen as epitomising this faceless aspect of dance in complete contrast to the lavish pseudo-artistic sleeve design and expansive liner-notes of the pop record of old. The layout of the club night is such that the DJ is often hidden away from public view in a DJ box, unlike the old stage presence-oozing rock performer. In early rave it was common practice for DJ names to appear on flyers for nights to attract fans who came for the music, often not knowing what their idol looked like. Indeed flyers often sold themselves on the technology of events, e.g. power of the sound system, etc. The self-parody that this image bred was seen in the club-wear t-shirt bearing the words 'faceless techno bollocks', spotted around dance music events around 1994–5. The DJ who is 'simultaneously the performer, marketer and composer of the music' (Langlois 1992: 229) has increasingly taken centre stage with the accompanying attention of specialist and mainstream media – magazines such as *Muzik*, *Mixmag* and *Ministry* (cf. Thornton 1995 on the niche media). These publications, implicitly aimed at men, contain lifestyle articles and personal profiles on 'name' DJs in much the same way as girls' teen magazines (McRobbie 1991; 1997), alongside articles of a more technical nature for the aspiring bedroom DJ. Acts such as Fatboy Slim or the Prodigy have crossed over to become household names selling out stadiums for their performances.[16] Thornton (1995: 29) remarks that in dance culture ' "liveness" is displaced from the stage to the dancefloor, from the worship of the performer to a veneration of "atmosphere" and "vibe" '. From my experience of attending the Creamfields outdoor dance festival in summer 2002 I would argue that this statement must be qualified with the recognition that some dance acts do combine elements of rock spectacle in their stage-show; in this case I could cite Kosheen or from earlier festival-going experiences the Prodigy (who I saw during the 'rock' festival Glastonbury in 1997), who also straddle the divide.

Dance culture has been said to depart from traditional youth cultures as distinct groups in the fact that it is more all-embracing; complicating attempts to align it with aggressively separatist definitions of 'subculture' usually based in the constituency of the male working class. An early hallmark promoted by rave champions was its inclusiveness (Melechi 1993: 36; Russell 1993: 126–7). However a number of variants of dance music exist with their own internally mediated structures and norms. Fikentscher (2000: 107) writes: 'the majority of those who identify themselves as participants in the New York dance underground are either minority (primarily black and/or Latino) or gay, or both … [under-ground dance music] provides the ritual through which collectivity and marginality can be affirmed and celebrated', a point also made in reference to rave's roots by Savage (1990). Thornton (1995: 25) meanwhile sees dance music as largely 'white, working, class, heterosexual and dominated by the lads'. Julie Burchill has written (*Guardian*, 17 April 1999): 'Dance music has given popular music back to the young, the working class, the female; all of those shut out of the debates about Bob Dylan and Keats, and none of them giving a damn.' Women have been more obviously present on the consumption side of dance music than in its (re)production. Female DJs do exist such as Sonique or Lottie who rose to the heights of commanding her own show on BBC Radio 1, but these are still largely billed as exceptional freakshow attractions, as opposed to the rule. Certainly at the outset of rave, women were often quoted as saying that they felt liberated by the non-aggressive ecstasy-fuelled climate of raves which made them a welcome antidote from the meat market-like atmosphere of the traditional disco which relied on alcohol as social lubricant. Pini's (1997; 2001) work, drawing on Angela McRobbie and Donna Haraway, takes gender as its corner-stone and her study of women ravers is a welcome counterbalance to the old studies of women situated within the contexts and confines of 'bedroom culture'.

Perhaps the main conclusion that can be drawn from the contradictory posi-tions on rave demographics sketched out above is that they all have validity if they are taken to apply to sectional audiences. The point is that dance music culture has a wide appeal across class and ethnic cleavages. Different publics will frequent different nights and venues that comprise this however, with a limited element of room for latitude in terms of crossover in between categories. In other words even if white working class estate youth *are* just as at home dancing in clubs as are people at the opposite end of the social spectrum – crusties, black youth, Asians, gays or the category that has been termed 'Sharon and Tracey' (Thornton 1995) – these groupings do not all dance at the same club nights. Music is a key factor of this differentiation, possibly a more important mediating factor than social strata, although both feed into this choice as do location, entry price, drink price, etc. Different musics are held to appeal to different groups. Jungle and garage for example are 'black' while some techno styles are more 'white' in terms of prin-cipal artists and audience base. MJ Cole has commented that when he has turned up for performance bookings, promoters are sometimes surprised to see that he is white and not black.[17] During summer 2002, which many in the music press saw as the height of garage, I attended a commercial outdoor dance music event, Creamfields on the site of the old Liverpool airport, a spin-off from the city's Cream club night. The acts and audience in attendance were very white.

Crucially, at different club nights the same physical space (venue) can take on a totally different atmosphere due to factors such as temporary internal decor and most importantly music. Reynolds (1997: 104) begins his analysis working backwards from the assumption that the 'rave myth of transracial, cross-class unity lies in tatters'. Whilst this is perhaps a little melodramatic, exclusivity and separatism persist in dance culture which is highly segmented with its own multiple elites. As one rave website points out 'unity doesn't happen just cuz [sic] a flyer says it will.'[18]

The musical properties of rave define many of its practices. For Stanley (1997: 50) the status of rave as a subculture of transgression is reinforced by the stolen sounds employed in the practice of sampling, i.e. using fragments of past recordings to assemble a new track (Beadle 1993; Goodwin 1987). Copyright has consequently become another legal issue in dance music. Sampled snippets are sometimes from related musical genres, for example the 1980s electro artist Gary Numan has been much sampled in contemporary electronic dance music. They can also be taken from less obvious sources, as in the use of old blues singers by Moby on his *Play* album. The cut-and-paste culture of sampling exemplifies collage and cross-fertilisation recalling the postmodern concept of 'bricolage'. The sheer volume of recorded music now in circulation *per se* enables sampling. No-one can listen to all the music currently being made – all anyone can ever do is to 'sample'. Toop (1995: 63) talks of the 'sampladelic' state where 'the dead are no more immune to this process [sampling] than the living', referring to dance remixes. Samples are almost akin then to quotation. McRobbie (1999: 132) comments:

> Current music styles leapfrog backwards and forwards in time, snatching phrases, chords and strains of sound from unlikely sources, placing one on top of the other, and by making issues of authorship and ownership irrelevant. 'Who is that by?' becomes an absurdly naïve question.

New technology also allows the use of samples that are not lifted wholesale from their original sources but imaginatively re-interpreted; as seen in the quote from Mathew of Manchester rap band HD in the next chapter. This state of affairs applies just as easily to the retreads of the musical past by Britpop guitar band Oasis in their 1960s-styled guitar music as it does to the more blatant sample culture of dance music. Both are as much about the creation of new configurations of sound as they are about recreation.

It is then the diversity of practice in contemporary dance culture set against a background of post-millennial uncertainty that complicates conceptualising it as 'another subculture'. Thornton's (1995) reworking of the term 'subculture' updated for the 1990s is useful here for the notion of 'subcultural capital', derived from Bourdieu's work (1979; 1984b) on cultural distinction. The fragmentation of 'acid house'/'rave' into multiple sub-genres makes any collective political response of dance culture to material inequality in the way that the old

106

subcultural dream might have dictated impossible. For the CCCS, the adherents of subcultures were always doomed to end up inevitably following the life-patterns dictated by their birth position. However theorists such as Beck (1992) and Maffesoli (1996) comment on the weakening of older structures and blurring of older divisions where social positions and identities are increasingly unstable. This can be applied in some measure to dance music and its wider setting. Careers in the cultural industries are more uncertain than in the pre-set apprenticeship or other trajectories of earlier times. It is however not yet clear if men and women for example can compete on more equal terms in these fora despite the democratising potential of the new media. It is easy to get carried away with ascribing agency to dance culture participants in the supposed fluidity and flux that passes for contemporary society when many of the old structures do remain. There is a need to find a medium between subcultural positions which place a disproportionate emphasis on structure and the romanticised postmodern accounts that overemphasise the agency of the individual in theorising contemporary dance and club culture.

Future directions and conclusions

Over a quarter of a century from the start of disco in the US and more than a decade after the subsequent advent of house and the UK's 'second summer of love', dance culture, frequently aided and abetted by illegal intoxicants, has arguably become the predominant form of youth cultural expression in much of the western world. However, noticeable changes have occurred throughout this period on a number of fronts, including in terms of musical style, fashion, event-structure and technology. A number of these shifts can be listed.

1   Although a much-noted feature of early rave-dance music that sometimes attracted criticism was its instrumental form, many of the acts that have been champions of the UK garage scene have been critically lauded for their lyrical content, conveying the sound of young urban Britain in accessible vernacular language. The critical acclaim received by Birmingham garage act The Streets is in large part due to the kitchen-sink realism lyrics of Mike Skinner, for example.

2   Mysterious limited-run white DJ-only label underground 12" single releases, usually bearing no information on the track or artist, that circulated in the DJ fraternity alone were long hailed as symbolic of DJ culture (Fikentscher 2000; Hesmondhalgh 1997). The equation of record box, mixer and two Technics SL1210 turntables has long been held as the key equipment for the DJ's trade; although vinyl has been in decline as a format since the 1980s. At the time of writing however there is evidence that new hardware is ushering in a gradual shift to CDs, using advanced new CD mixers that allow the mixing and scratching of MP3 files from laptops to take place. Further features such as sound-processing and precise millisecond control over CDs

and digital soundfiles then threaten the primacy of the 12" and vinyl in the DJ's armoury.[19]

3   After the glut of 1990s superclubs, a number of which ended up closing, UK club culture appears to be downsizing in the emergence of smaller-scale café-bars with late licenses and DJs providing background music at lower levels compatible with holding conversations in a more understated way than the 'go mental' major events of the superclubs or weekend extravaganzas. The constituency that patronise such events are often a more discerning crowd of 'middle youth' than some of the original rave events were aimed at.

4   Also aimed at the more discerning listener are the range of 'Back to Mine' compilations, designed for after-event listening, in which dance culture exponents such as the garage producer MJ Cole and Asian Underground artist Talvin Singh have selected/paraded their influences. Taking this a step further, the spread of sample culture can be seen in albums compiled around tunes sampled by dance artists, e.g. the Gary Numan compilation issued in the UK in 2002 to capitalise on the hits by Armand Van Helden and the Sugababes and Gut records' 2002 collection *A Break from the Norm* featuring the original versions of songs from which samples (or breaks) had been used by Fatboy Slim aka Norman Cook. These recordings compliment domesti-cised commercially available dance music mix CDs by name DJs and demonstrate how dance music consumption takes place on a wider scale than simply at dance music events. There has also been a noticeable rise in down-tempo chill-out compilations again designed for relaxation as opposed to straight 'dancing', despite being a variant of dance music and by-product of the club scene.[20]

Once upon a time, rave was a verb not a noun. Rave could be seen as the last subculture; signifying either 'most recent' or even as those pronouncing the end of youth culture contend, the final one. In many ways it is cause and effect of youth culture coming of age. For the dance music generation computer tech-nology, foreign travel and drugs have largely been normalised as they have grown up with all three. The late 1980s contribution to the great western post-war youth culture collection 'acid house' has mutated into the early twenty-first century version of the same, scooping up a bewildering array of musics and raising questions of politics, drugs and currents in youth culture. Both rave and the politics of its defence are as much about the essential continuities of opposi-tional youth culture as they are about any sort of rupture. It is easy to slip into postmodern clichés in talking about pastiche, cut-and-paste culture and recycling, however in the 'seen it all before' twenty-first century much youth culture is coloured by a sense of *déjà vu* for anyone old enough to remember (or care). The coming of crusty combining both punk and hippie elements of sartorial and polit-ical style/philosophy to a soundtrack of repetitive beats shows that rave did not kill punk, which in turn did not kill hippie. Contemporary youth cultures are cumulative rather than successive, constructed of a panoply of influences. Dance culture is about town (high-street club, orbital warehouse party) and country (open-air festival). It displays traits of Euro-centricism (Mediterranean holiday dancefloors) and anti-western values (Goa spiritualism). Its producers and consumers follow individualised life-paths in some respects but in others they are still constrained by structure, e.g. access to economic capital. There are also numerous crossovers between these geographies of dance, e.g. the way that certain clubs may attempt to recreate the feel of an open-air festival in an indoor city space. Garratt (1998: 11) rightly reminds us that dance culture is importantly far from a homogeneous entity: 'Club culture is restless, fluid, constantly changing and feeding off itself.' The changing nature of dance music culture in the past decade contains manifestations unseen before in post-war youth culture as well as retreads of the past. As Gilbert and Pearson (1999: 72) point out: 'British dance culture could be dated as beginning at just about any time. "Ravers" did not invent the practice of dancing all night with the aid of illegal stimulants.' Raving, despite attempts to legislate it out of existence, has remained an important point of reference for youth at both under- and overground gatherings.

Dance music, radical as it is in many ways, does contain many continuities with earlier musical forms. The repetitive hooks that most dance 12" tracks are constructed around are an enduring feature in pop, rap has used turntables in its creation from the outset and mixing is a longstanding feature of disco music. Crossovers between musical forms and the ways in which dance music properties have become suffused in the practices of traditional pop acts can be seen in the growth of DJ culture across genres. Wilson (2002: 45) in an *NME* article points out:

> There's no avoiding it, DJ culture still dominates the music world. From Slipknot to Judge Jules to Nelly Furtado, DJs are a permanent fixture everywhere you look. Dance acts have a DJ; hip hop acts have a DJ; pop acts have a DJ; even metal bands have a DJ.[21]

My own limited and sporadic experiences of DJ-ing have given me some insight into the dynamics of DJ culture, although I would not quite elevate myself to the status described by Fikentscher (2000: 26) of DJ as 'a new type of pop star'. In this chapter I have begun to hint at the ways in which dance music acts as an example of how cultural forms are regionally adapted and adopted by youth in various local contexts; and how the totality of different variants in circulation add up to a global youth musical culture. Hip-hop provides another example in which localised practices of global music are manifested. In contrast with the largely instrumental form of dance music which has enfranchised instrumental and non-English language music (Robb 1999), however, language is of key importance in rap. It is then to another breed of turntable and sampling culture utilising another 'new type of pop star' that we turn in the next chapter as we look at rap and hip-hop culture.

6

SELLING, SELLING OUT OR RESISTING DOMINANT DISCOURSES?

Rap and the uses of hip-hop culture

For years I have been very worried about these hateful lyrics that
these boasting, macho, idiot rappers come out with.
(UK arts minister Kim Howells quoted in the *Daily Telegraph*, 8 January 2003)

Weapon is my Lyric,

(Overlord X 1989)

This chapter continues the theme of transnationalism in pop and its relationship
with local hybridities by turning to rap and its position at the centre of wider hip-
hop culture. Rap can be seen as rebel music as much as commercial machine or as
educational tool. In this chapter then I will attempt to say something about, to
paraphrase Richard Hoggart, the 'uses' of hip-hop culture and the way that a
range of different rap scenes co-exist in different situational settings in the early
twenty-first century. This demonstrates how youth creatively fashion context-
dependent musical–cultural forms in street-speak vernacular tongues that reflect
their local environments, potentially providing a counter-balance to the negative
version of globalisation whereby a top-down process of cultural homogenisation
forcibly flattens cultural diversity. We saw in the introduction how 'being hard'
and 'not selling out' have been longstanding youth cultural qualities. In hip-hop
culture authenticity is of key importance with 'keeping it real' being the phrase to
connote this. Rap is closely associated with the US but I will, for comparative
purposes, take a closer look at rap music in contemporary France as well as
drawing on examples in the UK. Indeed I want to begin with a preliminary scene-
setting ethnographic episode that flags up some of the ways that hip-hop culture is
being played out in contemporary British urban settings today.

A Thursday evening in Spring 2003. I'm in a disused church converted into a
community centre and sound-recording studio in Longsight, an ethnically mixed
neighbourhood of inner-south Manchester, notorious for gun-crime and gang-
violence.[1] Tonight a hip-hop show is taking place. This is no informal 'jam'
however. The performers have taken part in the Cultural Fusion project financed
by the National Foundation for Youth Music in London and the North West Arts
Board leading to an NVQ (National Vocational Qualification) in music. Tonight
showcases some of the highlights. For their coursework these young people have

composed, recorded and performed live rap. Nicole, one of tonight's teenage female performers – carrying on the tradition of Queen Latifah, Missy Elliott, Kelis, Lauren Hill and Miss Dynamite – has been chosen to open the evening by speaking about the project from a participant's perspective. She addresses the invited parents, peers, siblings and friends in a broad Mancunian accent:

> Everyone who comes in and out of these doors knows. ... It's a good way of keeping us off the street. There's a lot of talented people in Longsight; singers, rappers, MCs. We've performed at the Zion centre [community venue housed in the opulent former headquarters of Manchester's Hallé orchestra], Urbis in town [multimillion-pound museum of metropolitan culture built with European funding, in central Manchester]. Respect to the tutors who've helped us. They haven't been like a lot of adults who talk down to young people. Big up to the tutors. Respect.[2]

She finishes to hooting applause. It is left to David Sulkin, a be-suited emissary from London to provide a word from the sponsors. Sulkin informs us that Cultural Fusion in Manchester is just one of the projects that the National Youth Music Foundation has supported over the past year, spanning hip-hop to chamber orchestras, with a budget of £32 million from the National Lottery. Following his contribution a presentation of NVQ certificates takes place. Some of the audience are getting fidgety. It's time for the performances to begin. The show and its mechanics will be returned to later but in the meantime this incident neatly high-lights the entanglement of rap with public sector sponsorship, informal and formal education as well as its use as a medium to keep youth on the 'straight and narrow' path away from 'the street' with all the associations that this entails. The excerpt from Nicole also shows rap slang in action. Before we revisit Longsight however I will begin by discussing some of the salient features of rap and hip-hop by way of contextual background. I will draw on the content of an interview conducted with members of HD, one of the Cultural Fusion rap groups, throughout this chapter.

Defining rap: the music and message

Stressing its function of social commentary and protesting against injustice, Rose (1994: 2) defines rap as: 'a black cultural expression that prioritises black voices from the margins of America'. Others have opted for 'the black punk' (Johnstone 1999: 290) for its grassroots articulation of anger. Associations of rap with ghetto music are in keeping with the old subcultural pre-requisite of authenticity. Rap can be both verb and noun. It has been traced as following on from black musical–oral traditions of storytelling, improvisation and call-and-response (Jones 1988) and earlier musical forms such as gospel, blues, jazz, soul and reggae. Nonetheless rap production eschews many traditional or authentic musical traits.

Since rap's beginnings in late 1970s New York, the basic hardware requirements have been two turntables and a microphone. DJs supply the backing track while MCs and rappers provide vocals. Techniques such as scratching and looping are then applied to the vinyl records that serve as sampling material. As can be said of the dance musics looked at in the previous chapter, recent years have seen the development of a range of software programs too which can be used to repeat and reassemble electronically sampled extracts and live instrumental passages. What HD term 'spitting lyrics', i.e. the delivery of texts, assumes central significance rather than the tune – unlike the dance musics discussed in the previous chapter. Rapping's spoken-word form dispenses with the traditional musical requirement of singing in tune. As Krims (2000: 73) puts it: 'The hip-hop sublime is the product of dense combinations of musical layers.' Importantly broader hip-hop culture includes the non-musical bodily expression of breakdance, sartorial statements communicated by hip-hip fashion, rap slang and the visual display of graffiti as well as rap music. It is performed at live gatherings, such as the Cultural Fusion event at Longsight and consumed commercially, as part of an important sector of the popular music market (Negus 1999). Offshoots include the garage style which is derived from both hip-hop and dance music culture.

Rap – and in particular the sub-genre gangster (or gangsta) rap – has also provoked outraged opposition from conservative campaigners for its supposed disregard of family values. Cashmore (1997: 170) highlights the inherent contradiction of rap's championing by liberal commentators and some of its less laudable sides: 'One can appreciate that rap was [sic] a genre to try a critic's conscience ... for all the apologia, rap was sexist, homophobic, anti-semitic and about as politically incorrect as it was possible to be.' Accordingly rap has over the years unleashed Stanley Cohenite 'moral panic' in America (Springhall 1998), often with racist undertones. Reactionary pro-censorship pressure groups such as the PMRC (Parent's Music Resource Centre) have been the most vocal in condemning artists like NWA (Niggaz with Attitude), Cypress Hill and Snoop Doggy Dog for supposedly promoting violence and guns (Lipsitz 1998). Rose (1994: 104) sees a clear agenda behind this: 'Rap's resistive, yet contradictory, positions are waged in the face of a powerful, media-supported construction of black urban America as the source of urban social ills that threaten social order.' Her argument, that by highlighting contemporary urban issues rappers provide valuable social critique, is echoed in comments attributed to various rap artists. The gangster rap artist Ice Cube of NWA has been quoted as explaining that the band's lyrics reflect their neighbourhood of Compton, Los Angeles where they hail from and where drive-by shootings, drugs and police brutality are part of the everyday landscape: 'NWA are reporting what's going on in our town – the fighting, the poverty, the drug selling – aren't fairy tales or scenes from a movie. This is our reality' (quoted in Johnstone 1999: 314). The high expletive count of many rap records that are accompanied by 'Parental Advisory' warnings could also be explained as employing the language of the street.

Authenticity has always been a desirable quality in both youth culture and popular music as we have seen from Part I of this book. For Shuker (1998: 20) it is 'a central concept in the discourses surrounding popular music'. Some of the defining features that he spells out are originality, creativity, sincerity, uniqueness, musicianship, live performance and independent label operations. Rap is a musical form that is often seen as embodying authenticity. The self-image of the music often stresses the need for this. The expression 'old school' for example refers to pioneering early rap which is seen as more 'real' than subsequent commercialised versions. The notion of 'keeping it real' referred to above is the opposite of 'selling out' – to lose touch with one's original ideals, usually provoked by material success. The fact that it is seen as emanating from the street or ghetto is testimony to rap's claims to being an authentically produced bottom-up popular musical form. Of course rap has steadily become a commercial going concern, widely available marketed by multinational record companies. Negus (1999: 96) for example talks about the rap industry as positioned 'between the street and the executive suite' as he warns:

> we need to be wary of the increasingly routine rhetoric and romanticization of rap musicians as oppositional rebels 'outside' the corporate system or as iconoclasts in revolt against 'the mainstream' – a discourse that has often been imposed upon rap and not necessarily come from the participants of hip-hop culture itself.

Crucially rap comes in many guises and it is hard to generalise about it in straightforward terms.

Interviewing the fledgling Manchester rap group HD in 2003 the realisation that commercialism was a necessary element of a financially-rewarding successful career, as a stage that was preceded with an underground existence, was voiced by Mathew and Ravelle:

RH: It's kind of seen that commercial rap is bad because it sacrifices purity …
MJ: Everyone don't want to be underground all their life. You want to start making [at least] a *little bit* of money so you're gonna have to step it up to … commercial. I couldn't just go straight into commercial without proving myself. … With hardcore you can get your street credit [*sic*] first, you can spit lyrics so when you *do* do commercial, if anyone tries to diss [disparage] you, you can tell 'em straight, 'look I've already been there, done that'.

The expression 'street credit', usually abbreviated to 'street cred', is interesting as it implies building up quantitative amounts of this, rather akin to economic capital, rather than the more vague, more qualitative notion implied by the alternative explanation 'street credibility', which is more in line with social capital.

RL: Sometimes you don't necessarily 'go commercial', it's just more people are buying it so more people say you're commercial. On an album you don't just get commercial tracks.

MJ: You just put out a few commercial tracks [as singles] to learn the fans to ya ... that's when they're gonna start listening to your album, [then] they might listen to a few of your hardcore stuff ...

Bourdieuan logic dictates that taste groups come with boundaries, e.g. 'commercial' rap for hip-hop fans who appreciate the music only on a superficial level and 'hardcore' for the more discerning. Taste is a classifying system in which people are differentiated from others who do not share the same taste but here the unequal distribution of economic capital in turn filters through to cultural capital. However the claims of HD above suggest that a single hip-hop act can combine a surface level commercial side for the wider public of pop chart followers (on singles) with a parallel hardcore, less compromising content reserved for fans who will seek out album tracks.

Although he is at pains to point out that hip-hop styles are constantly in a state of flux, Krims (2000) spells out a typology of rap genres based on musical style, MCing style and the issues addressed. 'Party-rap' is dance-centred, characterised by humour and a playful spirit. Historically it was the first rap style. Sonically it uses samples from disco and is fast tempoed. R'n'b-derived 'Mack' rap, meanwhile, depicts money and girls in its subject matter, signifying something of a loss of rap innocence from its 'party' beginnings. It contrasts with the more student-oriented politically correct style of 'jazz/bohemian' rap which often advocates Afrocentricity and rejects gangster rap sentiments. Exponents include De La Soul, who on their initial appearance in the late 1980s used hippie imagery such as the peace symbol and hailed that the 'daisy age' was upon us. Krims's final category is 'reality rap' which has prevailed from the 1990s onwards on both west and east coasts of the US. Here hardness and authentic 'ghetto centricity' are of central significance. These four categories are clearly not mutually exclusive. Most rappers would lay claim to describing 'reality' in some form or another. DJ Paul of UK Asian rappers Hustlers HC told hip-hop fanzine *Represent* (October–November 1994):

> We always try to do a release with one side political and one track non-political because that's how Hustlers are. Like if you see us on stage, we'll start off with all the political tracks, then we'll take it to just pure hip-hop, rappin', flexin' our styles just creating a really good vibe 'cos you don't want people leaving your show thinking 'ah man life is really fucked'.

Here we see a desire to fuse message rap with its more festive elements.

Since the Frankfurt School theorists of the early twentieth century described in chapter 2, commercialism has been frowned upon by popular culture theorists as it is seen as inherently anti-authentic – particularly in the well-known work of Adorno. As Frith (1989: 5) puts it 'Among left-leaning intellectuals the attitude is a generalised disdain for rock's commercialism and vulgarity.' Some musical forms have been about denying the importance of material wealth, such as what is commonly understood to be indie rock. Befittingly enough for a multi-million-dollar industry however, some rap styles make no attempt to hide that they are about unashamed conspicuous consumption. Krims (2000: 64) labels mack rap 'money-flaunting R&B song'. This open celebration of the spoils of capitalism is evidenced in the hip-hop expression 'bling bling' (*Guardian*, 21 May 2003). This term refers to the material spoils of flashy, ostentatious consumerism and is typified by the early twentyfirst century celebrity couple J-Lo and Puff Daddy, who commonly appeared in the media clad in jewellery and furs. Interviews with rappers demonstrate their remorselessness about making money. MC Ren of NWA for example has commented: 'We went into this business to make money ... criticism and controversy are cool, it all adds up to publicity' (*Melody Maker*, 4 November 1989). Rap can be seen to mirror its times. The growth of gangster rap, a subset of Krims's 'reality rap' category, has been variously traced to the Los Angeles disturbances of 1992 presaged by the LAPD's beating of black motorist Rodney King and to the 1980s Reagan government policy of funding the Nicuraguan Contra rebels, which inadvertently begun the flood of crack cocaine into US ghetto neighbourhoods. Similarly the emphasis on money by US rappers could be seen as consistent with the American value system that itself celebrates consumer capitalism, an ideology that prospered under Reagan and both Bush presidencies. Hip-hop fashion proudly parades the designer labels culture of sportswear accompanied by the wearing of jewellery. Run DMC were from the 1980s, for example, wearing Adidas gear and gold chains, practising the art of conspicuous consumption.

Postmodernism as a culture of pastiche and cut and paste is deeply inauthentic. Rap is often cited as an example of postmodern music for its intertextuality and use of source material recycling earlier musical eras (McRobbie 1990; Shusterman 1992a,b; Potter 1997; 1998). Krims (2000: 8) remarks: 'It seems at times that rap music would have to be invented by postmodern theory, had it not been there.' Postmodernists have seen something of a lost authenticity of modernity as inherent in rap. The 'break' or climatic part of a record is what rap records are constructed around. Appropriately enough the assembly of the new track takes place in a fragmentary fashion. Records are broken and lose their fixity as a final product, instead becoming ripe for manipulation. Chambers (1985: 169) describes a state of affairs where 'Instruments – drums, saxophones, guitars, studio mixers, microphones, turntables ("wheels of steel") – become extensions of your self, technology is socialized and bent to particular cultural rhythms.' A graphic example exists in the human beat box (human approximation of back beats with the vocal chords alone) which in the circumstances of urban poverty, is attractive as, like the air guitar and unlike conventional musical instruments, it costs nothing. Gilroy (1987: 211) comments: 'A patchwork or collage of melody, voice and rhythm is created when these sounds come together with rapped vocal commentary and chants which draw on Afro-America's older traditions of communication.' Back (1996: 192) goes further: 'The music is dependent on the rearranging of musical fragments intermixed by the DJ. ... The DJ is close to what Lévi-Strauss (1976) called a cultural "bricoleur", or a craftsperson who makes use – in this case of musical fragments in order to create new music.' Post-Fordist, post-industrial and postcolonial are other eras that hip-hop can be seen to have sprung from. It is a leisure product, provided for segmented markets and a product of twentieth-century migration.

Hip-hop redefines a range of relationships, including the means of musical production and reception which blur in the interactive element at concerts and live open-mic events where the audience can 'freestyle' and join in. Potter (1998: 41) comments: 'in their earlier stages, hip-hop relied on the tactical aural recycling of previously existing sounds, a reclamation of the *consumed* (the vinyl record whose value was supposed to be exchange-value) as a praxis of *production* (use-value)'. This was clear in early rap records such as the Sugar Hill Gang's celebrated track 'Rapper's Delight', in which the bass refrain from Chic's hit 'Good Times' was repeated or looped with minimal manipulation to serve as a backing for the main rap. However with the advance of technology, sampling has become more sophisticated so that within a tune the sound patterns can be radically reconfigured, as this following comment from Mathew of HD illustrates:

MJ: We do use samples but we mash 'em up. We might do a pitchshift on them and take em down an octave and so on. At the end of it we've took a sample but we've smashed it so much to bits that you can't realise that it's from something else.

Negus (1999: 158) highlights the intertextuality of rap with the example of the hit *Gangster's Paradise* that sold for its inclusion in the film *Dangerous Minds* as well as its sampling of Stevie Wonder. Indeed following the lead of Sinatra's Hollywood forays, rappers have graduated from the training ground of the promotional video to turn their hand to acting, for example Ice T in *New Jack City*, Ice Cube in *Boyz N the Hood* and Eminem in *8 Mile*. Will Smith's career as a rapper predates his incarnation as a cinema star.[3] This potentially demonstrates another mode of sampling.

Rap is usually understood to be a musical culture that was, in the words of Bruce Springsteen, 'born in the USA'. However as we have seen, this does not mean that its message is simply a restatement of good old thanksgiving and apple pie American values. Rap is identified with black youth and seen as emanating from the mythologised locale of 'the street', a site that is the opposite pole of suburbia with all its in-built connotations of whiteness. Rose (1994: 100–1) writes:

> Not all rap transcripts directly critique all forms of domination; nonetheless, a large and significant element in rap's discursive territory is engaged in symbolic and ideological warfare with institutions and

groups that symbolically, ideologically and materially oppress African Americans. In this way rap music is a contemporary stage for the theater of the powerless.

There is also a sense of double standards in criticism of rap music for violence and sexism when these sentiments have not been subject to the same degree of condemnation in other more mainstream white popular cultural forms. In 1994, during the week of his arrest for murder, Snoop Doggy Dogg was quoted by the *Melody Maker* as saying: 'Clint Eastwood and Charles Bronson they can kill up a million motherfuckers and create bad images for the kids, but once they get off screen everybody praises and loves them. But when we do our art in the studio, we get criticised for it' (Johnstone 1999: 355). Misogyny in rock lyrics is longstanding. The Beatles and Rolling Stones are now accepted as twin British institutions but tracks such as 'Run For Your Life' and 'Under My Thumb' have some very dubious lyrics. Both Mick Jagger and Paul McCartney have subsequently been knighted for services to Britain. The Prodigy's single 'Smack My Bitch Up' provides a more recent example of inexcusable sexism in pop from a white act who do not seem to have been tainted in the same way as all rap often is. Springhall (1998: 7) claims that moral panics in relation to popular cultural phenomena are often based on the way popular culture is seen as being of inferior status compared to high culture or art. Popular music for its critics is particularly debasing and rap, as a predominantly black popular musical form, has a higher threshold still to contend with (hooks 1994).

Rapping all over the world

Krims (2000) describes how, within the US, as rap spread away from its point of origin in New York, rappers elsewhere were conscious of asserting their distinctive regional identities which gave rise to new musical styles. Examples include the rivalry between the sometimes discordant sample-heavy tendency of east coast rap (as exemplified by Public Enemy) and more mellifluous west coast funk-derived sounds.[4] In the 1990s much was made of a southern US variety of hip-hop with a folk-music edge, exemplified by groups such as Arrested Development. The same point of local adaptation can be made of rap styles outside the US. There is an increasing body of 'homegrown' rap in European countries that one might normally imagine as whitefaced, with growing academic histories to match, e.g. Scandinavia (Ásmundsson 2001; Fock 1999; Vestel 1999), Germany (Bennett 1999; Cheesman 1998; Soysal 2001) and Italy (Wright 2000), as well as in the middle east and Pacific Asian rim. Mitchell (2001: 10), one of the most meticulous chroniclers of rap's internationalisation, makes a case for 'the locality, temporality and "universality" of hip hop' in the way that rap has been indigenised outside America. He argues that 'in most countries where rap has taken root, hip-hop scenes have rapidly developed from an adoption to an adaptation of US musical forms and idioms. This has involved an increasing syncretism and incorporation of local linguistic and musical features' (Mitchell 2001: 11). I want to address the hip-hop scene in France in particular here, a rap variant that I have written about previously (Huq 1999b; 2001) and which is attracting increasing English language scholarship (Lipsitz 1994; Mitchell 1996; Prévos 1997; 2001; Warne 1997; 2000).

Although it is relatively little known outside the French-speaking world, French language rap has made France the second worldwide market for rap after the US. English language studies of this phenomenon are on the rise.[5] Ambiguous attitudes to American cultural influences have been enduring in France, just as they have been in the UK (Bazin 1995; Hebdige 1988), revolving around repulsion at a perceived anti-intellectual inability to compete cerebrally with ancient/older established civilizations and simultaneous fascination for its hedonistic codes of youth cultural liberation. Rap in France continues this ambiguity, both in using US influences and resisting cultural domination. While the reaction of French cultural policy to a percieved threat of Americanisation has at times appeared defensive in nature, French rap and film have been beneficiaries of official initiatives to assert national identity. Governmnent-imposed quotas of French language output on national and local radio instituted in 1994 are a key factor in assisting the growth of French rap. The scene has ushered in a new generation of heroes of youth originating from former French colonies, including second generation French-Arab 'beurs' and African youth. Cannon (1997: 160) has described Senegal-born Paris literature graduate MC Solaar as 'France's first black superstar'. In the press he has been seen as carrying on the traditions of French performance art, seen in the way Solaar was labelled 'l'heriteur rap du dandyisme Française' (the rap heir apparent of French dandyism) by France's newspaper of record Le Monde (11 June 1997).

Poulet (1993: 312) writes: 'From the multiple ethnic communities of big cities in France are emerging new musical hybrids reflecting both their ancestral musical heritage and their French content.' French hip-hop is synonymous with banlieue music.[6] As in the US the text is inseparable from its (sub)urban context (Bazin 1995; Cannon 1997). An alternative suggestion advanced to explain NTM's controversial name[7] is 'Le Nord Transmet le Message' (Message Transmitted from the North), hailing from the group's humble origins in the north Parisian banlieue – a location where the band's Joey Starr was proud to claim he still lived in 2002.[8] Rather than 'making good' though, remaining in touch with one's proletarian roots are promoted outwardly. Lapassade (1990: 93) comments 'Le message du rappeur, c'est d'abord que le monde est devenu l'empire du mal. Le rappeur cherche à dire la désolation du ghetto ou de la banlieue, et loin de cacher ses origines.' (The message of the rapper is first of all that the world has become the bad empire. Far from hiding their origins, the rapper seeks to tell of this desolation of the ghetto or neighbourhood.) The group Ministère AMER produced the album 95 200 after the postal code of Sarcelles, another tough north Parisien banlieue, in the same way as NWA proudly proclaimed that they were 'Straight Outta Compton'. Bazin (1995: 92) writes of a further fissure in a rival north versus south Parisian banlieue civil war. Rap's academic theorists all note that it is rooted in lived urban expression: its dance is corporeal expression and its visual art – graffiti – practiced on such urban canvas as public transport, regrouping all the arts of the street (Bazin 1995: 237). For Cathus (1994) it is the power of street experience that gives hip-hop its aesthetic power. The term 'street credibility' is not so-called for nothing. If the street is rap's stage, it can be worked into a cartography of social relations.

Just as US rap has been categorised, French rap can be subdivided into the 1983–90 underground scene in Parisian banlieue districts and the years following 1990 which have been characterised by its move to being a fully fledged overground youth culture (Lapassade 1996). Along the lines of Krims' reality rap and party rap dichotomy, this second phase can be further bifurcated into 'hardcore' and 'cool' rap, tendencies represented by the combative, radical message music of NTM and Ministère AMER in the first category and the more consensual MC Solaar in the second (Bazin 1995: 214). Bocquet and Pierre-Adolphe (1997: 78) call the categories 'underground hardcore' and 'rap variety'. However as binaries always are, such demarcations are somewhat simplistic. Outfits such as the Marseilles mixed-race band IAM are somewhere between the 'cool/variety' and 'hard/underground' camps and others have crossed boundaries. NTM were long seen as a 'hardcore' act, although their most recent album has seen something of a shift in style with more peace-seeking lyrics than their earlier offerings, demonstrating the dynamism of French rap. Many leading acts are signed to large mainstream record labels. MC Solaar is currently on Warner Brothers having previously been with Polydor, NTM are on Sony and IAM are on Delabel/Virgin. The 1990 compilation *Rapattitude* issued on Virgin Records has been seen as marking the beginning of French rap's commercial recognition. The subsequent record company scramble to sign up anything seen as profitable at the expense of quality has been condemned by rap fans in France as it has been elsewhere. French rap has for some years boasted impressive export sales in particular to Francophone Switzerland, Belgium and Canada. Virgin issued two compilations of French rap for non-French audiences, *Le Flow* and *Le Flow 2*, in 1998 and 2000 demonstrating a concerted attempt to attain international crossover.

In France rap has not been immune from controversy. The group NTM [*Nique ta mère*, which translates as 'fuck your mother'] were sentenced to six months in prison and a F50,000 fine in 1996 for the ancient and little used or known offence of 'outrages par paroles', for offensive (anti-police) remarks made by them at a festival in FN (Front National) Toulon, in the South of France during summer 1995. A parallel can be drawn with the hustling offstage of NWA in Detroit in 1989 by the police after performing the track 'Fuck Da Police' (Johnstone 1999: 315). The NTM incident made a public example of two individuals whose immigrant origins were ceaselessly stressed ('Kool Shen' Bruno Lopez is of Portuguese stock and 'Joey Starr' in the media Didier Morville Antallaise Caribbean). The widely attacked decision was later partially overturned by the national justice department.[9] FN leader Jean-Marie Le Pen is on record as stating: 'Rap, tag [graffiti] sont des modes pasagères des excroisances pathogènes' – rap and graffiti are passing fads of pathogenic outbursts (*Le Monde*, 23–4 June 1996). Rap and anti-racist politics have been yoked together more than once. Campaigning uses of rap on benefit records suggest that music still has the capacity to offer anti-establishment oppositional societal critique in contradiction to arguments that youth culture /music has become commodified into part of the capitalist establishment.[10] Anti-racist organizations, student unions, pressure groups and trade unions demonstrated in support of NTM against the 1996 censure; similar alliances have been mobilized against racist immigration policy and against Le Pen in the period between the first and second rounds of the French Presidential elections in 2002. UK rap has similarly been used as a vehicle for promoting anti-racist messages. A 1993 newspaper profile of Matty Hanson, aka MC Fusion of the band Credit to the Nation, much feted by the media as the future of UK hip-hop for their campaigning stance and rap–indie crossover sound, remarks: 'He is rejected by the hardcore black hip-hop community for addressing the problems within rap: homophobia, misogyny and anti-semitism' (Forrest 1993). Contrastingly the black separatist rap of the Nation of Islam-supporting Public Enemy and their alleged anti-semitism are further reasons why, in the words of Cashmore (1997: 170), rap is potentially every 'liberal white's worst nightmare'.

French rap's political dimension has extended from its use in anti-racist campaigning to black identity assertion. Lapassade notes 'noirceur' (blackness) as critical to rap in general (1996: 52–65). Blackness in rap has been seen in Public Enemy's album entitled 'Fear of a Black Planet' or NWA's use of the word 'Nigger' which they see as a positive reclaiming of the word.[11] Africa has been a historic seedbed for rap on both sides of the Atlantic (Calio 1998; Toop 1999). Afrika Bambaataa's Zulu Nation collective, named after an eighteenth century South African tribe who fought white colonisation (Toop 1999: 56–59), for example idealise the continent as a model of peace, harmony and rights. The live performance of Paris-based Senegalese born rappers Djoloff (named after an ancient Senegalese kingdom) combines French and Woloff language lyrics, traditional African costumes, instruments and various anti-colonial political pronouncements, critiquing corrupt African dictators and third world debt. Accompanying the set-list from their Manchester concert of 2000, scribbled notes I have, compiled by the band themselves, include next to the song 'Ecoute' (Listen) the word 'colonialisation' for the song-title 'Metite', 'Malheur Africaine' (African Unhappiness) and next to 'Ninkilale', 'la dictature' (dictatorship). In interview in March 2000, lead rapper Mbegane N'Dour commented of integration:

It's all about making you into a French citizen to alienate your spirit, to wipe it out so you forget all your differences. France risks exploding because it's two-faced integration. They're all for us integrating to do low-level cheap labour but they don't want us to be lawyers, doctors, engineers, television presenters, parliamentarians or executives. Integration is the new colonialisation.[12]

Afrocentricism was a subject that early US rap theorists such as Rose (1994) were expansive on. Gilroy's (1993a) influential proposition of the black Atlantic is a sophisticated model of Afrodiasporic black cultures in western modernity that transgresses different national paradigms for thinking about history. Black identity is seen as unstable, unlike traditional and outmoded conceptions of cultural essentialism and national purity. Cultural, national and political influences all feed into this account which is transnational in character. This model for the development of black cultural production in the US and Europe could potentially then apply to France. The experiences of migrants however arguably differ in different nation-states due to varying circumstances. Mercer (1994: 251) situates minority cultural production beyond a single black diaspora: 'The terrain of postimperial Britain is the site of many, overlapping diasporas, including the Indian, Pakistani, Bangladeshi and broader South Asian diasporas, as well as the diaspora of Islam.' Islam has been another influence on rap in France in some of the work of Marseilles group IAM as well as in the US with acts such as the Nation of Islam-inspired Public Enemy and Sunni Muslim rappers such as Nas and Mos Def. Islam has also been used in rap in countries such as Algeria and by Palestinians in Israel who stress this aspect of their identity before blackness or Africa.[13]

UK-produced rap is not always in the English language either: recent years have witnessed a bhangra/hip-hop crossover. Mention has already been made in chapter 4 of the Manchester bhangra daytimer that I attended in summer 2002 and its split-level rap/garage room and Asian music policy. In 2003 the artist Rajinder Rai of Coventry in the UK, trading under the name Punjabi MC, had a large worldwide hit with 'Mundian Te Bach Ke' (Beware of the Boys), a bhangra–rap hybrid which sampled the bassline of the 1980s television adventure series theme tune *Knight Rider* and overlaid it with a bhangra beat and Punjabi lyrics. The song spent a lengthy run in the German charts and achieved the rare feat of making the UK top 10 despite its lack of English language lyrics. It had been played at bhangra gatherings as long ago as five years earlier but made the UK mainstream charts when it began receiving airplay from BBC Radio 1. Rai was quoted by the *Sunday Times* (12 January 2002) remarking 'A lot of people who buy it won't have a clue what it means.' Rai interestingly compares bhangra to hip-hop, invoking some of the same long-made claims of bhangra's relative lack of support from the mainstream music industry in limiting its success to a parallel marketspace. 'Bhangra started out in 1979 at the same time as hip-hop. Hip-hop is now a multimillion pound industry, and bhangra is … a £250,000 industry. [However] Bhangra is massive in the UK. It's bigger than hip-hop. We've got a party every night of the week.' This again emphasises the way that both bhangra and hip-hop are experienced live in communal gatherings. Well-known recorded

US examples of Asian rap crossover tracks include Missy Elliot's 'Get Yr Freak On', Truth Hurts, 'So Addictive' by and Bubba Sparks' 'Ugly' which have used Indian instrumentation as a bed for break beats and rapping.

Elsewhere in Europe rap has been played out by youth in several settings reflecting global influences as well as local circumstances; in each case mediated through different sets of experiences. Wright (1997) looks at the development of Italian rap from the country's network of social centres that were originally set up independently with anarcho-punk leanings. The musical style is described as reggae/raggamuffin infused, as 'street music' incorporating everyday soliliquies. In other countries, specific urban locales have been evoked as particularly significant in rap's development. Soysal (2001) for example names Kreuzberg in Berlin as a significant site for its 2 million-strong Turkish population that comprise 12 per cent of the population. This is in much the same way as Marseilles is held as synonymous with rap in France (Sberna 2002). He describes a Berlin-held local government hip-hop festival at which rappers from Paris and New York are invited to perform. Robins and Morely (1996) use the example of the Turkish–German rap act the Cartel who identify with black urban US culture over and above integrating into 'white' German society. It is claimed 'Like many other German youth looking for a way forward, the members of Cartel turn to American culture as a resource in the articulation of identity and projection. Their distinction then is that they are, in fact, between *three* cultures' (Robins and Morely 1996: 249, emphasis added). This recalls and rejects the earlier dichotomising logic of youth studies that revolves around binaries (e.g. Anwar 1976). The youth who 'use' hip-hop experience multiple realities and thus inhabit various cultures. The collective Kanak-Attack of Turkish origin are overtly political in their work (Cheesman 2002), providing an interesting parallel to French migrant youth as the main drivers of rap. The message of Turkish/German rap is however largely secular in tenor as figures show a lessening importance of religion in young minority lives, although of course there are always exceptions to every rule (Soysal 2001).

Chambers (1985: 169) has called rap 'the latest in the black urban soundtrack' but rap has emerged in a number of countries traditionally conceived of as white. Scandinavia has provided some interesting examples of rap in recent years, often reflecting migration; however this is a younger migration history than that of the UK or France. In Finland the group Kwan include female rapper MC Mariko born in middle Finland in 1979, who lived in the US from the age of two to eight. Co-rapper MC Tidjân was born in Helsinki in 1978 of Finnish-Senegalese parents but grew up in the US, Germany, Senegal and France. In interviews the group have highlighted this background (www.kwan-dynasty. com). Best-selling act Mr Paleface is, as his nom de rap suggests, white. His subject matter includes the police crackdown on graffiti.[14] Here we see that, as in France, the omnipresence of the police on the urban landscape makes them an obvious target. US equivalents can be found in 'Fuck Da Police' by NWA and Ice T's 'Cop Killer'. Mr Paleface has claimed that he was exposed to rap as an exchange student in Iowa in 1995 (http://paleface.fm. 10580/#). Fintelligents, meanwhile, are a white Finnish group who have existed since 1997 and rap in Finnish. I witnessed them live in December 2001 at the Gloria venue in Helsinki, a local government-owned youth concert hall. Jostling amongst the crowds outside the venue trying to get tickets for what had been a sold-out event I noted that their fanbase seemed ethnically mixed and young. Bomfunk MCs meanwhile are a Finnish musical export; the track 'Freestyler' of 2000 was a huge international hit. The song was performed in English but is more memorable for its rhythm than for its lyrical content. Gudmundsson (1999) has pointed out that Nordic pop acts such as Abba, A-ha and Aqua have only been able to succeed internationally by becoming 'artificial' pop. Although rap is in many ways artificial, many Scandinavian rap groups have not compromised linguistically, such as Denmark's Den Gale Posse (The Wrong Bag) and Rottweiler XXX, who dominated the Icelandic charts in 2001–2002 (Ásmundsson 2001). Sweden also has a well-developed indigenous rap scene.

The following excerpt of interview data shows that for Mathew of HD, foreign language rap is not entirely impenetrable.

MJ: Like Sïan Supa Crew, which is a French group, I like their stuff. I don't have a clue what they're saying but I can tell what the flow [delivery] is like. [It's the same with] MC Solaar ... but it's a lot harder for them to make it than us. The British obviously speak English ... but like the Americans can't [even] understand certain bits of our language.

In other words the linguistic disadvantage can be compensated for by more attitudinal characteristics of rap delivery. Furthermore the simple label 'English' in language terms masks a range of differences, e.g. US versus UK, Manchester versus London, etc.

The uses of hip-hop: rap in the classroom and the hip-hop university

We remain in Longsight, Manchester for this next section. The Cultural Fusion event demonstrated many of the features commonly ascribed to hip-hop. The sense of it as a group venture was clear in the way that the acts performed with mutuality, supporting their co-participants. Technical difficulties with the backing tape for example dictated that female vocalist Jamokee had to deliver an acapella version of 'Killing Me Softly' (introduced simply as 'the Fugees', although the song was originally done by Roberta Flack). Despite this potentially daunting situation she was met with encouragement from fellow-performers and others present, evidenced in supportive cries of 'go girl', 'show dem' from the audience, who even took on the role of filling in the twangy instrumental motif in between the verses. Of the nine acts of the show there was also much interchange.

Proceedings concluded with 'the Combined Cultural Fusion Choir' which encompassed all of the evening's performers. Interestingly the large number of girls performing seemed to counteract the popular perception of rap as a male preserve/macho genre (cf. Rose 1994), including the American-accented Rosie and MC SSB, an Asian girl named Sunita who included the phrase 'black/white/Asian' in the lyrics urging people of all races to unite. The use of hip-hop vernacular was much in evidence throughout. In terms of fashion, comfortable sportswear dominated with brand names and labels flouted openly.

The ethnically diverse, mixed-gender band HD, a sprawling be-capped and be-hooded eight-strong collective, turned out to be Cultural Fusion's most memorable act. The appearance of the group onstage moved a person sitting behind me to murmur 'So Solid', referring to the controversial UK garage/act So Solid Crew of thirty-plus members. The performativity and theatrical aspect of their music was clearly at the fore with the members ducking and diving, switching position and sharing chief vocal duties on the track 'Hyperlyrics'. The band noticeably stressed their origins on the track with the initials M-A-N-C-H-E-S-T-E-R repeatedly spelt out in a key refrain. Much analysis of rap music tends to concentrate largely on lyrics, a time-honoured tradition in popular music studies as we have seen in chapter 3. Importantly lyrics (text) cannot be divorced from their situation (context). Buckingham and Sefton-Green (1994: 64) noted in their observations of a group of young people on an A-level media studies course in the UK that rap for them was less about any relationship with black America and more a means of positive self-esteem offering a consciously political critique of racism and fixed notions of national identity. An interview that I carried out two weeks later with core members of HD both supports and contradicts elements of this claim.

When I interviewed them, HD had been in operation for two years as a loose grouping of friends rapping together and for eighteen months as a recording concern, initially in the institutional setting of a GMMAZ (Greater Manchester Music Action Zone) local community initiative at the Contact Theatre in Manchester's University district and then subsequently over the twelve months preceding the interview at Cultural Fusion in Longsight. The group were keen to stress that within their eight members they contained different personalities and rapping styles. These assumed identities were reflected in their pseudonyms.[15] Members fitted in their hours on the project around other school-level and further education commitments. Seventeen-year-old rapper and producer Mathew Jay, the self appointed 'leader', was undertaking a BTEC national diploma in music technology at college in central Manchester. Ravelle Leacock, also a rapper and producer aged seventeen, was doing A-levels in physics, art and environmental science with a view to a career in architecture. Marc Leacock, Ravelle's cousin aged twenty, was studying multimedia while Hamza Mbeju, seventeen, was a business student living in the white middle class suburb of Cheadle outside the City of Manchester boundary. Finally Rosie Garvey, fourteen and still at school, had been in Manchester for a year, having been sent there to live with her mother by her father who remained in Longbeach in the US where Rosie grew up. All lived with at least one parent. Intriguingly enough the initials HD stand for 'Helletic domains'. Mathew explained 'I came up with it. It means evil territory; like gang life and so on … [it comes] with the habitat.' At once we can see linguistic innovation and reinvention here in this neologism derived from the word 'hell'. Again the 'reality rap' aspect was stressed in a comment reminiscent of that of NWA cited earlier:

RH: Does your music reflect your surroundings in Longsight?

MJ: I wouldn't say Longsight but Manchester as a whole. We're just saying that our life; it ain't no fairyland. It's about spitting rhymes, about situations that you've been in, like depression or being angry but not like going on like you're flaming terminator when you've never done it. … All I write about is stuff that I've got opinions on and stuff that I've experienced.

To obtain NVQs there are no examinations but project requirements are assessed and moderated by internal and external examiners. Participants are required to undertake a minimum of 30 hours of music production and performance. However Owen Thomas, project director and internal verifier for the ONC told me 'you'll get them doing 40 and 50 because once they come here I can't them out of the building'. Some Cultural Fusion candidates are former young offenders. The idea of music as a positive outlet was reflected in a number of comments from HD members who attended the project on weekdays.

RH: Longsight's the kind of area with a bit of a reputation isn't it?

MJ: That's why Cultural Fusion's a good way of getting us away from that. I think music's made a huge impact on my life. It's what I live for. Music's my saviour at the end of the day … being able to come here and trying to achieve my dreams … it keeps me focused and keeps me out of trouble.

Sara Cohen (1997: 31) noted in her Liverpool study 'The [music] scene offers a social life, a sense of purpose, and dreams and aspirations outside any responsibilities of work, family or home. It becomes an important source of collective and individual identity.' The interviewees of Fornäs et al. (1995) and Finnegan (1989) also make similar statements. Rosie also sees the Cultural Fusion project as a positive influence in her life, as does Mathew.

RG: Last year I was really immature. I've changed a lot. I was bad. I was always getting into trouble with the police and stuff. I came here and thought 'what's the point in rebelling when you can go places with your life?' I just thought 'I'm just gonna change.' I didn't wanna be some little person … a black high school dropout.

RH: What do you make of that whole media label of Manchester as Gunchester?

ML: When I was young I used to get mixed up in that shit then I was seeing a social worker and I'm here now. It's kept me off the streets so I think it's a good thing.

As the only band member from outside the Longsight area, Hamza contrasted the locality with the dreariness of white suburbia.

HB: I prefer Longsight to Cheadle. Cheadle's like dead. After 7.00 pm you don't see anybody. It's like 'where did everybody go?'

Studies of pedagogy in hip-hop are a growing area of rap scholarship (Dimitriadis 2001; Weaver et al. 2001; Weaver and Daspit 2001). Various links can be made between the Cultural Fusion project in action and recent developments in educational theory. We have also seen how reflexive biographies and individualised trajectories are also been played out by the members of HD. Here work and education are fused in a process of situated cognition or 'learning on the job' (Lave and Wenger 1990).

Among Owen Jones' objectives for the programme that he spelt out to me were developing youth, giving them a platform and providing employment. HD members Ravelle and Mathew had at the time of interview already begun tutoring younger children in Cubase technology through Cultural Fusion, which they were remunerated for under the government's Connexions youth training scheme. Other interviewees were mixed on the possibilities of rap as an occupation – from a distant possibility to a worked out educational route.

RH: Could it even turn into a career for you?
ML: I'd like to use it as a career but I'm not good enough. I need to be better.
RG: I'm not in it for the money right now because I'm young. I just do it because I like it but [eventually] I see it as a career, definitely.
RH: Would you need to go through some more training?
RG: My school's trying to get me work experience in a studio for sound engineering and they recommended that I go to Salford Music College after I finish.

Mathew asserted that he had taken up his college course to qualify himself in studio management to insulate himself against the possible outcome of not succeeding in signing a recording contract. If a deal was not forthcoming he could run a studio as an alternative. This shows a rationalised response to risk. This new type of risky career structure (cf. Beck 1992) alluded to by McRobbie (1999) and Banks et al. (2000) is thus formalised within the educational qualifications framework of college courses which are responding to the new economy.

Remarks such as those of the band on the importance of music to their lives and the possibility of it becoming a career recall Finnegan's (1989: 5) comments:

far from music-making taking a peripheral role for individuals and society – a view propagated in the kind of theoretical stance that marginalises 'leisure' or 'culture' as somehow less than 'work or society'

– music can equally well be seen as playing a central part not just in urban networks but also in the social structure and processes of our life today.

Although it is recognised that to go into music in studio management or full-time tutoring, qualifications are needed, part of the attraction of rap is that you don't need any formal training to get started. Members use a mixture of skills learned at school, on the job, through listening to other recorded rappers and improvisation.

RL: I sort of play the piano. I've not got any grades or anything but I am able to play different tunes. I read a bit of music as well. At school I was like shown … that's how I learn, by looking at something.

RH: As a producer then you construct the tracks with software? Doesn't that do away with the need for formal musical knowledge?

RL: You don't even have to play the instrument because when you go to Cubase you can just do it all from the computer … but you have the option to play it manually. I play manual.

The performance aspect of this creative process was also stressed in keeping with the Cultural Fusion objective of confidence-building.

RH: What's in your heads when you're performing live?

MJ: It's just like the energy that you get on stage. If you're just stood there people are gonna think 'What's he doin'?' But if you're moving and getting into it and showing you're not shy and showing that you're enjoying it on stage it's gonna make them [the audience] feel good and enjoying themselves.

RH: Do you ever take part in those sort of competitions like in the film *8 Mile* where different rival crews are rapping and trying to outdo each other?

RL: The only time we ever battle is like when we're messing [around] between us or sometimes we sit and rap or we'll be on the bus or wherever and we just do it.

This again demonstrates the portability of rap. The rapper's main tool is the vocal chords, unlike an instrument that might be lost or stolen.

Rap has also been used in a learning context in teaching the French language, even though breaking with linguistic convention is one of the most noteworthy features of French rap. Recognition of the educational potential of rap by the part-industry, part-government financed French Music Bureau, essentially a running campaign to export French music worldwide, is evidenced in the regular issuing to French teachers of a compilation CD series entitled *Génération Française* with an accompanying book (*livret pédagogique*) containing full lyrics, background information and suggested classroom activities for

French language students from beginners to advanced. All volumes have included a spread of offerings including liberal amounts of rap.[16] Baker (1993: 62) notes how in the US, rap has also been broadcast and used for educational purposes on children's television programme *Sesame Street* to teach children the alphabet. In a more direct use of rap in the classroom, in both 2000 and 2001 the London French Embassy office of the French Music Bureau organised UK tours by French rappers Sïan Supa Crew and Djolof tied in with French language workshops delivered by the groups to French classes in local schools. Children were given tuition on how to rhyme in French and deliver the resulting lyrics in a rap style. As a result of publicity on Channel 4 television's Planet Pop programme and articles in the *Face* magazine and the *Times Educational Supplement*, the French Music Bureau was besieged with calls from other schools clamouring for rap bands to come to their language lessons. Even without the appearance of big name stars from France, the deconstruction of rap texts in a classroom context in this way is much more acceptable to pupils than traditional grammar exercises and there is also an argument to be made for it highlighting how language cannot be divorced from culture. After all French hip-hop arguably says much more about contemporary French society than many outdated textbooks relied on by schools that still propagate images of France that equate with the Eiffel Tower or baguette-carrying moustached men in berets with striped jerseys.

French rap is being used to export the French language overseas in spite of its disregard for grammatical formalism and its diverse source-material which runs counter to attempts to safeguard 'pure' French. Yet youth culture was seen as a chief offender in the ill-fated 1991 Loi Toubon, an ultimately unconstitutional legislative attempt to replace (supposedly) Anglicised vocabulary with defined French words, sometimes created for this purpose, e.g. 'le balladeur' in place of the (strictly Japanese) word 'le walkman'. French rap is performed in a streetspeak version of French, including African, Arab, gypsy and American roots, and viewed with disapproval by traditionalists for its disregard for traditional grammar rules and liberal use of neologisms. Verlan, a cryptic form of back-slang which reverses the syllables of individual words and switches their vowels round, is an important constituent component.[17] There is accordingly a burgeoning literature on *le Français branché* (cutting-edge French) (Ball 1990; Verdelhan-Bourgade 1990) paralelling the work of Hewitt (1986; 1990) and Rampton (1995) on the lexicon of Black British youth. The twin edited collections of rap lyrics of Bocquet and Pierre-Adolphe (1997) and Perrier (2000) were both issued in poetry collection series, in keeping with Lapassade's (1990: 5) labeling of rap as 'la nouvelle poesie orale des metropoles' (new urban oral poetry). The codification of this slang has taken place in specialised French dictionaries (Andreini 1985; Festin 1999; Merle 1999; Pierre-Adolphe 1995). Perhaps only when these new words enter the *Robert* or *Petit Laurousse* (standard dictionaries) will we be able to state that *le Français branché* has found a place at the centre of the French language rather than languishing on its margins.

Nicole from Cultural Fusion's comment towards the start of this chapter is telling. Rap can be used in formal and non-formal education; often for the purposes of keeping youth off 'the street'. An example of the co-option of rap for official purposes by the French left in France can be seen in the week-long 'Université du Hip-hop' festival held in Strasbourg. This was organised in summer 1996 by Été Jeune, the local council youth arts and cultural service, as an activity for young people to occupy themselves with during the summer holidays. Here no formal qualifications were achieved but the event does demonstrate the use of rap via progressive municipal involvement in youth cultural activities extending beyond the obvious local state-sponsorship of concerts. A range of graffiti, fanzine-writing, rapping, scratching and DJing workshops took place over the festival's eight day duration. Public debates also took place with plenary speakers and panels. Among the attractions, an entire HLM (Municipal Housing Estate) in the neighbourhood of Illkirch was sanctioned as a graffiti-permitted zone for the week. The event aroused some suspicion for countervailing the dispossessed/ protest aspect of hip-hop (Cross 1993; Rose 1994; Toop 1999; Vulbeau 1992) as voiced in this following interview extract from Mr E, a 23-year-old graffiti writer:

> France is a police state. It's centralized, everything is controlled: the administration, the papers,[18] everything is had [recorded]. Pirate radio gets very quickly fucked up by the state for example. Hip-hop's been on the French scene since the early eighties. The media didn't believe it or push it [at first]. Regular people couldn't get to it. In 1996 it's getting popular, so they want everything under control.

French academic theories of rap, whilst noting its connections with immigrant youth culture, see it as part and parcel of integration (Lapassade 1990: 13). As we can see it is being integrated in more ways than one.

Although Strasbourg has a public image derived from postcard depictions of the European Parliament and its picturesque cathedral, the city is a diverse one. Its banlieues were the scene of serious youth unrest in 1995 that were relatively fresh in occurrence when the 'hip-hop university' took place. As with similar disturbances in northern England in 2001, various explanations have been advanced as to why the 'riots' occurred and what to do about them, e.g. FAS (1996). Indeed car-burning at New Year's Eve has established itself as an unofficial annual youth ritual in some of Strasbourg's banlieue neighbour-hoods. Some readings might label the municipality of (then socialist) Strasbourg as a benign regime, a containment function can be seen in the objective of its youth arts and cultural service (Été Jeune) in the programming of the Université du Hip-hop to channel (potentially riotous) youthful exuber-ance and fondness for hip-hop into a municipal framework, thus avoiding any risk of it spilling over into unwanted anti-social behaviour. With the pathology of rap and youth already presumed the hip-hop University's function to provide youth with a supposedly 'constructive' summer leisure activity comes across as a patronising attempt to pacify them. The use of the banlieue of Illkirch as a site for the graffiti display for example is questionable as its far flung location means that none of the people who 'matter' in Strasbourg, e.g. ambassadors, European parliamentarians, Council of Europe dignitaries, etc. would have seen it. Other noteworthy aspects of the festival included a bus donated by the local transport authority for use for graffiti, although this has not been seen in circulation. Such obviously artificial attempts to manage and control the culture seem to sit somewhat incongruously with the resistive capacity of hip-hop.

Despite assurances denying any hidden agenda, such as Été Jeune's publicity officer Linda Boukkakiou telling *Repères de Strasbourg* (17 December 1996) that Strasbourg youth are lucky to have a town hall supporting such activities, an interview I carried out with Leo, a Strasbourg based commercial hip-hop promoter, brought in to the Université du Hip-hop organising team, highlighted tensions. Interestingly, at a time when the arts community in the UK clamours for increased funding, her complaints were of too much support given to rap from officialdom to the extent that it is being neutralised:

> This town is run by the socialists. They've done a lot for social provision but there's a whole policy of 'assistata' [spoon-feeding], it's pretty bad for helping youth manage for themselves. There's a lot of problems in the quartiers [neighbourhoods] here – fights, racism. The political powers just throw money at it. They'll put an assistant [youth worker] on the ground but it'll be someone who doesn't know the terrain, doesn't understand.

Perhaps the Université du Hip-hop is best understood in the context of the French statist tradition of arts sponsorship at both local and national levels. The first French minister of culture André Malraux instituted a national network of local youth centres (*maisons de la jeunesse et de la culture*) in the 1950s and the socio-cultural centres as successors to these have in recent years been the sites of hip-hop activity. Ménard (2000) dates the involvement of officialdom in hip-hop back to the acceptance of graffiti into art galleries by Jack Lang, Mittterand's minister of culture in the 1980s, as an attempt at social integration. The municipality of the north Parisian district Saint Denis, labelled the geographic cradle of rap in France (Mayol 1997: 204), was running hip-hop events from the early 1990s backed by a Ministry of Culture initiative FAIR – Fonds d'Action et d'Initiative pour le Rock (*Le Monde* 31 October 1991). This history then situates the hip-hop university as a pop festival within defined parameters or limitations rather than a more sinister social democratic engineering project. The official organisation of rap – now widely practised by the local state in France via various festivals (Ménard 2000) is contrary to the subcultural valorisation of the concept of 'underground'. Yet the fact that rap was the musical style chosen to anchor the event is testimony to the music's outreach capability and arguably achieves a repositioning away from the underground. In France both local and national government have employed rap to exploit its potential integrative functions.

In both Manchester and Strasbourg the uses of hip-hop are multiple. The locally situated hip-hop scenes that occur there are far from simple exercises in US mimicry. When I interviewed DJ Rebel of the Marseilles group Soul Swing during the Université du Hip-hop, he remarked: 'For too long, it's been said that France only copies America. It's time to say that we're not in America. We rap in French, our maternal language. We have a vision of rap that's French not American.' Yet the US still has a hold on practitioners of rap outside its borders. At the Cultural Fusion evening acts rapped in both American and Mancunian accents. Dubet (quoted in Calio 1998: 27) has observed 'New York fascine plus qu'Alger' (New York fascinates – French youth – more than Algeria), stressing the exoticism of the American dream as opposed to one's own more tangible roots. Buckingham and Sefton-Green (1994), quoted above, talk about how tenuously the youths they studied were linked with black America. Similarly Afrocentricism was not a preoccupying lyrical concern for HD, although the group members I interviewed all had African-Caribbean heritage in one way or another:

MJ: Africa is just the motherland of all black people. That's all I know. Is our music inspired by that culture? Not really.

RL: I don't think those topics are irrelevant but where I am now I choose to write about stuff that's happening around me in Longsight.

MJ: What I think really affects my lyrics is that England as a place is really ethnic. ... I think it is more equal now for ethnics and like white British.

RL: I like the Asian hip-hop crossover.

The band also rejected the much-made claims that rap is necessarily a black music form (Baker 1993; Rose 1994), instead seeing the strength of one's lyrics as a marker for the right to participate and citing Eminem as an individual who had opened it up.

Interestingly Rosie firmly denied that there was any issue about her as a rapper being a female in man's world although this may be in part be due to the focus-group dynamic of the interview and the fact that she was the only female respondent amongst five. I want to finish this section with a quote from Rosie about the differences between the UK and US:

RG: When I first came here and started school, the three questions were like 'Have you got a gun?', 'Have you ever seen someone get shot?' and 'Have you ever seen anyone famous?' It's never like 'what was your school like?'

The irony that the likelihood of being shot in Longsight is high, if the media are to be believed, was not lost on Rosie.

Conclusion: rap as postcolonial locally situated youth culture in global context

At the time of writing rap has been engendering moral panic anew in the UK, this time for supposedly glamorising violence. In many ways this is simply the latest instalment in the story of the running popular music tradition of shocking one's elders. Bill Haley and Elvis Presley for their suggestive hip-swivelling, the Rolling Stones' menacing pouts that provoked the plea 'lock up your daughters', punk's nihilism and the supposed drug culture of acid house are all in some degree precursors to controversy over rap and hip-hop culture. Indeed rap itself has repeatedly courted controversy.[19] The same year that Culture Minister Kim Howells spoke out against rap in the UK, rap acts took an unprecedented number of nominations at the UK's annual music industry 'Brit' awards. Eventual winners included both 21-year-old black Londoner Ms Dynamite and white US rapper Eminem.[20] While rap lyrics have been held responsible for inciting violence, essentially much rap in the UK and US contains messages based on the enduring popular musical themes of romantic love – such as the bestselling act Ja Rule. HD were all vehemently critical of recent press specualtion that hip-hop bred a culture of violence, citing the Cultural Fusion project as a positive example of the application of rap. As Ravelle commented 'Urban music is a scapegoat.'

Rap then has become a key part of twenty-first century global culture; produced and consumed by youth of culturally diverse origins, as well as from more 'mainstream' moorings. Cross (1993: 64) writes that rap evokes 'new soundtracks for urban survival'. Its high profile fans include somewhat incongruously the heir to the British throne Prince William and the fictional youth culture anti-hero Ali G. While the UK rap/garage collective So Solid Crew attracted criticism for glamorising violence in their lyrics, the music journalist Peter Paphides (2002: 5) explains their appeal thus: 'tracks like "Haters" and "Ride Wid Us" glamorise a life that most of us can only live vicariously'.[21] It is one thing to buy a record and another to actually interact with the people and ideas that it conveys. When two teenage girls were shot dead over the New Year holiday of 2003 in Birmingham in the UK, the incident fuelled a moral panic over 'black on black' crime – a term that has attached itself to gang rivalries such as those alluded to in Longsight. Rap's supposed incitement to violence was also invoked; it was alleged that the assailants were playing Ms Dynamite on their car stereo. Yet this in itself demonstrates the fallacy in assuming 'hypodermic syringe'-type media message reception models in the vein of the Frankfurt School. Ms Dynamite has resolutely propounded anti-violence messages, e.g. in her vocal opposition to the 2003 Gulf War.[22] There can easily be a disjuncture between listening and action. Youth construct their own meanings; in the case of HD's Mathew listening to French hip-hop it is primarily the beats, i.e. rhythm, that are of importance. When I interviewed 2Phaan of UK Asian rappers Kaleef he challenged the potential limited appeal of political tracks and connected it to the relationship between black performance and white pleasure (cf. Chambers 1976; Jones 1988): 'Yeah, there is a danger of it falling on deaf ears. It's just for the white kids, to ease their consciences so they can spin a record, put it to the back of the pile and then say "That's it. I've done my bit for the Pakis for the day." '[23] Claims that rap can break down barriers between different ethnic groups need to be kept in perspective then. There is also intra-rap strife, e.g. the shootings between east coast and west coast US rappers as portrayed in the film *Biggie and Tupac*. In France there are divisions between north and south Paris as well as between Paris and Marseilles.

French hip-hop has been highlighted in this chapter as a case study to demonstrate its uses as a powerful counter-balance to the centralising and integrationist French nation-state and as an agent of it. Many aspects of contemporary French rap are contradictory. It is as much an agent of political mobilisation – seen in its use in anti-racist/anti-immigration law campaigning – as it is a contested terrain of culture in the service of social control, with its aesthetics up for grabs to be interpreted by 'tolerant' leftist patronising patronage (Université du Hip-hop) and far right attacks (censorship via demonisation as anti-social urban malaise). The vision of France proposed by French rap is not a monocultural and fixed entity but multicultural and dynamic; characterised by diversity where the new tricolore is black, blanc, beur.[24] This inclusiveness applies to numerous rap scenes in local multicultural contexts. Some continuities with twentieth century musically based youth culture do persist, however. Rap continually finds itself caught in the paradox of juggling credibility with mass acceptance. This highlights a tension. Practitioners want to obtain mainstream success without a loss of any 'cool' cachet. The youth cultural quest for authenticity is eternal and endures from time to time and place to place.

As we have seen rap can through various mediums contribute to youth identities in articulating multiple messages for example in the celebration of capitalism or in the positioning of young people outside the dominant order, or even fulfilling both roles at once. The growth in rap scholarship serves as a legitimising influence on the music. The number of different approaches taken by commentators who have written about it in terms of Afrocentricism, postmodernism, multiculturalism and education, to name but a few, is perfectly in keeping with a music which is multifaceted and is often described as polyvocal (e.g. by Rose 1994). However the academicisation of rap need not indicate that in over a quarter of a century the message of rap has necessarily been blunted. Most of the music described in this chapter is commodified rap; it has been mediated through the music industry at large with its recording and marketing arms. However this does not detract from the fact that rap and hip-hop culture still have the capacity to comment on social situations offering a version of reality for their listeners and even to challenge contemporary power relations. All of the above then serve as diverse and healthy examples of the uses of hip-hop.

7

WHITE NOISE

Identity and nation in grunge, Britpop and beyond

Teenage angst has served me well, Now I'm bored and old.
(Nirvana, 'Serve the Servants', 1994)

Oasis is necrophilia.
(*Modern Review*, October 1997)

The last of the chapters of this book addressing musical forms with transnational appeal, before my concluding thoughts, differs from the others presented in Part II as the sounds it concerns are to a greater extent than any of the others of preceding chapters only very loosely describable as a discrete musical category. After looking specifically at musical forms that clearly cross geographical territorial borders and where minority ethnic identity is often a factor articulated by its practitioners, this penultimate chapter looks at a set of styles that I have placed under the generic heading 'white noise', as their main proponents are of *majority* white ethnicity; something that their critics have seen as problematic. Furthermore, although they have enjoyed international export sales, the two styles that make up the bulk of the chapter are specifically located in two nation-states that critics of globalisation see as spreading a common language and culture unnecessarily over the world's surface: grunge music from the US and Britpop from the UK. I am going to link these two musics to recent theories of whiteness and broaden my discussion to span authenticity in contemporary musical practice and the wigger – a term derived from the conflation of the words 'white' and 'nigger' – before concluding with some remarks on identity and nation in grunge, Britpop and beyond.

Whiteness: the ethnic identity that dare not speak its name?

For western scholars whiteness was for many years the ethnic identity that dared not speak its name. The now-outmoded expression for non-whites as 'coloureds' provides something of a clue as to why. Whiteness has been absent in ethnic studies as it is almost an absence, a given accepted 'normal' identity that passes without comment. As whiteness' best-known theorist Dyer (1997: 3) states:

'whites are everywhere in representation [therefore] they seem not to be repre-
sented to themselves as whites. ... At the level of racial representation, in other
words, whites are not of a certain race, they're just the human race.' It goes
without saying that whiteness is the majority identity in the west. Majority populations are always seen as coherent and non-problematic while minority
populations are posited in opposition to them – the practice known as 'othering'.
Whiteness is potentially a deeply problematic subject in the left-leaning social
sciences, as it is inextricably bound up in notions of white supremacy – something that sits uneasily with, for example, the emancipatory agenda that was at the
core of cultural studies' original remit. Nonetheless this academic silence has
been breached in recent years. As Giroux (1997: 90) states ' "Whiteness" is no
longer invisible.' This new strand of 'whiteness studies' has emerged against a
backdrop of anxieties about globalisation. For Gabriel (1998: 63):

> whiteness is neither a set of values nor a set of physical properties which
> we can apply with certainty to some groups and not others ... for long
> periods whiteness has been inscribed in the unwritten normative struc-
> tures of both the US and England. ... In both countries, whiteness, like
> some slumbering beast, has stirred only in moments of apparent and
> imminent danger.

In contrast to this Dyer (1997: 57) remarks that it is consistently 'presented as an
apparently attainable, flexible varied category, while setting up an always move-
able criterion of inclusion, the ascribed whiteness of your skin'. However it can
never be all-inclusive: 'Whiteness as ideal can never be attained, not only because
white skin can never be hue white, but because ideally white is to be nothing'
(Dyer 1997: 78). Whiteness is paradoxically rendered invisible by its very
ubiquity.

As long ago as 1979 Said wrote that white western culture defined itself in
opposition to its non-white others. Since this observation and Dyer's (1997)
pioneering essay in *Screen* that began its serious scrutiny, whiteness has
burgeoned as a subject of academic scrutiny in recent years with an explosion of
published works on the subject, largely emanating from the US (e.g. Fine *et al.*
1997; Frankenberg 1994; Hall 2002; Hill 1997; Newits and Wray 1997;
Roediger 1991; 1994; Seshardi-Crooks 2000; Ware 1992; Young 1990). Of
course whiteness goes further than pigmentation. The underlying aim of a
deconstruction of white hegemony is central to whiteness studies, in which
white academics largely outweigh blacks – exceptions include hooks (1992) and
Morrison (1993). In an example of this desire of whites to put the world to
rights Dyer (1997: 298) writes, 'if the white association with death is the logical
outcome of the way in which whites have had power, then perhaps the recognition of our deathliness may be the one thing that will make us relinquish it'. The
(white) educationalist Giroux (1997: 91) however, although recognizing this
potential of white critique in highlighting injustices, argues for a move 'beyond

positions of guilt or resentment' towards a more critical whiteness studies that provides a more 'nuanced, dialectical, and layered account of "whiteness" that would allow white youth and others to appropriate selective elements of white identity and culture as oppositional'.

Indeed during the 1990s the arguments began to surface that white masculinity was in crisis and that the white male had become a victim. At the time of writing this argument has almost become commonplace in certain sections of the media and has reached beyond academic texts to inform popular writing such as the much-media-hyberpole-accompanied book of 2002 by US film-director Michael Moore, *Stupid White Men*, which is a reaction against these analyses that aims to provoke.[1] Analyses of whiteness proliferated at the historical moment that they did in response to a general late twentieth century sense of anxiety about identity which has continued to pervade media discourse into the twenty-first century. Pfeil (1995: 236–7) has commented:

> in effect … the deal that subtended the definition of the white straight middle-class man as protector–provider, and that together with intense discrimination against women in both employment and income opportunities, guaranteed their subordination as mothers and wives … is now decisively and perversely off.

An article in UK monthly music magazine *Q* profiling the band Limp Bizkit (Wilkinson 2001: 99) quotes the Australian writer Robert Hughes (1993), making similar remarks about the heroic status of the victim in post-politically correct America where white men clamour for inclusion in this category. Many studies largely draw on films as examples of this new articulation of whiteness (Dyer 1997; Giroux 1996; 1997; Pfiel 1995). However music can be taken as another site for this.

Born in the USA: grunge and riot grrrl as soundtracks to Generation X

Back in the introduction I referred to US studies of Generation X and the slackers. I wish to return to this idea in addressing the grunge youth culture that emerged from America in the early 1990s. Musically grunge is loosely onomatopoeic: fuzzy, distorted-sounding rock relying on a traditional bass/drums/guitar line-up. The sound and sentiments were a hybrid of heavy metal (powerchords) and punk (independent ethos, verse/chorus structure). Although there is no 'grunge manifesto' among the underlying themes of grunge philosophy that could be listed is a sense of frustration with suburban life and possibly a reaction to the pomposity of less self-consciously ironic 1980s heavy metal. Rather than the naked violence or sharply focused violent anger of other angry, young white musics such as the UK early 1980s Oi movement (Laing 1985; Sabin 1998), the grunge credo was more about a feeling of death by slow suffocation, or to paraphrase the CCCS, resistance through *withdrawal* rather than rituals. This sentiment is mirrored in the suicide at the age of 27 of Kurt Cobain, lead singer of the archetypal grunge ensemble Nirvana, who has indisputably become *the* emblematic figure of grunge. Cobain thus joined the circle of rock stars to have met an early end and assured themselves mythical status in the same way as Jimi Hendrix, Jim Morrison and Sid Vicious.[2] Other similarities can be seen between grunge and earlier youth musical cultures. An inevitable institution-alisation of grunge, as befell the new age travellers described in chapter 5, followed. Epstein (1998: 17) comments that grunge became subject to its 'co-optation ... into the marketing of a particular music. ... The alienation of youth becomes a marketing strategy, which of course only alienates the youth in ques-tion.' Grunge's anti-fashion dress codes and self-identification are not entirely without precedent. However, in other ways grunge represents a rupture with previous equivalents. Weinstein (1995) interprets it as a supremely ironic musical style which revisits and recaptures youth cultural history. Its rejecting and recy-cling of the past in equal parts is consistent with it as a style that reflects a 'coming of age' of post-war pop and youth culture. Indeed we can trace a line between grunge and early white US alternative bands such as the Velvet Underground, the Violent Femmes and the Pixies. The music was also in timbre and texture unrelentingly white.

Cobain was reportedly a reluctant figurehead of the grunge movement, uncomfortable with his role as a spokesperson for a generation and the weight of the burden of representation upon him. This ambivalence to his status can be seen in the way he was photographed wearing t-shirts with slogans such as 'grunge is dead' (Crisafulli 1996: 102) and even 'Corporate Rock Magazines Still Suck' on a *Rolling Stone* cover (Moore 1998: 258). An anarchic streak can be seen in the photograph of the band on stage with the close-up of a sticker adorning Cobain's guitar with the words 'VANDALISM: BEAUTIFUL AS A ROCK IN A COP'S FACE' (Crisafulli 1996: 28). Yet this call to arms existed alongside a more world-weary attitude to the music industry. Most leading grunge acts were signed to major record labels, sometimes compromising indie credibility, e.g. in the case of Pearl Jam. Nirvana's recognition of the irony of this can be seen in the song title from the *In Utero* album 'Radio-friendly Unit Shifter', which is presumably what the band feared becoming on their signing to the David Geffren Corporation following indie beginnings on the Sub Pop label, hence the 'harder' sound on this album as opposed to the more polished sounds of its predecessor, the ground-breaking *Nevermind*. My inclusion of a couplet from Cobain at the start of this chapter, with the awareness of the limitations of lyrical analysis, is not an isolated example.[3] Perhaps this tendency to quote Nirvana can in part be explained by the fact that there are a limited number of interviews with Cobain or indeed other band members available and that the ambiguity of their lyrics, reinforced by 'the end' of the story known to all, makes them ripe for interpretation in this way. The fact that his suicide note has repeatedly been scanned for 'clues' as to his motives meant that the scrutiny of his actions continued even in death. Nick Broomfield's feature-film *Kurt and Courtney* (1998) continued the intrigue. While grunge will always be seen as synonymous with Nirvana and more specifically Kurt Cobain, other grunge acts include their contemporaries Alice in Chains, Soundgarden and Pearl Jam. Following Nirvana's demise two other groups with Cobain connections rose to prominence. Hole, led by Cobain's widow Courtney Love, had been in existence since 1989 but their actions were more noticed by the world's media after 1994, after which attempts were made to situate them within the riot grrrl scene. The Foo Fighters formed by Nirvana drummer Dave Grohl continued in a melodic grunge vein.[4]

In many ways grunge is inseparable from its constituency and context of white youth in the US suburbs. The music is widely seen as originating in Seattle but the sense of suburban alienation gave it a far wider appeal. Theories of grunge as the soundtrack to a dispossessed generation coincide with concurrent US youth research focusing on similar subjects such as the suburban despair chronicled in the ethnography of Gaines (1994). Just as the skinhead sartorial style of heavy Doctor Marten's brand boots and belt-and-braces jeans with t-shirt was traced as signalling the white skinhead's identification with the threatened-with-extinction race of the British working man (Clarke 1976; P. Cohen 1972), grunge's aesthetic of anti-fashion charity shop chic has also attracted comment. Weinstein (1995: 68) interprets the uniform of ripped jeans and lumberjack shirts as coming from the Pacific US northwest and standing for 'identification with the homeless and destitute'. A deliberate aesthetic of 'slumming', devoid of class motives, however could be another explanation. This dressed-down ethos was captured in the Nirvana song-title 'Come As You Are'. Needless to say it was only a matter of time before mass-produced torn denims began to appear on catwalks and subsequently in high streets the world over. In grunge and its drop-out sentiment we can see a reaction to the Reagan–Bush axis with its central belief that 'greed is good' which, as we have seen in the previous chapter, some aspects of the rap movement have subscribed to in the philosophy of 'bling bling'.

Weinstein (1995) itemises among significant factors that are relevant to grunge's circumstances of production: the realties of environmental decay, AIDS and divorce. Again, however, it is important to stress that the style was in many ways one of ambivalence rather than outright rage. For Weinstein (1995: 68): 'Its anger is self-humiliated, not the rage of the self-righteous who are repressed because the individual is unwilling or unable to express it fully.' The Sex Pistols defiantly called their debut, indeed only 'real' studio, album *Never Mind the Bollocks* and included direct sloganeering on its tracks, e.g. the rabble-rousing 'Anarchy in the UK'. Nirvana chose the abbreviated, more nonchalant, equivocal *Nevermind* as the title of their second album which catapulted them to superstardom. Some of the song-titles suggest introversion rather than revolution, e.g. 'Drain You' and 'Stay Away'. While grunge's musical message and its sonic textures are both somewhat hazy, realities and realism also underpin it. In keeping with the concurrent slacker film-title *Reality Bites* and the common phrase of youth culture vernacular at the time 'get real', grunge is the product of a generation who are rooted in a sometimes cynical realism. As Weinstein (1995: 69) reminds us there is change and decay all around these youth, 'Yet the hook baited with a dollar bill is always there, waiting for the baby.' The slackers and Generation Xers of grunge are in many ways unshockable after having had the youth cultural excesses of earlier decades replayed to them through the ever-saturated all-encompassing mass media. Epstein (1998: 19) states: 'these youth think of themselves as being realistic and, conversely, view their parents' generation's activities in the sixties and seventies as being highly unrealistic'. The myth of the golden age is punctured in their eyes.

Existing alongside grunge and outliving it was its girl cousin riot grrrl, which originated in Washington and has provoked a growing number of academic analyses (Kearney 1997; 1998; Leonard 1997; Gottlieb and Wald 1994),[5] which usually cite 1991 as its year of inception. The music has often been interpreted as part of a lineage including punk and grunge (Robb 1999; Sabin 1999). Certainly its guitar-based succinct song structures based around a fairly orthodox three-chord thrash has echoes of both. It is also similarly anti-fashion, however it is gender that is usually uppermost in considerations of riot grrrl – evidenced in the fact that, in his description of musical terms, Shuker's (1998: 144–6) description of the movement is included under his entry for gender. Its groups included the all-female line-ups of Bikini Kill, Hole, L7 and Babes in Toyland. In fact early gigs sometimes even had a 'women only' admittance policy. Riot grrrl has been seen as a post subcultural 'network' (Leonard 1997), drawing on Deleuze and Guattari's notion of horizon-tally rooted rhizomes, for its linking other forms of expression besides music, including most importantly fanzines. It has been seen in some ways as the realisa-tion of many earlier youth cultural 'dreams': the 'punk dream' (Leonard 1998) for its autonomy traits and also McRobbie's (1990) stated aim of seeing one day an all-girl subculture that transcends the need for boys (Kearney 1997; 1998). Lyrics sometimes illustrate this, although the riot grrrl philosophy is about self-assertion and direct action. Just as the US rap group NWA reclaimed the word 'nigger' as a term of self-appellation, riot grrrl reappropriates 'girl' into an active word with the female performer at the centre rather than peripheralised in the movement. Leonard (1998: 114–16) comments: 'Whilst some young women of colour were active in the network, the grrrl revolution tended to be confined to white, middle class women.' This constituency overlaps to a great extent with that of grunge. In the UK paradoxically, riot grrrl's most long-lasting product was the all-male Cornershop, who emerged from the Wiiija label which had been home to a number of riot grrrl acts, transcending sharing the bill at early concerts with acts such as Huggy Bear to become pop institutions by the beginning of the new century.

Grunge's sonic combination is ostensibly close to the perfect formula for both youth cultural street credibility and commercial mainstream success worldwide for fusing the urgency and immediacy of heavy metal hooks with punk's laudably anti-rockist, inclusive ideals and incisive structure. However its lineage is more complex than a strictly dual heritage would appear to suggest, as is the case with all the musical cultures discussed in this book. Just as Asian Underground is not only defined by the equation of Indian subcontinent plus UK, other elements have fed into grunge: the 1960s garage rock of the Stooges and MC5 are obvious candidates for inclusion. The 1980s styles hardcore, thrash metal, skatepunk, death metal and above all 'alternative' have been listed as proto-grunge styles (Weinstein 1995: 65). This last category is a term widely used in the US to cate-gorise bands such as REM, Sonic Youth and the B-52s. American college rock is among its mainstay methods of getting its music heard (Epstein 1998; Weinstein 1995). Epstein (1998: 21) says of alternative music:

> [T]he musicians shunned the trappings of what they saw as corporate rock. Gone were the elaborate stage sets, snazzy costumes, and multi-millions dollar productions. In their places, these bands relied on their music and their identification with their listeners ... [thus] rock regained its sense of community.

Here we can see clear links with earlier pop music theorising. In a comment very probably influenced by the on-set of dance culture, Frith (1994: 237) has written that 'Rock was a last attempt to preserve ways of music-making – performer as artist, performance as "community" – that had been made obsolete by technology and capital.' Although until recently grunge could be taken as an exemplar for this remark, more recent pop history has begun to throw up a collection of post-grunge white US music styles that take rock as their template. Despite Frith's (1994: 237–8) contention that 'there is something essentially tedious these days about the 4:4 beat and the hoarse (mostly male) cries for freedom', post-grunge pop forms can be seen in the rise of riot girl with its upfront gender politics setting a feminist, autonomous agenda where girls are the subject not object of rock on a scale unseen since some of the fringe operators of punk. The UK band that came closest to approximating the grunge sound were Londoners Bush who significantly did not achieve anything approaching their impressive US success in their home country. Perhaps this can be explained in part as due to the onset of another by-product of grunge – the similarly whitefaced English language guitar-driven sound of specific national derivations which became known as Britpop. Britpop evokes a contemporary representation of nationhood that differs from the way in which (also white) grunge music talked culturally about alienation in a characteristically American way, and it is this to which I turn next.

I'm so bored with the USA: Britpop and beyond

The UK's response to grunge, Britpop first entered the national consciousness in 1995 (A. Bennett 1997; P. Bennett 1998) when reports of the summer's Oasis versus Blur 'Who's the greatest?' duel elevated it to mainstream newspapers and evening television news bulletins during a slow news period.[6] This phoney war, reminiscent of earlier 1960s Beatles versus Stones or 1970s Pistols versus Clash rivalries, was interpreted as symbolising both the UK's age-old north–south divide and class war with the supposedly uncouth Mancunians Oasis counterpoised against Southern sophisticates Blur from Colchester, Essex – which became subsumed into 'London' in the accompanying commentary.[7] The scales appeared to tip one way and then the other. When both bands simultaneously released singles on the same day, it was Blur's 'Country House' which reached number one, however Oasis compensated for this when their album *What's the Story?* later outsold Blur's *Great Escape*. In its 1960s beat generation-style, standard verse-chorus, power-chord guitar pop. punctuated by the odd string section and nod to punk attitude, musically Britpop displayed a high degree of derivativeness. U2's guitarist the Edge has remarked of Oasis 'You get the feeling you have heard the songs before, but they still surprise you.'[8] The *Modern Review* (October 1997) was less kind, claiming that they were 'the musical equivalent of the three part costume drama, pillaging the past to nullify the future; reactionary, uncreative and impotent'. Rather than being based around shadowy DJs like dance or avowedly denying its own importance like grunge, Britpop was a high visibility scene which positively thrived on the star system and dominated the popular press – Jarvis Cocker of Pulp ironically became a household name for his stage invasion in protest at Michael Jackson's supposedly self-aggrandising (UK music industry) Brit awards appearance of 1996. Britpop is often posited in opposition to dance music (P. Bennett 1998) and branded as anti-grunge (P. Bennett 1998; Shuker 1998: 36; Storry and Childs 1997).

Britpop has been read as continuing a British hatred for America originally voiced by Richard Hoggart (1958). Dawson (1997: 320–321) for example claims: 'The marketing of Britpop bands like Oasis and Blur has been a recent overt form of cultural resistance to the Americanisation of music. America as an inevitable future has made an uneasy combination of influence and resistance for youths who see this choice as no choice.' The British music industry seized on Britpop as the impetus to revive sagging fortunes following the early 1990s grunge-led American chart-sales hegemony. Britpop's indie identification signifies autonomy from the negatively viewed major record labels, conveniently hiding the fact that many of its most successful exponents are financially backed by the multinationals. Of the US$32 billion global music fiscal cake in 1996, 16 per cent of ownership rested with Sony whose umbrella sheltered Oasis (in its 49 per cent ownership of Oasis' one-time 'independent' base Creation Records); a 14 per cent share was held by Polygram whose subsidiary Island is home to Pulp; and 13 per cent was owned by EMI, whose artists include Blur (on offshoot Food Records).[9] This seemingly confirms Adorno's fear (1991 [1941]: 87) that the standardising effects of 'the culture industry' deceptively convince people that less is more in terms of choice resulting in conformity through supposed individualisation: 'What parades as progress in the culture industry, as the incessantly new which it offers up, remains the disguise for an eternal sameness.' However this hegemony cannot be forced on an unwilling public. Significantly for a music with implications for national identity, Britpop was slow to travel abroad, provoking

Oasis' Noel Gallagher to remark in a moment of frustration that the Americans 'don't get it' and Damon Albarn of Blur similarly to comment 'what we do is a little too coded for the Americans' (quoted by P. Bennett 1998: 13). The distinctly non-Britpop Spice Girls, aggressively marketed to 8–12 year olds with a message of safe sex and loving your mother, were however the biggest grossing UK pop act on an international level in 1997, with the album *Spice* netting US$16 million (Christopher 1999).[10] The band's girl power message owed much to riot grrrl.

Buttressed by glossy supplement revelry in a neo-swinging London and endorsed by Tony Blair with a photo-opportunity of Noel Gallagher at 10 Downing Street, Britpop's concept brought to mind the 1960s 'I'm Backing Britain' and 'Buy British' consumerist campaigns spurred on by then-Labour Prime Minister Harold Wilson, who had decorated the Beatles with MBE awards. Oasis's widely reported rock 'n' roll excesses, weddings, tantrums and Labour Prime Ministerial patronage replay earlier moments in pop history and run counter to the ethos of 1980s independent rock austerity and self-denial evidenced in the celebration of celibacy and vegetarianism of the Smiths, the worthy troubadour Billy Bragg or the down-to-earth US alternative scene. Medved (*Sunday Times* 28 February 1993) remarked of John Lennon's 1966 'Beatles are bigger than Jesus' outburst: 'Today comments like Lennon's could never cause controversy; a contemptuous attitude to religion is all but expected from all mainstream pop performers.' Consequently Noel Gallagher's 'Oasis are bigger than God' boast of 1997 only caused a minor ripple, nothing on the scale of Lennon's public apology thirty-one years earlier. Gallagher's later claim that drug-taking was considered by today's youth as akin to 'having a cup of tea in the morning,' caused something of a tabloid stir, even if it was up to a point borne out by research on the normalisation of youth recreational drug use (Parker *et al.*, 1998; Shiner and Newburn 1999). By 1998 Noel claimed to have given up drugs: 'I thought there's no need to live up to this "thou shalt act like a rock star" thing.'[11] Noel later claimed that, whilst being honest, he had made the claims under the pressure of living up to his media representation as 'an authentic working class person'. When asked how he felt as being a 'spokesperson for his generation' he answered 'I'm not comfortable with it. Oasis shouldn't be anyone's life. I've just got a big gob on me.'[12] This shows Gallagher's inbuilt need to conform to the burden of representation; although in this case this is not a burden of ethnicity – no-one could satisfactorily be able to stand up for all whites or even be expected to, unlike expectations of bhangra performers discussed in chapter 4. Gallagher here is subject to a representational burden based on his identity as a northern male member of the working class subsequently 'made good'.

As well as its demarcation from grunge, Britpop is often counterpoised with contemporary dance music, another high visibility 1990s musical scene (Huq 1997; 1998a). Peter Bennett (1998: 14) for example claims that dance has no stars, is based on club-based consumption and home listening rather than live performances, and is 'mainly produced by technicians'. Given its surface-level musical conservatism, Britpop's variant of nationalism then largely proved to be its most 'controversial' feature. Britpop critics (Fisher 1995; Gilbert 1997; 1998; Savage 1996) have seen its problematic white ethnic identification and use of the union jack flag as inappropriate to multicultural Britain.[13] Gilbert (1997: 19) for example attacks the need for pop to take representational form commenting 'Britpop is nothing more and nothing less than the organised cultural reaction to all that is threatening about rave.' Britpop has been contrasted unfavourably with the new Asian dance music (Hutnyk 2000; Huq 1996) and seen as the polar opposite of jungle which has an avowedly 'dark' musical texture (Collin 1997: 252; James 1997). Blake (1998: 150) writes of this dichotomy: 'It is one of the profound failures of New Labour that its symbolic representations of "Cool Britannia" have tended to stress the more nostalgic, monocultural Britpop at the expense of ... genuinely new forms.' With unintended irony, the so-called late 1960s 'British invasion' era of UK male guitar-group pop export,[14] which Britpop drew comparisons with, occurred simultaneously with the high tide of racist anti-immigration politics known as Powellism in the UK after its proponent Conservative MP Enoch Powell. Like Nirvana's *Nevermind* album sleeve-shot of a baby chasing a dollar bill, Britpop exhibits healthy elements of the irony and playfulness integral to postmodernism, e.g. Blur's album title *Modern Life is Rubbish*, showing more of a love/hate relationship with Blighty than simply a one-way celebration. Certainly the vignettes of lower-middle class life on Blur's 'London trilogy' albums[15] or Pulp's recorded output can be read as satirical insightful commentary on contemporaneous British social mores. Oasis's open parading of influences demonstrates an attitude to music-making that the *Modern Review* might have labelled as necrophilia but that could also be read as sharing much with sample culture as described in the previous two chapters. This can be seen to form a knowing position of empowerment replaying the Foucauldian power/knowledge couplet, rather than impotence.

Redhead (1990: 13)[16] asserts that pop replicates many power relations of everyday life and Cosgrove (1991: 185) goes as far as to call it 'an exclusively masculine world, steeped in male ritual ... not a million miles from the industrial trade unions and the spirit of industrial trade unions and authentic labour'. The lineage of the ostentatious laddish masculine tendencies of Britpop and its articulation of masculine identity can be directly traced from the eighties phenomenon 'the casual', a refined Thatcherite variation on an age-old theme: the lad. Oasis marry the two; projecting a deliberately raffish macho image alongside appearance-conscious casual tendencies (e.g. sporting designer labels, the spoils of popular consumer capitalism). Nevertheless in spite of this and McRobbie's claim, 'Men, dispossessed of the kind of jobs they would once have done ... now jealously guard music as about the only field still relatively free from the encroachment of female competition' (*THES*, 16 August 1996). Britpop's ranks have included a number of high profile strong female role models, including Elastica's Justine Frischman, Sleeper's Louise Weiner and Echobelly's Sonia Madan – the latter also being Asian. This has strong parallels with riot grrrl. This liberated feminism, exhibited by both styles, is unlike old-style 'women's lib', or at least the negative associations with which it was tainted by the 1990s, for it substitutes hedonism in the place of austerity (Croft 1997: 182; Gilbert 1998; McRobbie 1997: 197). However it arguably would have been impossible without the pioneering work of feminists such as Germaine Greer (1971). Female Britpop role models like riot grrrls reverse the 'female dummy' stereotype as portrayed in Robert Palmer's 'Addicted to Love' video of the 1980s, where the self-aggrandising male is centre of attention backed by largely lifeless perfunctory females.[17] These performers take leading roles in groups, sometimes fronting male minstrels, with a female presence on a par with the wave of female post-punk epitomised by bands such as the Slits, Blondie and the Raincoats. The Spice Girls philosophy 'girl power' provides a further example of how the turn of the century 'babe' is infinitely more gutsy than yesterday's fawning violet. The early twentieth century provides further examples such as the Russian pseudo-lesbians Tatu and UK talent show victors Girls Aloud who also express female autonomy even though they are both to some extent manufactured acts.

Variations on whiteness: wiggaz with attitude

In recent youth cultural practice authenticity skirmishes have become entangled with ethnicity in the advent of the wigger, the white youth who refashions him/herself as black. Examples include the UK comedy figure turned filmstar Ali G, acted out by a middle class white Cambridge-educated Jew who occupies an ambiguously positioned ethnicity loosely modelled on the middle class white kid playing at being black (Malik 2002: 103–4). In the US the most obvious example of recent years is white rapper Eminem. Both are seen as melanin-deficient pale imitations of the genuine, i.e. *black*, article, or in youth culture parlance the 'real deal'. The term wigger initially appeared in the mid-1990s in the US. An article filed by the Washington correspondent of UK 'serious' daily newspaper the *Independent* from 1993 offers a fourteen-point guide delineating 'tips on how to spot a wigger'. Among these are the following: (i) middle or upper class family backgrounds; (ii) hip-hop tastes in music and street fashion; (iii) open-minded former-hippie parents; (iv) fluency in Malcolm X and black history. The marketing consultant Marian Salzman of BKG Youth, whose clients at the time included Levi's, Nintendo and Pepsi, commented: 'To put it simply, black is where it's at. This is the most important new trend to hit fashion and it may turn out to be the biggest trend of the Nineties' (David Usborne, 'Wiggers just wanna be black', *Independent* 22 August 1993). Of course the wigger has existed for longer than simply the past decade. There is a long history of middle class white youth identification with black youth culture. The Rolling Stones long predate the term and were white suburban British youth at the inception of the band rather than genuine urban street urchins. Hardy and Laing (1995: 808) cite the blues of Muddy Waters and Chuck Berry as key influences and specify that 'At the heart of the band was Jagger's mannered but powerful black-influenced singing and Richard's incisive rhythm guitar.' Is this then appreciation or appropriation?

Arguments against the cult of the wigger are closely bound up with its supposed inauthenticity; their inability to articulate the black experience when they come from a category of oppressors (white majority) rather than the oppressed (black minority). The black journalist Gary Younge argues against wiggers for demeaning the black experience (1994: 35):

> [T]here is more to being black than just frightening your parents with outrageous clothing and alternative language. I know, I have been black all my life and am tired of the racist stereotyping that says all blacks are genetically equipped for singing, dancing and a handful of sports ... there is an awful lot about being black that is hardly conducive to making a fashion statement. You get beaten up at school, have dog shit shoved through your letter box and turned down for a good few jobs.

Alleyne (2000), whilst not addressing wiggers centrally, deals with the interrelated theme of what he calls 'white reggae' which he attacks as tantamount to pseudoreggae for its political neutrality and 'propensity for adopting reggae-oriented material on the basis of aesthetically pleasing surface qualities rather than explicitly political or deeper musical content.' The argument that commercialism necessarily compromises authenticity is a recurring one in both academic discourse and commonsense opinion on youth culture and popular music, as we have seen. Here it is argued that reggae has been used simply as exotic trimmings to mainstream pop with the effect of devaluing the original meaning of reggae itself. Alleyne (2000) comments: 'It has often been mistakenly assumed that international exposure for reggae has been and is wholly beneficial, with little consideration given to the negative influence of the record industry's capitalistic impulses.' The commercial success of artists including the Police and Bob Marley (the latter having submitted to the forces of commercialisation) are cited as an example of a watered-down version of reggae ultimately resulting in limiting the impact of other more deserved artists. The Beastie Boys are another, more recent, example of arguably middle class wigger groups. Indeed to be middle class in pop has long been viewed with suspicion; to be white-aspiring-black and middle class doubly damns the artist, the implication being that they know nothing of suffering. Prince William's appearance wearing a reversed baseball cap and making a Bronx-style pointed-fingered hand-gesture on a royal tour for example was widely lambasted.

Perhaps we could draw up a list of black artists and their white equivalents:

Duke Ellington	Glenn Miller
Luther Vandross	Rick Astley, Mick Hucknall
Run DMC	Beastie Boys
Ice Cube	Vanilla Ice
Ice T	Marky Mark, Eminem
Stevie Wonder	Jamiroquai

146

Muddy Waters   Eric Clapton
Michael Jackson   Justin Timberlake

Many of the latter category are often described in terms of the former.

Indeed the whole genre of blue-eyed soul would be a candidate for inclusion in such a list. There is always something of a nagging doubt that such musics cannot ever be authentic however, that these white versions will always be pale imitations. In remarks that recall the sort of guilt surrounding whiteness studies that Giroux attacks, Shepherd (1994: 223) has commented:

> The situation of white Afro-American-influenced music is different in the sense that although many white people have suffered considerable material and intellectual (and to some extent, emotional) dispossession, they have never been outside the social system in the same way as black people.

Indeed the attempt by the white music buyer to find the holy grail of authenticity is one explanation behind the rise of world music and neo-folk forms.

At the time of writing, another born-in-the-USA metal-influenced post-grunge youth musical style, nu metal, is making its presence felt, notably for its abrasive quality and stylised rebelliousness. Lyrically many of the same emergent themes of grunge have resurfaced in nu metal, whose proponents include Korn, Offspring, Limp Bizkit and Slipknot. Papa Roach's hit of summer 2002 'She Loves Me Not' for example revolves around the lyric 'Life's not fair', revisiting the age-old theme in vernacular popular song of romantic love and articulating the sense of injustice voiced in numerous examples of punk, grunge and other 'alternative' musics. There are also various examples of youth culture shock tactics in nu metal, as seen in punk posturing and the extreme edges of heavy metal, such as Ozzy Osbourne's stage shows. Examples exist in Amen's album title 'We Have Come For Your Parents' and Slipkot's distinctive serial killer masks worn onstage. However nu metal is arguably even more hybridised than grunge's punk-metal stylings, as hip-hop sensibilities are also utilised in its sound, with scratching and raps alongside recognisably grunge elements. Q's (July 2001) retrospective review on Slipknot's 'parent-annoying' self-titled first album of 1999 for example commented:

> Giddily meshing the crunch of thrash metal with samples and turntables, this independently released debut – which has since sold a hefty one million copies in the US – was a terrifying, some might say, unprecedented racket.

The band Korn have a similar sound and sport dreadlocks. Indeed many nu metal bands and fans dress themselves wigger style attired in shorts, baggy jeans or combat trousers, long-sleeved t-shirts, trainers and other items of street-smart style.

In a profile of Fred Durst, lead singer of Limp Bizkit, his love of black music is stressed and seen as contradictory to his outward physical appearance (R. Wilkinson 2001: 96):

> He is a mass of contradictions. He's a lyrical nihilist who prays daily, a self-proclaimed 'redneck fucker from Jacksonville' who adores black culture … he spent his youth trying to dress like Michael Jackson and breakdancing.

Durst was allegedly bullied at school for being a 'nigger-loving rap fan' and wearing an earring (R. Wilkinson 2001: 99). A realist streak is also uncovered:

> He distrusts the press but, in interview, he's astonishingly candid. Ask him how much he earned last year and, without hesitation, he tells you. 'Before taxes I earned close to $1 million', he says.
>
> (R. Wilkinson 2001: 96)

The hard rock–rap crossover can be seen to have started some years earlier with for example Run DMC and Aerosmith's joint hit of 1986 'Walk this Way'. The early work of the Beastie Boys also shows something of a crossover of these two styles. Perhaps the wigger can importantly pave the way for a growing cultural understanding. Roediger (1998: 362) for example recognises that wiggers can caricature blackness with a 'tendency towards essentializing views of black culture as male, hard, sexual, and violent'. Nonetheless quite apart from the fact that the majority of hip-hop sales are made to white youth, a general movement of cultural forces is likely to see the erosion of such entrenched boundaries and stereotypically held views. Roediger (1998: 362–3) cites increases in mixed marriages and greater two-way interaction between black and white youth as positive factors counteracting old stereotypes. Such interactions are bound to occur regardless of the wigger trend; however the growth of the scene can be no barrier to this sort of mixing and cultural fusion.

Accusations of Britpop hankering after a mythical imagined (exclusively white) past of England in what Fisher (1995) calls 'a more-or-less conscious attempt to minimise black influences in music' were succeeded by arguments around the same themes of 'little Englander' cultural introversion and retrogression, hinging on the legitimacy of the white-boys-with-sitars pop sensation Kula Shaker. The band's use of Indian imagery and revival of hippiedom's fascination with all things Asian was inevitable given that every other aspect of the decade had been disinterred but some saw them as neo-colonialisists. The Beatles' Indian experimentation for example can be accused of not engaging with 'real' Asian youth beyond the anointed gurus such as Ravi Shankar (hardly young even in the 1960s). Gilroy (1993c: 6) for example disapprovingly notes the existence of 'whites who borrow comprehensively from black forms and styles yet whose pleasures and decisions do not actually extend to associations with real live black people.' John Pandit of Asian

Dub Foundation was typical of the detractors (*Melody Maker*, 28 June 1997): 'What the f*** [*sic*] is this? You've got Kula Faker telling Hindu people about Hindu religion.'[18] Hutnyk (2000: 92) similarly claims that

> Cool Kula Crisipian's search for the alterity of Asia through music ... means that we could be talking about 'whiteness in crisis' here ... it posits a nostalgic regret for an imaginary India that was not plundered by British imperialism but which cannot really admit to that history, and so now warbles on.

However this rather one-sided white view of Kula Shaker is not universally held. Other Asian artists that I have interviewed, although at times expressing boredom at being asked to comment on the 'Kula Shaker question' rather than their own music, have expressed positions from ambivalence to support. Talvin Singh in 1998 commented: 'People ask me what I think of Kula Shaker, and I'm like, "What's the big deal? It's got nothing to do with my music." '[19] Detrimental's Inder however voiced a different view in describing watching Kula Shaker on television with his mother:

> My mum, said '*white* people?' She just couldn't believe white people singing Govinda [sacred Hindu song]. It just tripped her out man. She wasn't sure ... I said 'Mum. We are doing the opposite. We're doing rap and reggae and all that. Why can't they do it? As long as they do it with the utmost respect.'[20]

Discussion: identity and nationhood in grunge, Britpop and beyond

In contrast to the consistently improving social and material circumstances known by successive generations of post-war youth, in contemporary America it has been argued that *downward* mobility is a common future for many of this cohort from the middle class for whom the American dream lies in tatters. Moore (1998) lists declining employment stability and the replacement of this with transient low paid service sector jobs and graduate under-employment as key reasons for this and sees these factors as feeding into the nihilism, cynicism and cultural exhaustion at the heart of contemporary US youth cultures and postmodernism. He contrasts this with the earlier 'golden age' of youth culture and argues that it is economic reasons that dictate this:

> Sustained downward mobility, after all, represents a threat to what has served as a crucial narrative among the relatively privileged in our society: in postwar America, progress has been tightly bound to the experience of upward mobility such that 'we are true optimists, always

assuming that the world – or rather our corner of it – will continue to provide more for us than it did for our parents, and more for our children than we have today'.

(Moore 1998: 259)

For Giroux (1996: 117) a racialised representation of youth can be seen in the US media's depiction of the apathy of 'Generation X', i.e. white youth and the contrasting menace of 'youth' as potential muggers, killers and criminals which is a shorthand for, or euphemistic description of, black youth. He reports that a 'siege mentality' has grown up amongst US whites in recent years around a conservative consensus led by figures such as television evangelists Pat Buchanan, Pat Robertson, the congressman Jesse Helms and former Speaker of the House Newt Gingrich. We can see a parallel here with conservative attempts to reassert Britishness that were in circulation at the time of the rise of Britpop. Giroux (1996: 99) warns of a white moral panic:

> the elements of this panic are rooted in a growing fear among the white middle class over the declining quality of social, political and economic life that has resulted from an increase in poverty, drugs, hate, guns, unemployment, social disenfranchisement and hopelessness.

This engenders the belief that 'national identity' is in crisis. In the US this has cohered around rites such as Thanksgiving, the pledge of allegiance to the US flag, and the prayer to the star-spangled banner in schools, although these institutions have less and less of a hold on the American people at a time of increasing cultural diversity.

Can we construct a list of characteristics that can be associated with 'Britishness'? Three recent books aimed at overseas readerships on this somewhat nebulous concept, while all admitting the impossibility of arriving at watertight definitions, have provided hints at what some of the features of this might be. Interestingly all three have pop music imagery on their jackets, although they vary in their treatment of the subject in their content (Christopher 1999; Oakland 1998; Storry and Childs 1997).[21] National identity in the UK is increasingly complicated; not least for the reason that the four nations that make up the British Isles, so often conflated by those outside the UK into a monolithic entity called 'England', are now subject to a degree of self-autonomy with devolved parliaments possessing limited powers. Whether this has the effect of tempering Scottish and Welsh nationalism remains to be seen although some claim that a musical resurgence of minority Welsh language youth music is now underway (Llewellyn 2000). The resurgence of the cross of St George flag, increasingly displayed at occasions such as the 2002 World Cup, whereas once it was the preserve of neo-fascist English nationalist political parties, may also be a possible by-product of this.[22] However, to see debates on Britishness only in terms of widening the stereotyped images attached to it (Oakland 1998: 66) to include the multiple identities that are Scotland, Wales and Northern Ireland is reminiscent of an earlier age where 'equal opportunities' was equated simply with employing more women, ignoring sexual orientation, disability and ethnic minorities.

Dawson (1997: 324) concludes Storry and Childs with the following observation:

> Official British culture has been slow to acknowledge multicultural iden-
> tities, but ... contemporary British people do not understand their
> identities in simple and singular ways ... both British cultures and
> British identities are today forged by mixtures of people and ethnic prac-
> tices which only forty years ago would have been regarded as, in both
> senses, 'foreign'. The term 'British' will only survive as a worthwhile
> label of identity if it can be used to embrace all of these multicultural
> identities while recognising and valuing the differences between them.

The Parekh Report (2000: 56) comes to similar conclusions: 'Britain needs to be, certainly, "One Nation" – but understood as a community of communities and a community of citizens, not based on a single substantive culture.' Quite apart from the fact that Britain only has a weak tradition of citizenship given that its inhabitants are loyal subjects of the monarch, these are noble sentiments.

Nonetheless, both increasingly indistinguishable 'sides' of the UK's party polit-ical duopoly seized on Britpop as a sign of Britain's cultural robustness when in power.[23] This typifies political consensus in a post-ideological era. Analogies have been drawn between Britpop harking back (in anger) to a fixed, mythical and resolutely white Albion of the 1960s, Major's 1950s-based dream of an England of warm beer and 'old maids cycling to Holy Communion', and New Labour's retrogressive and safe approach (Blake 1998; Fisher 1995; Gilbert 1997; 1998; Savage 1996). 'For when you analyse the formal entrails of Britpop, what you see is a perfectly rehabilitated national identity, perfectly tailored for a Blairist future', claimed Pat Kane in the *Guardian* ('Pop Goes the Future in a Blur of a Sound', 17 August 1995). Adorno-ite fears of mass-produced popular culture ultimately reinforcing dominant values can be seen in reading Britpop as consensus music that your mum and dad can like, mirroring the climate of 1990s UK politics where the left governs using right-wing policies. Prime Minister John Major's chief education adviser Nicholas Tate repeatedly stated that all children should be taught 'the value of Britishness', claiming in a widely reported speech in 1995: 'There is a mistaken notion that the way to respond to cultural diversity is to try to bring everything together into some kind of watered down multicul-turalism. The best guarantee of strong minority cultures is the existence of a majority culture which is sure of itself.'[24] This was defined narrowly as being constituted by English language, history and Christianity. Conservative govern-ments from 1979 to 1997 had retracted from the 1960s/1970s-established ethic of multicultural education in measures such as the introduction of a daily act of Christian worship in schools, stipulated by the 1988 Education Act. The Labour administration's initial support of multiculturalism from 1997 was evidenced in early Prime Ministerial pronoucements[25] and the cabinet minister Robin Cook's declaration of the Indian-derived dish, Chicken tikka masala, as equating with Britishness.[26] However later Home Office-endorsed reports into the summer unrest in several northern cities that had been dubbed 'race riots' by the press blamed multiculturalism. Home Secretary David Blunkett's introduction of citizenship classes almost shows Labour policies as coming full circle with the position of the Conservatives a decade earlier.

Music, like boxing, has always been popularly conceived of as an exit-route from the ghetto, by which working class boys can 'make good', i.e. break out of the CCCS-style social reproduction cycle (Willis 1977) pre-ordained at birth; however as class boundaries undergo reorientation, many involved in grunge and Britpop are from lower-middle class suburban origins. Best and Kellner (1998: 77) describe the popular 1990s MTV animated series Beavis and Butthead as symptomatic of white suburban *ennui* in media saturated times:

> Beavis and Butthead are, of course, young white boys, so the oppressiveness of their situation is nothing in comparison to the racism and violence in display in films like *Boys N the Hood* or *Menace II Society*. Yet the series underscores the terror of the suburbs, the oppressively boring and normalizing atmosphere of white, middle-class suburbia and its shabbier underclass counterparts.

Importantly Britpop and grunge, between them and each internally, highlight creativity and diversity within majority 'white' populations. Los Angeles-based 1990s rappers House of Pain for example continually stressed their immigrant Irish identity. Consistent with the traditional received pop wisdom of working class origins equating with authenticity/hardness – a direct parallel with CCCS academic discourse – Britpop bands often downplayed middle class roots, for example Suede and Blur, groups from London's prosperous commuter-belt hinterlands who adopted mock working class London cockney ('mockney') accents in their singing voices.[27] McRobbie's (1996) implication that pop musicians are drawn from the manual class beset by industrial decline ignores the historic trajectory of middle class youth culture (Bracewell 1997), e.g. mods and punks, via that one-time veritable hothouse of UK pop culture: the art school (Frith and Horne 1987; Longhurst 1995), from which Blur also graduated. Just as the Beastie Boys have also claimed that as white boys in a black genre they have had to prove themselves more than other rappers (Johnstone 1999: 291–2), Eminem's autobiographical film *8 Mile* told a triumph-through-adversity tale of the white outsider competing in the closed black arena of Detroit hip-hop jams. In an interview on the subject Eminem called his home-town the 'whitetrash capital of the world' and rejected accusations that he had portrayed the setting with disproportionate poetic license: 'You can't tell me. I grew up there. You're gonna say I'm giving the city a bad name? Dummy the city already had a bad name' (Davis 2002). Here the rapper's authentic whiteness is stressed.

Conclusions

Stuart Hall (1990: 225) persuasively makes the case for culture and identity as dynamic processes underscored by complexity as opposed to fixed entities:

> Cultural identity … is a matter of 'becoming' as well as 'being'. It belongs to the future as much as to the past. It is not something which already exists, transcending time, place and culture. Cultural identities come from somewhere, have histories. But like everything else which is historical, they undergo constant transformation. Far from being eternally fixed in some essentialised past, they are subject to the continuous 'play' of history, culture and power.

Britpop has also found its historians (Harris 2003; Robb 1999; Thompson 1998). If we take the term to literally mean British-produced pop, a case can be made for emergent multicultural modern metropolitan musics such as bhangra, Asian Underground, UK garage and jungle being a more representative pop soundtrack to contemporary Britain than the retrograde and arguably whitefaced Britpop. Gabriel (1998: 29) also comments that through its export to the US British bhangra is well placed to 'play mischievously with the traditional understandings of "Britpop", "world music", "cultural imperialism" and "Americanisation".' Of these new postcolonial sounds, which also include raï in France and rap throughout Europe (which we looked at in chapters 4 and 6), Fock (1999: 75) comments: 'This music is challenging the western interpretation of modernity, presenting new spaces, new ways of navigating modern societies across traditional regional borders across new borders of traditions.' In a rhetorical remark Asian Dub Foundation's John Pandit has commented: 'Why is it that British reggae and bhangra aren't regarded as Britpop?'[28] thus drawing attention to how the term Britpop seems to contain an unspoken element of whiteness in its equation. Lipsitz (1994: 130–1) has enthused:

> in venerating Mahatma Gandhi and Bob Marley rather than Winston Churchill or George Frederick Handel, Apache Indian creates problems for nation states and their narratives of discrete, homogeneous and autonomous culture, but he solves the problems for people who want cultural expressions as the lives they live every day.

This is probably overstating the case of one musician who was arguably a transient fad; however such musics surely have a justifiable case to be considered as 'Britpop', given the intrinsic Britishness that they are characterised by.

Interestingly it is always overtly 'multicultural' musics such as Asian Underground or French or German rap that are characterised as hybrid. Yet both grunge and Britpop are intrinsically hybrid too in their use of earlier pop in their stylings. Furthermore, just as national cultures are problematic to describe the mixed musics of Asian Underground and less obviously nu metal, these demonstrate the difficulty of classifying musical styles by ethnic or even stylistic origin. If the early 1990s 'baggy' Madchester scene saw a chorus of 'there's always been a dance element to our music' claims from a clutch of guitar bands through dance mixes, the adoption of wah-wah pedals, etc. (Russell 1993: 153), by the end of the decade the inverse assertion was being manifested with dance acts engaging in distinctly non-dance and conversely 'rockist' practices, e.g. the Prodigy touring with a lead vocalist.[29] Redhead (1997a: 106) acknowledges the Oasis–Beatles connection but claims nonetheless, 'Strangely enough, Oasis are responsible for translating the ecstatic dance culture into guitar pop.' For all the claims of their problematic ethnicity, the band are of Irish immigrant stock. Furthermore, crossovers have been many: Noel Gallagher has appeared on records by (white) dance act the Chemical Brothers, (black) junglist Goldie and Anglo-Asian band Cornershop. Blur's 1999 album *13* featured a black gospel choir on its opening track and lead singer Damon Albarn has since undertaken various world music projects. Recorded musics are cumulative (i.e. co-exist alongside one other) rather than successive (replacing and superseding). The modern listener is influenced by pop's past as well as its present and future with the entire canon of pop music at their dispersal. These new forms require new terms. In the UK for example, the notion of music 'of black origin' has appeared in recent years.[30]

The macro Britpop versus grunge (or dance) and even the micro Oasis versus Blur tussles that the media colludes in constructing are entirely consistent with traditional pop rivalries and equally so with dichotomies in cultural studies. Genres in pop in some ways are as much about border maintenance as anything else (Fock 1999). Their artificiality can be seen in the difficulty of situating a band such as Cornershop. With an Anglo-Asian line-up, the band's ethnicity makes them natural candidates for inclusion in discussions of the new Asian dance music, as we have see in chapter 4. However their signing to an independent label and rise to prominence around 1995–1997, coupled with quintessentially 'English' lyrics in much of their output, could qualify them as Britpop. To further compli-cate matters are the band's initial pro-riot grrrl identifications. Certainly as someone who has seen them on numerous occasions from 1993 to 2002, I can unreservedly state that Cornershop's fanbase is more white indie fans than anything else, in keeping with grunge and Britpop.[31] However my attendance at various musical events from the early 1990s to the present has demonstrated to me that audiences are becoming more diverse; I am no longer usually the only Asian (female) at pop concerts. Conversely, attending Asian Underground and, to a lesser extent, bhangra events presents less of an opportunity to play 'spot the white person' than it once did, as they are present in increasing numbers along with youth from all sorts of other ethnic backgrounds.

The age-old problem of 'alternative' musics is needing something to react to. Perhaps grunge and Britpop both represent the moment that the divide between alternative/indie musics and the musical mainstream was finally eroded, following earlier attempts in musical scenes such as the Madchester indie/dance crossover. Toynbee (1993) for example comments on how Kurt Cobain's photo-genic good looks made Nirvana pin-ups in teen magazine *Smash Hits*. Whereas once alternative music had attracted comments such as 'jangly-guitar "indie" music beloved by the students of the late 1980s, the journalists who wrote for the inkies [UK serious music press] and hardly anyone else' (Blake 1996: 207), by the late 1990s this was no longer strictly the case. If we consider them in purely economic terms, despite 'indie'-type associations, many of the bands in both grunge and Britpop were signed to major labels. Indeed, just as we have seen with Asian Underground in chapter 4, a large number of both types of acts were taken on by 'the majors' after stirrings of initial success from both scenes, which saw various bands who were formerly independent recording atrists 'poached' away from their earlier contractual homes. The example of Nirvana has been discussed above while perennial grunge mainstays Pearl Jam have always recorded for Epic and Britpoppers Shed Seven were signed straight to Polydor. Existing in a space in between straight 'indie'/major polarities are the examples of Oasis and Blur given above. By the time Oasis became the UK's biggest band, probably around 1996, the underground had become overground with the band representing in many ways the 'last' alternative band in the true sense of the word. Meanwhile, while Blur, Oasis and others who sailed in the good ship Britpop had dragged indie from the alternative margins to the mainstream, youth musical cultures were diversifying into ever-more permutations. Without wishing to slip here into clichés of postmodern pastiche and fragmentation, it must be stated that youth by the 1990s had an unprecedented level of choice at their disposal in terms of alter-natives available. However these are not simply picked 'off the peg'. Choices regarding musical taste by the young (and old) are made in ways that are multiple and not mutually exclusive, locking the choosers into a subcultural commitment model. Furthermore contemporary media-literate youth have a high level of awareness in our knowledge economy as to what they are letting themselves in for in their listening. This awareness of pop's past informs their interpretation of pop's present, and arguably its future. We will return to these themes in the final and concluding chapter.

8

CONCLUSION

Rethinking youth and pop beyond subculture

Age is a funny thing in music. For young people now rock and roll
is old peoples' music.[1]

(Simon Frith 1995, aged 48)

Unwrap pop's layers and what we are left with is the same old
meat and two veg that have kept generations of pop pickers well
satisfied. The emotional appetite that pop satisfies is constant. The
hunger lasts forever.

(The Timelords 1988: 21)

This book has attempted to delve beyond subculture by addressing music and
music scenes not only in terms of audiences or ordinary participants but also of
the creative and commercial entrepreneurs who make the music. The journey
through contemporary youth culture and pop music set out in the introduction is
nearing its end as we embark on the concluding chapter. Here it remains for me
to draw together some of the threads that have emerged from the cacophonous
jumble of musical youth cultures encountered on the way and suggest what these
might say about youth culture and pop music in multi-ethnic modernity and the
reconfigured relationship between them. While a number of common themes
have emerged from the preceding chapters, drawing them together in a single
conclusion is not easy. Glib as it may sound, perhaps the only thing that can be
stated with certainty is that youth culture and its relationship with pop music are
essentially *complicated*. They are complicated by a number of social, cultural and
economic factors, themselves forever changing in content and form. In our inter-
dependent world pop consumers and producers have aged enough to see a
dissolution of the traditional youth–pop association. Also there is much more
music out there. As a result there is an unprecedented degree of cross-fertilisation
between musical styles, with a far greater number of media for their reception
than ever before. At the same time youth diversity in modernity cannot be
ignored in our considerations of youth culture. Theory in these de-traditionalised
times consequently needs a serious 'rethinking'. Finally the institutionalisation of
pop that we have witnessed reflects the place of youth culture in an ageing world.
I will take these points one by one in the remainder of this chapter.

Pop consumption and production in an ageing world

Featherstone (1991: 100–1) notes: '[A]s youth styles and lifestyles are migrating up the age scale and as the 1960s generation ages they are taking some of their youth-oriented dispositions with them … adults are being granted greater licence for childlike behaviour and vice versa.' There has been something of a process of juvenilisation apparent in recent years as a result, as the attractiveness of the state of youth is repeatedly projected by the media. The economic purchasing power of youth has long been identified (Abrams 1959) but alongside teenage and obvious youth markets is now a post-youth generation to whom various products to preserve youthfulness are promoted including hormone replacement therapy, vitamins, cosmetic surgery and pop music. According to Burnett (1996: 26), perhaps somewhat surprisingly 1992 turned out to be the best album selling year ever for Eric Clapton, Rod Stewart and Neil Young, each of whom sold more albums that year than in any other time ever in their careers – due to revived interest in their back catalogues from young and old alike following MTV 'Unplugged' appearances. The same applies to the repackaging of classic dead artists on reissued new CD compilations. Jimi Hendrix and Jim Morrison have enjoyed sizeable posthumous sales for example as have the more recently deceased Kurt Cobain and rapper Tupac Shakur.[2]

The political potential of youth culture as a means of resisting dominant social norms and the adult order is complicated by the fact that youth culture itself has to an extent now been appropriated into later life or 'middle youth' by the adults reared on it. Culturally, youth no longer have sole rights to pop music; however, this is the demographic inevitability of an ageing population, not a cause of pop implosion. Whereas Ozzy Osbourne was once seen as a rabble-rouser wildman of rock, by the early twenty-first century he had become the cuddly middle-aged figure at the centre of a domestic reality television sitcom, 'The Osbournes', based on his family antics. Importantly music and fans from previous generations do not evaporate but themselves age. This is borne out by industry statistics (www.ifpi.org.uk) repeatedly showing an ageing pop music consumption base. Thus the 1980s marketing-speak term 'yuppie' – young urban professional – now sits alongside DINKY (dual income, no kids yet) and OPAL (older people with active lifestyles) – all categories fostered by demographic change and more individualised life trajectories. There are increasing numbers of older people in most developed countries. Most have now grown up with youth culture.

Colin MacInnes (1967) wrote: 'Singers, actors, models, dress designers, photographers, all in their teens and early twenties, have earned more foreign currency for Britain recently than hundreds of adult grumblers who lament their style, and earn us absolutely nothing.' The old production-based economy centred on manufactured goods is in decline in many western nations while the high-tech service-based creative and cultural industries thrive. According to Banks *et al.* (2000) risk-taking and trust-building are central to cultural entrepreneurship in this new post-Fordist economic sector where diversity at every level contrasts starkly with the unchanging, standardised Ford Model T production line. We saw in chapter 6 how the members of HD are hoping to make a living from music through college courses to equip them with the skills to reinforce their knowledge of rap production, which they have already begun to formalise through their involvement on the Cultural Fusion programme. As they work towards vocational qualifications, their learning takes place in a non-traditional educational context (cf. Lave and Wenger 1990 and Richards 2003). The members of HD are not simply following in their parents' footsteps in terms of their educational routes (cf. Beck 1992 on individualisation). Indeed, as Redhead (1997b) remarks of post-industrial Manchester, 'cotton has been replaced by popular culture'. However in other aspects of HD's lives the old structures prevail. While Beck talks of people living more independently in risk society, all the members of HD were living in the parental home when I interviewed them.

For some of the interviewees of Ruth Finnegan and Sara Cohen, through playing amateur concerts, pop provides an additional means of economic support to their main income stream. Furthermore there are now professional musicians who have been employed in pop for their entire working lives. In an interview with Peter Hook of New Order, conducted around the release of the second album of his side project, the band Monaco, he reflected on how he had repositioned himself as a performer since beginning with the band Joy Division in the late 1970s:

RH: Did you think you'd still be at it all these years later?
PH: No. I thought musicians died at 20-odd. Never thought I'd be doing it at 44. When we went on *Top of the Pops* doing 'What Do You Want From Me?', I was 41 years old and I was looking at these kids going 'yeaaahhh' and they're like 14. It's a bit of a strange position to be in. Couldn't really envisage that [in the beginning] because we were all ... [going] 'get off you old fart', shouting at Deep Purple, all that lot and here we are all now old farts – fantastic![3]

Hook concluded our interview with the excuse that he 'had to go to work'. When I looked puzzled he explained that this meant New Order rehearsals (for the 2001 studio album *Get Ready*).

When I interviewed DJ Fritz, who had notched up seventeen years playing gigs on the Manchester bhangra scene, he told me that weddings for what he called 'the status-conscious Asian community' provided him with his most lucrative bookings. Furthermore he did not consider it in any way a 'sell out' to play them. As he put it: 'That's where the money is. [After all] it pays the mortgage.' Again Fritz reflected on how the audiences seemed to be getting younger which made him feel old. Approaching the daytimer I had accompanied him to, on spying the teenage girls gathered outside the venue, he self-deprecatingly remarked 'Hope they don't think I'm a paedophile or something.'[4] The simple economic motive of working in music can be overlooked by the interpreters of pop seeking purely artistic motives. Simon Reynolds' quest to uncover extra layers of cultural significance in Bally Sagoo's work was for example roundly rebuffed: 'When I suggest that ... "Chura" [a love song] ... might have a political dimension – demonstrating to the racists and BNP that Britain is now a multicultural society ... he shrugs. It's clear that Sagoo's main interest in crossover is maximum market penetration.'[5] When I asked DJ Fritz if he would ever play Womad, my question aimed to probe at the difficulties of appearing as an exotic performer at this much reviled white person's 'world music' festival (Hutnyk 2000). The unhesitating reply was 'Of course I would if I got paid.' This again shows that researchers can all too often make assumptions and draw the wrong conclusions from the actions of the researched.

Expanded horizons: musical styles and scope

Today's musical consumers – youth and older members of society alike – are at liberty to select their listening material from a far wider choice than was ever available to previous generations with the proliferation of genres, meta-genres and sub-genres. Musical practices and preferences vary enormously. Occupying the mainstream we see 'safe' products such as tried and tested rockers from earlier decades and manufactured boy/girl bands peddling pop standards. Simultaneously however, at the margins there is a greater degree of diversity than previously witnessed during any so-called golden moments of pop of the 1960s, 1970s, etc. due to the dramatically wider choice of listening material available to the average listener via a widely increased range of media.[6] This book has highlighted some examples. It is paradoxically the advance of technology and global capital in the music industry that has facilitated the rise of the world music scene. If indigenous musics were to remain indigenous, they – along with the local hybridities that they articulate – would only have a limited sphere of influence. Distributed through the multinational phonographic industry however, they have had a much wider diffusion than would otherwise have been imaginable, empowering them to engage in a process of postcolonial negotiation. However unlike that described by its critics (e.g. Jenkins 1997), positive globalisation should seek to enable the opening up of genuine two-way traffic rather than one-way exploitation. In this way the local dimension of these cultural products can be highlighted as opposed to being lost under the weight of global dominance in production and distribution terms by the US.

Refuting pessimistic claims of 'crisis in pop' of the 1990s, Grossberg (1994a: 41) argues 'it is not so much of the "death of rock" as of rock becoming something else'. This includes Britpop, nu metal, rap, raï, Asian Underground, bhangra and dance. Importantly these are themselves all far from monolithic categories but rather shorthand descriptive terms. Contemporary pop is characterised by a diversity of practices and styles. The musical practices and styles looked at in Part II in turn can all be individually interpreted as characterised by diversity. Indeed even the internal Britpop squabbling behind Oasis versus Blur battles was importantly framed by *difference*, not similarity. Contemporary musical styles frequently overlap. The hybrid form nu metal described in chapter 7 provides an obvious example. In another example, in 2003 Madonna, usually seen as a pop artist, turned to rap in her hit 'American Life'. Moreover Grossberg's 'something else' incorporates youth culture (di)versions outside music. To give a young person a record token (a traditional parental birthday/Christmas offering), today might be ill-advised when they might rather spend the amount on other things, e.g. mobile phones, software, 'chemical generation' fiction (Redhead 1999), etc. Although this suggests a deprioritising of music, there have always been other cultural objects available to youth, e.g. fashion and angry young man novels (Glover and Pickering 1988). It is just that there are now more of these, symptomatic of technological advance.

It is tempting, if a little simplistic, to look at youth cultures as a succession of styles. Thus the 1950s saw youth culture in its infancy, with the hedonistic impulses of rock 'n' roll a reaction to wartime austerity. The 1960s hippie movements were a result of student protest and the 1970s punk movement a reaction against both the pacifist leanings of flower power and the pompous excesses of 1970s progressive rock. 1980s materialism accompanied the spread of influence of postmodern theory with the advent of pop videos – befitting a more knowing audience adept at decoding media messages. The 1990s meanwhile saw brutalism and a lack of subtlety in musical styles such as grunge and techno. Of course more complex genealogies and counter-examples can always be found. The twenty-first century could be seen as a mix of all the above. Yet part of the problem with our longstanding preconceptions about pop music is a false understanding of pop time as linear (cf. Beck on individualisation being reflexive rather than linear). Redhead (1990) suggests that it has always been cyclical. Similarly Wicke (1987: 75) writes:

> Rock developed not through an arbitrary linear progression of styles, but organically through its respective cultural contexts of use, embedded in the concrete structures of everyday life and specific social experiences and forming a multi-layered totality composed of parallel streams and separate 'scenes' diverging more and more widely.

Perhaps then a topography of continuous loops of influence provides a more useful metaphor; and one that now occurs literally with the technology available to loop and re-sequence sounds. As Frith (1996: 88) points out 'It is virtually impossible to say where a new term (house, rave, rap, garage) first came from.' We cannot then definitively state that rave music began in 1988 or Britpop in 1995 given the complex lineages of both.

Genre skirmishes are healthy and normal in pop but the media creation of binary oppositions such as the Britpop versus dance wars[7] serves only to construct a false dichotomy when both essentially inhabit the same space, with overlapping fan-bases and musical practices that borrow from each other. While ostensibly very different sounding musics, for their respective audiences they represent perfect pop in an imperfect world. Frith (1996: 274) comments: 'Pop tastes do not just derive from our socially constructed identities; they also help shape them.' Identities themselves are ever more fluid in post/late/high modernity. Musical identity is a complex construct that is multi-dimensional. There is no inherent contradiction in liking Britpop *and* bhangra – or in being in one's forties and doing so.

Toop (1995: 261) calls sampling technology 'the most extreme contemporary example of a music which absorbs into itself the music which surrounds it', yet the retrogressive and arguably consensual sound of Britpop is at least equally prone to cut and paste earlier musical moments in new configurations as the more obvious examples of dance or rap music. Robb (1999: 129) has remarked: 'Noel Gallagher is the curator from the great museum of British pop, his memory filing away a whole run of classic British pop moments from over the decades. The key to the Oasis sound is ... a whole slew of influences.' *Q* magazine (July 2001) meanwhile, on Antipodean eclectic merchants of dance music The Avalanches, comments: 'The Avalanches have plundered record shops the world over and built their own good music out of the booty – like especially cheeky Australian magpies.' Among pop successes of 2003 were dance artist Richard X, who sampled 1980s electro pop including the Human League, Gary Numan and The Darkness, a group whose aesthetic and music owed much to 1970s glam-rock. Contemporary musical eclecticism fuses elements of the global and local invoking multiple meanings. Modern listeners critically engage in the reception of music which itself can provide political resistance, e.g. to racism in rap or legislative clampdown in dance music. However this is not a necessary precondition for contemporary youth musical cultures.

Beck (1992: 11) claims that 'risk society is by tendency also a self-critical society'. The youth of the twentieth century are a media-saturated generation who have grown up against a background of ideas about *déjà vu*, intertextuality and self-reference. In some ways they have 'seen it all before' but in others they are actively using past pop resources in a process of reinterpretation to create new end products. When I asked HD about their listening habits, an array of different musical styles were named including classical, jazz and hip-hop of commercial and hardcore persuasions from both the US and the UK. Their modes of access included radio (pirate and official), HMV (high street music store), MTV and MP3. Ravelle told me: 'Some of the stuff [I listen to] I don't even know who's it by but I just like it so I listen to it.' Such a statement is rendered possible by the large amount of music now in circulation and what Grossberg (1994a: 45) terms 'the density of musical practices in daily life'.

There are an ever-increasing number of media for the reception of pop's text in addition to officially logged 'record sales'. Examples reflect continuity and change, e.g. the growth of 'golden oldie' radio programming. In 1996, an age ago in pop time, Burnett (1996: 60) presciently predicted, 'The potential for transmitting via cables, satellite or telephone lines means that home listeners will have access to the equivalent of a *global jukebox*.' The controversy surrounding the music industry's response to the technology of MP3 and Napster provides a twenty-first century example. The threat presented to music retail sales, particularly when coupled with the enhanced copying possibilities offered by the CD burner saw swift action from the multinationals in their enactment of encryption software. Claims of 'crisis' in the contemporary pop music industry are often disproportionately focused on sales of recorded music alone. The word 'intertextuality' has repeatedly been used in this book. Napster file transfer is another example of this, in keeping with the way in which mobile phones, palmtop computers and PCs are now increasingly compatible; all interacting with each other. We have seen how bhangra is just one of many musics that has been sold massively on 'democratic mobile cassettes' (Schade-Poulsen 1995: 95) that are frequently bootlegs. Anachronistic though they are now starting to seem, tapes were, on their introduction, themselves a technological innovation.

The discourse surrounding new technologies in music is frequently polarised between wide-eyed promise about utopian possibilities on the one hand and techno-fear on the other. Both camps would do well to bear in mind that technology does not itself drive change. Society harnesses technological change. We can trace the advent of an era of more interactive listening back to CDs, which allow listeners to play tracks in the order that they wish. Despite fears of pop being supplanted by cyberspace, it is important to remember that new technologies are cumulative, not successive – existing alongside rather than superseding one another, e.g. music video, the CD, CD-ROM and the internet. In 1985 when the compact cassette format overtook vinyl sales it looked unassailable; buttressed by widespread Walkman[8] use. However it was soon eclipsed by the Compact Disc, now itself being challenged in the supremacy stakes by MP3 soundfile transfer, DVDs and minidiscs. These innovations however can be seen as the next step of a continuum dating back to the invention of the electric guitar and beyond. As we have seen technology also affects pop's production as well as its distribution.

When interviewed on his view of the growing number of music media UK drum and bass artist MJ Cole commented:

> I'm really pro-internet, sending MP3 files to friends and stuff but for us as artists we do lose money. I was doing a [record] signing in America and someone brought a burnt MP3 version [of my album] up... I wrote 'buy the real copy' [on it]. There's two halves of me. [Part of me thinks] yeah it's out there, I'll have a bit of that but then I put a lot of time, sweat and tears into it. If I'm not getting the money. ... When you're making an album you can get quite paranoid. All it takes it for one person to go into a chatroom and say 'I've got this ...'[9]

Cole's ambivalent position recognises the democratic liberatory potential of music technology and indeed is not averse to accessing MP3 files of other artists for his own use. However this recognition is tempered with his own role as an artist and the capacity for digital theft of his material in this way.

Against this background, Paul Simon's claim that 'every generation sends a hero up the pop charts' might appear to be something of a historical observation when the top forty singles charts are of lesser significance than previously.[10] Then again charts have been compiled in a number of ways over the years. The first pop charts in the UK registered the sales of sheet music. By 1952 *Melody Maker* had switched to concerning itself with sales of 78 rpm records which were overtaken by 7″ singles and then CDs. In discussing pop's propensity to recycle itself, Shuker (1994: 247) describes 'the pleasure of finding that rare item in a second hand store bin; and the intellectual and emotional pleasures associated with "knowing" '. We can see a parallel in the thrift store chic of grunge fashion. The attraction of retrospective nostalgia in dance music can be seen in the popularity in the UK of 'school disco' type club nights, referred to in chapter 5. These can also be seen as a reaction against smart corporate superclubs with strict door-entry policies and élitist guest-lists. Jumble sales, car-boot sales and charity shops represent unmonitorable music consumption where the Britpop or 1990s dance music creator can mine/scan the past for inspiration; underlining that pop's past is not pickled in aspic but open to interaction. Illegal music copying also does not show up on any statistics. When I interviewed Mbegane of Djoloff he pointed out to me that the punitive price of CDs now puts French rap out of reach of the means of many *banlieusards* who often access them by pirating copies. Indeed for rap to have attained the levels of commercial success that it has in France, it has necessarily had to a reach wider audience than simply the underprivileged, and it now has a huge following amongst white middle class youth (cf. Negus 1999 on US rap). Moreover talking about 'generations' in pop is of historical value because of the multifaceted composition of contemporary youth cohorts; they are not just singular entities but diverse groupings.

De-traditionalisation and institutionalisation: youth culture and pop music in the twenty-first century

While the case studies that I have presented illustrate that popular music still has considerable influence on young people, importantly modern music listeners – old and young alike – are not simply prepared to accept what is foisted upon them by the multinationals of the contemporary music industry. Even if we accept that youth are targeted by sophisticated marketing strategies or that youth culture has become big business, youth consumers still have the final say. As Negus (1999: 29) points out, 'The media or music industry cannot simply "construct" a market, or "produce" a type of consumer, nor determine an artist's meaning and try as they might they continually fail in attempts to do this.' Punjabi MC had a hit with 'Mundian Te Bach Ke' when it was released as a single by a record label with major distribution, aided by its discovery by BBC Radio 1 in 2003 – half a decade after it was originally played in bhangra clubs. This demonstrates both the complexity of assuming hegemonic flows between industry and public and the plural environment in which bhangra is listened to.

From teen publications to specialist magazines aimed at more 'discerning', i.e. older, music fans, the space devoted to critical comment and reviews in the music press demonstrates the way that the reception of musical texts by listeners is done in a critical, reflexive way. Rimmer's (1985: 108) study of pop fandom denies that his subjects are cultural dupes: 'Pop fans aren't stupid. They know what they want and ultimately, all the media manipulation in the world isn't going to sell them something they haven't got any use for.' In an age of increased media literacy and saturation the reception of musical texts is influenced by multiple factors including the listener's self-image, social/material circumstances and the mass media. Quite unlike the old-fashioned Frankfurt School hypodermic syringe model which dictated that the public are powerless to resist messages pumped out by the media, contemporary youth construct their own meanings but they do not do so in a vacuum. People do not uncritically swallow 'the trash served up for the ostensible or real needs of the masses' (Adorno 1991 [1941]: 38). Our preferences and practices are subject to numerous external factors. Structural determinants such as ethnic origin, gender, sexual orientation or financial means may be among the factors that impact on our choices — contrary to some of the tenets of individualisation theory. Importantly people's access to new choices is frequently mediated by circumstances beyond their control. We must therefore temper predictions of the end of class/gender inequalities with the advent of individualisation and all the fluidity and flux that this engenders. Such structures affect musical–cultural choices as they do other arenas of social relations.

Although decades have elapsed since the first studies of youth culture and of pop music, both remain iconic in contemporary culture. We began with three chapters looking at differing theoretical and methodological approaches relating to the study of youth, culture and pop. Subcultural studies, individualisation, postmodernism and postcolonial studies have all been part of the diagnostic apparatus applied to youth culture with varying degrees of success. The choice to span different disciplinary boundaries in Part I was therefore a conscious effort to work towards a toolkit of theories for twenty-first century youth and pop, rather than one totalising grand theory. There is a need then for a degree of theoretical eclecticism given that, now more than ever before, there is no singular experience of youth. If we look at the historical evolution of youth cultures in the twentieth century, it is self-evident that all youth cultures are a product of their times, as are the theories that classify them. Increased life expectancy, globalisation, continued anxieties about national identity and the fundamental shift from an industrial/labour-dependent society to one of leisure feed into our understandings of both. Paradoxically the complicated relationship between youth culture and pop music in multi-ethnic modernity exhibits tendencies of continuity and change, and on various levels of de-traditionalisation as well as institutionalisation.

Both Gramscian sociological constructs placed on pop that situate its actors as locked in a symbolic ideological struggle and the reduction of pop to simple commodity form following the Frankfurt school are overly simplistic and deterministic. Expectations of youth culture and pop often rest on the false assumption that youth are an amorphous mass of passive consumers with unitary leisure interests with a generational culture of revolt against their elders. Resistance through rituals and political opposition through style ignore the fact that people may not all be equally 'active' in their adherence to, or may even move between, subcultures. Redhead (1990: 229) points out: 'Such [subcultural] notions are not capable of capturing the changes in youth culture and rock culture from at least the late 1970s onwards. They are, moreover, unsatisfactory as accounts of pop history and youth culture in general.' Indeed music is conspicuously absent in the treatment of both mods and skinheads in Hall and Jefferson (1976). Postmodernist clichés of inauthenticity and pastiche or the concept of tribalism too can mean everything and nothing. We need to develop a more culturally sensitive model encompassing elements of individualisation with an awareness of structure between subculture and risk. We also need to rethink concepts for different national and local contexts. Many CCCS studies have been very British in their insistence on social class as a determining factor. There is a need to develop theoretically mixed models which are not confined by geography and are capable of bending to local realities, nuances and differences. Here I would nominate the word 'scene' as a more palatable alternative to subculture, as it invokes a socio-spatial dimension. Reimer (1995) for example points out how traditional subcultural analyses of gender and class are less important than age in the leisure patterns of Swedish youth and how Bourdieu's (1984) concept of distinction is also difficult to apply to Sweden where there are not such obviously dichotomised high culture/low culture divides as in France. Similarly Gudmundsson (1999) attests that punk in Scandinavia sprang from different material circumstances to its UK 'dole queue rock' origins and was instead more a reaction to Nordic progressive rock.

It is a function of age to decry the state of current youth culture. In the late twentieth century popular commentators bemoaned supposedly increasingly safe, retrograde tendencies in the charts, consigning resistance in youth music cultures to the historical scrapheap. At the start of the twenty-first century the popularity of manufactured pop acts constructed from TV-based competitions, e.g. the phenomenally successful *Popstars* and *American Idol* television series would appear to have accelerated this decline. The appearance of artists from seemingly nowhere who suddenly sell out stadiums reverses notions of 'paying ones dues', yet the advance of recording technology and the ability to release music straight to the internet by-passing record companies is one of the reasons why the old trajectories no longer hold. Furthermore manufactured pop acts such as the Monkees have always short-circuited old established processes. In the same way moral panics about youth repeat themselves. In 2001 young Asians were highly visible in a wave of urban unrest in some of England's northern towns, their actions agitated by far-right white youth. Two decades earlier it had been young British Afro-Caribbeans under the spotlight in similar circumstances.

The new millennium begins with the same pessimistic prognosis of pop as a spent force that the last one witnessed, but then as Adorno (1991 [1941]: 26) pointed out, pessimistic attestations of the decline of music and musical taste are enduring tropes, as old as music itself. The now sizeable academic and accompanying non-academic literature on rap music and hip-hop culture serves as an indication of its coming of age as an art form. Rap has been seen as in essence poetry set to beats. Indeed parallels have even been drawn between US rapper Eminem and Shakespeare.[11] Recent years have seen a similar entry of punk into the realms of respectability (Sabin 1998)[12] and a historicism of dance culture. These rehabilitations demonstrate that, throughout history, once threatening musical youth styles have always eventually become harmless cultural artefacts, entering into accepted orthodoxy. All of the musics discussed furthermore underline the hollowness of homogeneity that was identified in chapter 3. We have seen throughout the course of this book how youth cultures are, in some ways, constructs that simultaneously embody national traditions and say much about postcolonial negotiations in multi-ethnic modernity. Despite automatic associations of blackness with hip-hop Eminem is a hugely popular white rapper with black and white youth alike – second in line to the British throne, Prince William, is reportedly a huge fan. Furthermore diversity within majority populations is manifested in the craft of numerous white artists from all genres, e.g. the Los Angeles rap group House of Pain who repeatedly stressed their Irish immigrant origins in their identity articulation.

Despite attempts to write it off, the currency of pop as a youth cultural signifier remains undeniable if not quite undiminished. Pop music is no longer 'youth music' but then the association between the two was a historical intersection. The Frankfurt theory of a 'culture industry' where 'more' (in quantity) inevitably means less (in quality) is mistaken. The chapters of this book have shown that for young people in multi-ethnic modernity, pop music is a form of social practice to be created as well as a cultural text to be consumed. In both cases youth are adept at constructing their own musical meanings in keeping with the reflexive biography notion of individualisation. Today's youth musics are more than ever before post-subcultural pop, as a growing academic literature acknowledges (Stahl 1999; Bennett and Harris 2003; Muggleton and Weinzierl 2003). Redhead (1990: 8) points out: '[P]opular music … is more pervasive than ever in our supposedly postmodern culture … [it] seep[s] out of our television sets … radio … [o]n the train or bus it leaks from turned up Walkmans … forever selling, soothing, celebrating, hustling, commiserating and titillating.' This subliminal presence, in addition to music's more blatant and deliberate manifestations is also identified by Blake (1997a: 10), who writes: 'in the age of mechanical reproduction, the era of the car radio, concourse muzak, the juke-box and the walkman, [music] is a virtually ever-present component of everyday life in the late twentieth century'. Perhaps rather than mourning its death, we should be celebrating pop's all-pervasiveness, which demonstrates its potency as an unparalleled popular cultural symbol heavily vested with meaning for old and young alike in an ageing world. In conclusion then, today's youth musical cultures are beyond strict territorially bonded units, beyond straight individualist analyses, beyond the classifying system of youth equating automatically with pop and above all, beyond subculture.

NOTES

Introduction

1 'Bush blows in on a chill wind of change', *Guardian*, 20 January 2001.
2 For a front cover picture of Blair with Fender Stratocaster electric guitar, see 'Ugly rumours stages a comeback', a reference to the student rock band that the Prime Minister played in at Oxford University in connection with Blair picking up a guitar, apparently impromptu, at a school visit in Hartlepool, northern England, *The Times*, 8 September 2001.

1 Rethinking subculture: a critique for the twenty-first century

1 The *NME* gave Hebdige's *Subculture* a rave review. The 1988 reprint includes gushing back cover recommendations from *Rolling Stone*, *Time Out* and the *New York Times*, indicative of the popularisation of popular culture critique of the 1980s.
2 This is still a potent sign as seen in the abuse that Kula Shaker (a white band using Indian instrumentation) were met with after the band used it in the stage set of their 1998 tour. The fact that Kula Shaker appropriated it in its inverted original Hindu form, i.e. non-fascist version, shows how re-signification can be effected creating further confusion/complication. The artistry of this group is returned to in chapter 7.
3 Willis (1977: 14) 'The term ear'ole itself connotes the passivity and absurdity of the school conformists for the lads. It seemed that they are always listening, never *doing*.' Asian youth are taken to be 'ear'oles' by extension which explains why they are so disliked (Willis 1977: 49).
4 An example is Hebdige (1979: 122), who propounds elitism when he writes 'the distinction between the originals and the hangers on is always a significant one in subculture ... the mods had an intricate system of classification whereby the 'faces' and 'stylists' who made up the original coterie were defined against the unimaginative majority'.
5 Hippiedom did, however, attract a passing interest in some published studies (Leech 1973; Musgrove 1974). Clarke *et al.* (1976: 57–71) do include 'counter-culture' as a subsection but this movement is largely dismissed, not seen to have the same function as supposedly all-pervasive working class subculture for the reason that 'they [hippies] inhabit a dominant culture ... they represent a rupture inside [it]'.
6 Although perhaps the rash of journals that erupted in 1997–8, including *Cultural Values*, the *International Journal of Cultural Studies* (Blackwell) and the *European Journal of Cultural Studies*, may well be explained as providing outlets for academic articles by

authors conscious of the 2001 British Government imposed Research Assesment Excerise RAE deadline. For an interesting treatment of the institutionalisation of cultural studies see *Cultural Studies*, 12 (4) (1998).

2 Age and culture: diversifying discourses beyond subculture

1 'Reflexive sociology' has also been used by Bourdieu (1992), although his application of it differs from that of Beck, Giddens and Lash. Bourdieu (1992) argues for more ethnomethodology in the fusion of sociologists' horizons with those of their respondents.
2 What British people would call the 'Asian' community is more accurately constituted from former imperial possessions of British-ruled India, i.e. present-day India, Pakistan and Bangladesh.
3 See for example 'British, Asian and hip', *Independent on Sunday*, 1 March 1998; 'Asian Wave', *The Times*, 23 August 1997. Choque Hussien, lead-singer of Leeds Asian Underground outfit Black Star Liner bemoaned to me that 'It's all become *Independent* and *Sunday Times*. For god's sake let's get *Daily Mirror* about it' (interview conducted by myself at the Roadhouse, Manchester, February 1999 and published in 'Not so Quiet on the Eastern Front', *City Life*, 3 March 1999).
4 The 'out' categorisation cannot be applied to either Freddie Mercury or Indian-born Cliff Richard.
5 See Huq (1998a).
6 Sample comment: 'Along with labour markets, consumer commodity markets move out as shopping malls and centres find locations that blacks have to travel distances to shop in and are rarely hired to work in' (Lash 1994: 62). This observation, referring to the US, seems to neglect upward mobility. In the UK many of the staff at out-of-town shopping facilities are of Asian origin. The siting of Manchester's Trafford Centre in the middle of the north-west's motorway network and at the centre of a sprawl of suburbs (now the preferred residential base of the successful and aspiring Asian) makes it well placed for Asian staff and clientele, to say nothing of its cinema complex being the only one in Manchester to show Asian films.
7 I say this as a female British Bangladeshi – the category that official statistics show are the least likely to succeed in the UK educational system – yet I have got as far as writing this book.
8 As Cohen and Ainley (2000: 91) point out, 'You only have to look at the bibliographies of "Rethinking Youth" and "Rethinking the Youth Question" to see how little cross-referencing there has been, despite so many potential points of convergence (Cohen, 1997; Wyn & White, 1996).'

3 Theorising youth pop music: meanings, production and consumption beyond subculture

1 For example the following definitions are offered by Hardy and Laing (1995): 'Pop – a broad term normally used for the softer, even more teenage-oriented sounds that emerged as ROCK 'N' ROLL in the early 1960s'; 'Rock – a general name for the wide range of styles that have evolved from rock 'n' roll.'
2 This notion was echoed later by the Jesus and Mary Chain in their 1993 hit 'Reverence': 'I wanna die like JFK, I wanna die on a sunny day. I wanna die like Jesus Christ. I wanna die on a bed of spikes.'
3 Personal conversation, March 1995.
4 Personal conversation, March 1995.

5 See Sabin (1999) on punk and a similar historicism of a decade of dance culture in the deluge of books celebrating the tenth anniversary of the 'second Summer of love' (Anthony 1998; Benson 1997; Broughton and Brewster 1998; Bussman 1998; Collin 1997; Garratt 1998; Harrison 1998; Reynolds 1998a; 1998b).

6 'A reader from Colorado', who gives Reynolds (1998b) three out of ten on the amazon.com website.

7 For example, in the UK Liverpool University has an Institute for Popular Music and the John Lennon Research Centre. Strathclyde University has a similar department. At Salford University 800 applications were made in 1996 for 40 places on the BA Popular Music and Recording course (*Times Higher Education Supplement*, 8 November 1996). See also 'Peer Review' by Robin Wilson and Elizabeth F. Farrell, which reports on a new Center for American Music at the University of Texas at Austin, from the *Chronicle of Higher Education* at http://chronicle.com/weekly/v49/i17/17a00701.htm

8 I will use musicological analyses least here. Two examples, however, are Schaeffer's (1977) acoustic ecology and Attali (1989). There are now a set of sound generalist secondary source textbooks to recommend to the interested reader, including Bennett (2001), Longhurst (1995), Negus (1996) and Shuker (2001).

9 Available in English as *Selections from The Political Writings of Antonio Gramsci* (1977).

10 This term was not used by Finnegan herself but was subsequently common currency amongst journalists, particularly in relation to Labour's inability to gain power at general elections in the 1980s and early 1990s as the constituency that the party needed to attract in order to regain power. It is as much an attitudinal description as a geographical signifier, although some 50 miles north-west of London, Milton Keynes would appear to qualify for a 'middle England' description based on this second criterion.

11 See for example Simon Bowers, 'B-ware: boost for Kylie as EMI purges second-string artists', *Guardian*, 16 March 2002, p. 27; John Casey, 'EMI vows to hit the right note next year', *Guardian*, 25 May 2002. See also 'EMI's US Bid to Put Robbie on Track', *Daily Express*, 21 May 2003; 'EMI in black after 1,900 job cuts', *Daily Telegraph*, 21 May 2003; 'Background noise spoils EMI's song', *Daily Telegraph*, 21 May 2003; Simon Bowers, 'EMI music unit sinks to tune of 13%', *Guardian*, 21 May 2003.

12 See for example 'Why Napster is the good guy (and the RIAA is not)', 28 May 2002 at http://zdnet.com/anchordesk/stories/story/0,10738,2867844,00.htm, in which it is claimed that traditional retail is too inflexible: 'If I want one song, I have to pay for a dozen more I don't want. I have to pay for the cost of the media, the CD jewel box, and the liner notes.' See also Martha Irvine, 'Students Defend Piracy on the Web', Associated Press 21 March 2003.

13 'All Saints march in as Europe's best', *The Times*, 17 November 2000.

14 For early 1990s examples, see the claim of Caroline Sullivan that 'The current crop of pop idols is the most pallid, personality-free and conservative ever' (*Guardian*, 21 November 1990) and of Simon Reynolds that 'backward-looking rock is in danger of devouring itself' (*Guardian*, 11 November 1990). A twenty-first century version of the same argument can be seen in Charlotte Raven, 'Why pop music ain't what it used to be', *Guardian*, 6 March 2001, which decries pop available to contemporary youth ... 'while the rest of us just have our memories and the grim consolation of sounding like our mothers when we say that pop records all sound the same'.

4 World in motion: bhangra, post-bhangra and raï as second generation sounds in inauthentic times

1 Olivier Cathus (2001) 'Khaled: La grande variété internationale' at http://gredin. free.fr/musiques/disques/58.khaledkenza.html. This comment can be roughly translated as 'Khaled is like Johnny Hallyday, beyond reproach/ rational discussion.'

2 Hebdige (1979: 58) declares: 'Less easily assimilated than the West Indians into the host community ... sharply differentiated not only by racial characteristics but by religious rituals, food taboos and a value system which encouraged deference, frugality and profit motive, the Pakistanis were singled out for the brutal attentions of skinheads, black and white alike.'

3 http://www.sadieo.ucsf.edu/music/bhangra.html

4 By the end of 1997 a clutch of compilations bearing the tag had been released including Talvin Singh's East London Monday club-night spin-off *Anoka: Soundz* [sic] *of the Asian Underground* and the Sony Corporation's *Eastern Uprising: Dance Music From the Asian Underground*.

5 After their existence for at least half a decade Cornershop were nominated as 'best British newcomer' at the 1999 Brit [British Music Industry] awards and 'Brimful of Asha' was shortlisted for best video. The Mercury Music prize in 1998 had shortlisted ADF's album *Rafi's Revenge* and Cornershop's *When I was Born For the Seventh Time*. Back in 1993 Apache Indian's *No Reservations* album had also been shortlisted for the Mercury Music prize. At the 1994 Brit awards he was nominated in the categories of best British newcomer, best British male solo artist, best dance act and best single for 'Boom Shack-a-lak'.

6 E.g. *The Times* article, 'Caught in the Culture Trap' (8 April 1997), which asserts: 'Few Asian girls cross the East–West divide without paying a price.'

7 One of the acts performing, RDB, began by asking the crowd where they came from before issuing a roll-call of towns that included Blackburn, Oldham, Burnley, Bradford and Sheffield, as well as Manchester. A young girl standing near me, with a clearly local accent, kept shouting in an ironic 'spoiler' way 'India'.

8 A reveller attending Bombay Jungle, a weekly bhangra night at the fashionable Wag Club in central London explains ('Bombay Nights: London's young Asian community is learning to let its hair down', *Independent*, 24 May 1994): 'For once Asians can conduct themselves in a way they would never dream of doing in front of their parents. Coming to the Wag reassures me that I'm not the only one suffering an identity crisis.' See Lawrence (1982: 132–3) for criticism of this psychological line.

9 Interview conducted by myself at Wiiija Records, London, 23 May 1995.

10 Interviewed conducted by myself at Community Music Centre, Farringdon, London, 3 August 1994.

11 Interview conducted by myself at 'Festival des Artefacts', Strasbourg, France, 5 September 1997.

12 This is, of course a play on words of the Spike Lee film *Do The Right Thing*. It is also a 1991 song by French rappers IAM, who will be returned to in the next chapter. A brief treatment of this song along with an English translation of some of its lyrics can be found in Prévos (1997: 151).

13 The single reached number fifteen in the UK and seventeen in the US charts.

14 The biography issued by UK press agency APB for the UK release of *Meli Meli* in April 2000 waxed lyrical about Mami's roots in Algeria (where he was born in 1966), but neglected to say that he has lived in Paris since the age of nineteen.

15 http://www.sadieo.ucsf.edu/music/bhangra.html

16 Fun-Da-Mental have played at the Socialist Workers Party (SWP) summer school and donated tracks to compilation albums for both criminal justice and anti-racist charities. *Time Out's* (25 March 1998) review of their album, *Erotic Terrorism*, however

criticises it for being message over music: 'It's a dour, shouty, funkless, tuneless, unfocussed, alienated, *depressing* din … in Fundamental's case, good intentions + no tunes = no challenge to anyone.'

17 Interview conducted by myself at Community Music Centre, Farringdon, London, 3 August 1994.

18 Interview conducted by myself at The Vibe Bar, 1 October 1998.

19 In Conversation event, Bridgewater Hall, Manchester, 21 May 2002.

20 The name of the group 'Zebda' is itself interesting. It plays on 'beur' which is the word in the French slang youthspeak 'verlan' (described further in the chapter of this book on rap) for 'Arab'. 'Zebda' meanwhile is the Arabic word for butter, which is 'beurre' in French, pronounced the same as the word 'beur', i.e. French-born Arab.

21 David Toop in *The Times* (25 January 1993) muses of this juxtaposition: 'Ragga's obsession with guns and sex do not make a particularly neat fit with the stereotyped, shy, law-abiding academically conscious Asians.'

22 http://www.state51.co.uk/hottips/295/bhangle2.html

23 The single's release provoked a rash of 'Those people in *that* song in full' explanatory articles in respected rock weeklies such as the *New Musical Express* and *Melody Maker*.

24 Mention could be made of exceptions to this rule: the one-hit wonders Sheila Chandra, Joyoti Mishra (White Town) and the group Babylon Zoo. 'Spaceman' by Babylon Zoo (fronted by Jas Mann) made number one in 1997, but largely for the reason that it was featured in a Levi's television commercial. As the *Guardian* (2 February 1996) pointed out: 'Early eighties fusion artist Monsoon, fronted by Sheila Chandra, and Bhangramuffin hitman Apache Indian were both restricted in mainstream terms because others were unable to separate their ethnicity from their artistry. Mann's good fortune is that he "happened" before this constriction could be applied.' Similarly mystery initially cloaked the identity of the performer of the 1997 number one 'Your Woman' by White Town. It later emerged that this was 'Asian porky bloke' (self-description in the *Guardian*, 3 October 1998) Joyti Mishra, a computer programmer who had produced the record in his bedroom. He retrospectively claimed, 'I'm never going to be a teenage pin-up and at least I got to number one solely on musical ability.' Both acts promptly disappeared.

25 This term will receive a fuller treatment in the next chapter. For now 'urban' is a fair approximation of its meaning.

26 As recently as 1996 very different comments were being made in the press: 'no Asians have made the big time as stand up comics. Thank heavens for that. The image of a gentle, doe-eyed girl in a sari doing what Jo Brand [sometimes crude UK alternative comedienne] does is horrible' (Sue Arnold, *Observer*, 9 June 1996).

27 The dolaks are drums and the tumbi is a horizontally played stringed instrument plucked like a harp.

28 Interview conducted at Community Music Centre, Farringdon, London, 3 August 1994.

29 Atlas's earlier album 'Bastet' (1999) had included 'La Vie en Rose', originally sung by Edith Piaf. Among her other collaborations in France is the Arabic language track 'Ness', recorded with the French raï group Sawt El Atlas (from Blois) in 2000 and featured on the album *Donia*.

30 Email exchange, 19 August 1999.

31 Although he was displeased with the fabricated *Loaded* magazine quote from him (September 1998), claiming 'to me a pair of tablas is like a pair of tits'.

32 Telephone interview, 19 August 1999.

33 A parallel can be drawn here with the much-mentioned Apache Indian/Maxi Priest collaboration that brought together bhangra and reggae (Back 1996; Gilroy 1993).

34 Khaled has also appeared in concert with female French singer Mylene Farmer and on the subsequent *Live à Bercy* CD with the pair dueting on the chanson 'La Poupeé Qui Fait Non' (The Doll Who Goes 'No').

35 These texts in specifically addressing the British second generation experience draw on theorists of wider postcolonial movements who also represent a new generation in the social sciences which it has not been possible in the scope of this article to examine any further, e.g. Bhaba (1990; 1994), Said (1978; 1993) and Spivak (1988).

36 Email exchange, 19 August 1999.

37 'Indian Simmer: has the Asian Underground gone off the boil?', *Time Out*, 18 February 1998.

38 This spurred the release of Bhosle CDs and Bhosle-featuring Bollywood compilations on various world music labels, featuring tracks that had long been available in British high streets through Asian retailers on CDs and cassettes distributed by specialist Asian labels. E.g. *The Kings and Queens of Bollywood* (Nascente, 2001) *The Best of Asha Bhosle: The Golden Voice of Bollywood* (Manteca, 2000). An 'Asian' equivalent can be found in the form of *Hum Tumhare Liye: Classics Revival* (Gramophone Company of India/Dum Dum, 2000). Bhosle incidentally had collaborated with 1980s UK synth-pop duo Blancmange on the single 'Ave Maria', recorded under the auspices of 'West India Company' on London Records in 1984.

39 http://www.rfimusique.com/o2cf_fr/groli...fr_base?INPUT-%3Eaffiche_ biographie(14)

40 According to his 1995 press release issued by Island Records his sell-out Indian shows earned him the epithet 'The Gandhi of Pop'.

41 Caroline Sullivan, 'Hippy Dippy Shaker', *Guardian*, 19 February 1999.

42 Press release biography by David Toop (1998), issued for the *OK* album.

43 *Melody Maker*, 28 June 1997.

44 Sony's 1994 signing of Bally Sagoo led *The Late Show* (BBC2, 12 October 1994) to ponder whether Asian youth who had bought his recordings on cheaply produced cassettes for £2 a throw would be willing to part with perhaps seven times that amount for a commercially manufactured CD of the same product. Four years on however, despite the *prima facie* 'safe bet' for Sony of an established artist producing popular tunes remixed, Sagoo had been dropped from the label, victim of what Banerji (1990: 144) had earlier called 'the price trap'.

45 Other areas where bhangra is consumed in the UK include Southall in West London (Gillespie 1995; Baumann 1990; 1996), Newcastle (Bennett 2000) and Manchester – where at the time of writing daytimers take place on a regular monthly basis between two promoters.

5 Deconstructing difference in dance music: subculture and club culture at the turn of the century

1 See e.g. the following comment from the Bishop of Woolwich on rock 'n' roll: 'The hypnotic rhythm and wild gestures have a maddening effect on a space loving age group and a result is a relaxing of all self-control' (*The Times*, 13 September 1956, quoted by Davis 1991).

2 Remark made at PRS-sponsored 'In Conversation' event at the Bridgewater Hall, Manchester, 21 May 2002.

3 See 'School Disco' in *Ministry* magazine (April 2002, p. 46) which reports on the 2,500 strong crowd at London's Po Na Na club at a schooldisco.com event. The article observes that no visible drug-taking took place and that cheap alcoholic drinks instead dominated proceedings.

4 Figures from the *South Bank Show* documentary on Moby, shown on ITV (7 July 2002).

5 The *NME* (16 June 2001) ran the cover headline 'UK garage takes US by storm'. The paper reported that Craig David, Artful Dodger and Oxide and Neutrino were leading the 'US two step invasion'.

6 Remark made at PRS-sponsored 'In Conversation' event at the Bridgewater Hall, Manchester, 21 May 2002.

7 *Faking It*, Channel 4 (17 April 2001); a series in which people are transposed into situations diametrically opposed to their chosen lifestyles and then entertainment value is derived from witnessing their struggle. Indeed a cursory flick through a publication such as the London monthly *DJ* magazine shows dozens of music production courses advertised in the classified section.

8 See e.g. the article 'From dusk till dawn' (*Guardian*, 4 November 2000), which profiles club entry, drink and flight prices in cities including Cape Town, Tokyo and Buenos Aires. Also 'In the Club', a feature on the Lisbon club-scene (*Guardian* Travel Supplement, 27 April 2002). The 2001 Channel 4 UK television series *Around the World in 80 Raves* also emphasised the appeal of clubbing worldwide.

9 See 'Clubbers face police crackdown as Cyprus takes on drugs paradise' in the *Guardian* (11 August 2001), which reports 'Dozens of Britons arrested to prevent Ayia Napa becoming the new Ibiza'; C. Butts, 'The Beat Goes On' (*Guardian* Travel Supplement, 25 January 2003, pp. 6–7). On Goa see 'They come in search of paradise' (*Observer*, 25 May 1997).

10 See e.g. the cover headline 'Ecstasy: my tragic girl's wasted life' (*Daily Mail*, 9 May 2001) about the case of teenager Laura Spinks, who died after taking tablets at a club in Cambridge.

11 Press (1995: 798) writes: 'in the public imagination, squatters, ravers and travellers blur together in the "crusty", a smelly drug-addled parasite ready to take over your house while you're on vacation ... [i]n reality there is no generic squatter or traveller; instead there is a multitude of 'tribes' ... in search of a less restrictive, more communal way of life'.

12 As Debby of ravers' pressure group Advance Party was often heard to remark at the time: 'I guess that's goodbye to Ravel's *Bolero* then.'

13 Hetherington (1998: 329) argues, however: 'New Age Travellers are a hybrid phenomenon. They remain a youth culture, in the sense that that was how their way of life originated and because most, though by no means all of those who travel and live on the road, have tended to be relatively young – but they are more besides.'

14 See 'La Justice durcit son attitude envers les organisateurs de raves' (*Le Monde*, 31 January 2002, p. 10), translatable as 'The legal system hardens its attitude towards rave organisers'. Also 'Liberté, égalité, fraternité: but no free raves' by Jon Henley in the *Guardian* (26 May 2001).

15 Fontaine and Fontana (1996: 95) write 'Le raver tente d'échapper au monde des normes et des valeurs et de sortir de lui même, de son propre conditionment', which can be translated as 'the raver tries to escape from a world of norms and values and escape their own self and the conditioning of themself.' They conclude 'Le ravers, et leurs danses frénétiques risquent alors d'être récupérés par la société qu'ils fuyaient' (1996: 96). A loose translation would go something like 'the ravers and their frenetic dances run the risk then of being appropriated by the society from which they flee'.

16 Britain's Channel 4 had a 'Fatboy Slim night' – an evening of television programmes based around the Brighton DJ – on 14 July 2001.

17 Remark made at PRS-sponsored 'In Conversation' event at the Bridgewater Hall, Manchester, 21 May 2002.

18 http://www.hyperreal.org/raves/spirit/vision/Perfect_Party.Culture.html

19 See 'What You Need to Be a DJ', *NME*, 14 December 2002.

20 See 'Calm Down: How Chill Out Became the Biggest Success Story of 2001' in *Ministry* magazine (January 2002), which warns that the market maybe becoming saturated with titles such as *Chill Out Session* (several volumes), *Ibiza Chill Out*, *Urban Chill*, etc. According to the article seventeen chill-out compilations with the word 'Chill' in the title were released in the months of July and August 2002 alone.

21 Surveying BBC 1's flagship weekly chart show *Top of the Pops* as a one-off exercise in Spring 2003 (11 April 2003), I noted that four of the seven acts featured included a DJ.

6 Selling, selling out or resisting dominant discourses? Rap and the uses of hip-hop culture

1 Longsight was featured on the BBC national news the week of 5 May 2003 on an item about Manchester police's firearms amnesty and local gangs.

2 Fieldwork note: I attended the Cultural Fusion presentation at Slade Lane, Longsight, Manchester M13, 29 April 2003. I interviewed the group HD at the same venue during rehearsals on 7 May 2003. All interview transcript material is taken from this second date.

3 See 'Making the "Easy" Jump From Hip-Hop to Screen' in the *New York Times* (12 May 2002) by K. Sanneh, who alleges: 'In many ways hip-hop isn't much different from stand-up comedy – both reward quick wits and expressive roles. So maybe this crossover was inevitable.' The growing number of hip-hop-themed feature films, from Spike Lee's *She's Got to Have It* and *School Daze* through to the documentary *Biggie and Tupac* and well-known French urban fable *La Haine*, have not (only) been marginal art-house efforts but boast a number of big screen successes. *Bulworth* (1998) starred Warren Beatty and centred on the story of a US senator who becomes possessed by the spirit of hip-hop.

4 The gentle tones of West Coast rapper Ice Cube's hit 'It was a Good Day' sounds innocuous enough to the untrained ear but the lyrics talk about the violence of gang-land; maudlin instrumentation providing the backing to lines such as 'I didn't have to use my AK [gun]. I must say today was a good day' intoned in a 'matter of fact' way. This deceptively commercial musical backing married to cutting lyrics is another variant on the strategy of reeling fans into the rapper's 'hardcore' world as described by Mathew and Ravelle above in their discussion of commercial versus selling out.

5 Predictably all the studies of French rap (Bazin 1995; Cachin 1996; Cannon 1997; Lapassade 1996) copiously acknowledge and reference large quantities of US rap; a compliment unsurprisingly not returned in US endeavours (Cross 1993; Rose 1994; Toop 1990).

6 The word 'banlieue' means literally 'suburb', although many British commenators (e.g. Hargreaves and McKinney 1997; Thoday 1995) leave it untranslated, as it has negative ghetto-type associations that the word 'suburb' is devoid of.

7 The band name 'Nique ta mère' recalls the US term 'motherfucker'. Lapassade (1996: 54) analyses it under a heading 'les malheurs de ta mère' (unhappiness over mother), claiming that insulting one's mother contravenes one of the ultimate taboos. Badache (1995) sees the insult 'nique ta mère' as symbolic of a crisis of masculinity among youth who have been consigned to the margins of society.

8 On the television programme *Tout Le Monde En Parle* (Everybody's talking about it) (TF1, 7 February 2002).

9 *Le Monde* sided with the group in an editorial titled 'A dangerous judgement' (17–18 November 1996). *Liberation*, under the headline 'NTM: le rap au trou' (rap in a hole) (16 November 1996), editorialised this as 'A judgement stupefying in severity.' Pop magazine *Les Irrockuptibles* (20 November 1996) called it 'NTM bâillioné' (NTM gagged), invoking quizzically-cum-sarcastically the old Charles Trenet classic song-

title 'La Douce France?' (Gentle France). *Télérama* (27 November 1996) called the sentence 'inattendu et stupide' (unexpected and stupid), blaming the balance of political power in the French judiciary for having turned NTM into martyrs.

10 The single '11 Minutes 30 Against the Racist Laws' of March 1997 assembled fifteen rap groups including IAM, Assassin and Djoloff to demand 'the abrogation of all the racist laws concerned with the stay of immigrants in France' and 'the emancipation of all the exploited of this country whether they be French or immigrants'. Royalties raised went to the pressure group MIB (Mouvement de l'Immigration et des Banlieues). The project was organised by film director Jean-Marie Richet who's work includes *Etats des Lieux*, classed alongside *La Haine* as a 'rap film'.

11 MC Ren has claimed 'When we call each other nigger it means no harm, in fact it's a friendly word. But if a white person uses it, it's something different. It's a racist word' (quoted in the article 'Why is America Running Scared of Niggers [*sic*] With Attitude?', *Melody Maker*, 4 November 1989). A parallel can be drawn in the reclamation of the word 'cornershop' by the band from a pejorative term stemming from small-scale Asian commerce in the UK.

12 Interview with Djoloff conducted at the Green Room, Manchester, 7 July 2000.

13 For a profile of Islamic rap in the US see http://seatlepi.nnwsource.com/pop/108750_muslimrap.shtml, a 2002 article from the *Seattle Post* by D. Prvaz entitled 'Muslim rap: local group rhymes about Islam, Mideast politics' profiling the group Sons of Hagar. For Palestinian rap see 'Israel's Arabs Find Revolution Rap', an Associated Press report of 29 June 2002. For Algerian rap details see Burkhalter (2003).

14 His real name is Karri Miettinen.

15 The band's pseudonyms also show frequent deliberate mis-spellings and wordplay in the tradition of London garage rap group Big Brovas (Brothers) or even the Beatles: Mathew Tearror; Ravelle Wiz d.o.m; Marc Vizion; Hamza Big Shade; Rosie Universal. When I asked about the meaning of their track 'Hyperlyrics', Mathew told me: 'That one's like statements. The lyrics are stating like who we are and what we do. It's like to get that vibe; characters mixed together.'

16 Volume 4 for example includes the celtic rap of Manau from Corsica, Tolouse's Zebda and Djoloff as well as raï artists Faudel and Sawt el Atlas. Suggested classroom exercises include oral, written and creative writing.

17 The word is derived from 'a l'envers' (back to front), verlanised. Other commonly used examples are 'meuf', from 'femme' (woman) and 'keuf' from 'flic' (cop).

18 The 'papers' referred to are the generic term for state-issued identity cards/residence cards (*carte d'identité/carte de séjour*) that are obligatory for people to carry on their person at all times. The demand 'Vos papiers s'il vous plait' (papers please) is a significant threat reminding all immigrants of the state's power.

19 Headlines such as 'Rap Culture has hijacked our identity' by Joseph Harker (*Guardian*, 6 March 2003 and 'UK hip hop "needs ethics code" ' (http://news.bbc.co.uk/hi/english/entertainment/newsvid_2073000/2073162.stm) serve as updates of earlier versions, e.g. 'Has Rap Gone 2 Far?', a cover story from *Melody Maker* (5 February 1994).

20 See F. Gibbons, 'Rappers hit the Brits big time' (*Guardian*, 14 January 2003, p. 5). In terms of official recognition, it took until 1996 for the appropriately named Alliance Ethnik (*sic*) to become the first French rappers to be named best group at France's Victoires de la Musique awards.

21 Three members have been arrested for firearms possession and one was jailed in 2002. In November 2001 two people were shot at at a London concert of theirs. They have argued in their defence that they are only articulating what amounts to unpalatable social reality in their music. The band's Asher D has been quoted in the *Sunday Times* (12 January 2002) as saying 'A lyricist is in the same category as an author.

Every writer has got a good imagination. We're not murderers 'cos we talk about guns and we don't hate women 'cos we talk about hating chicks.'

22 See 'Ms Dynamite is right – our society needs a miracle' in *The Independent* (21 January 2003).

23 Interview conducted by myself at the Forum, Kentish Town, London NW5, October 1995.

24 This update of the blue, white and red national flag gained currency after the multicultural French world cup-winning football team of 1998. It is alleged that 'black' is a more acceptable alternative to the more pejorative French word for the same colour, 'noir' (Ball 1990: 30).

7 White noise: identity and nation in grunge, Britpop and beyond

1 The book was for example serialised in the weekend supplement of UK left-liberal 'quality' newspaper the *Guardian* (30 March 2002).

2 Cobain's suicide note asserted: 'its better to burn out than to fade away'. Two years later parallels were drawn with rapper Tupac Shakur, killed in a gangland shooting (see obituary in the *Independent*, 17 October 1996). The mystique of the incident is so much that 'Tupac Alive' stories even began to circulate (*Muzik*, January 1997) in the same way as the long-running Elvis sightings. See also: 'Who Killed Kurt Cobain?', *Guardian*, 1 June 1998.

3 Weinstein (1995) begins her article with the following lines from the band's best-known hit 'Smells Like Teen Spirit' (1992): 'I found it hard/ It's hard to find/ Oh well whatever/ Nevermind' and 'I feel stupid and contagious/ Here we are now/ Entertain Us'. Santiago-Lucerna (1998: 189) starts his piece on grunge with 'I miss the comfort of being sad' from 'Dumb' (1993). Moore (1998: 258) opts for the song 'Territorial Pissings' from *Nevermind* with its opening sarcastic pronouncement, 'Come on everybody/ Smile to your brother/ Everybody get together/ Try to love one another right now', which he describes as 'sickeningly off-key'. Crisafulli's (1996) book is based on 'the stories behind every Nirvana song'. Numerous websites also exist deconstructing the meanings of all that poured from Cobain's pen.

4 Whilst I was based in England throughout the duration of grunge, my attendance at the Reading rock festival in the South of England in 1995 a year later confirmed Cobain's induction into rock-star myth. This type of three-day open-air event is always a useful barometer to gauge youth cultural fashion trends. My observation at previous and subsequent events has shown that t-shirts of previous year's events are *de rigueur*. In this way a t-shirt commemorating Reading 1989 or the other major UK rock event Glastonbury of an earlier year confers on the wearer the 'proof' of having attended and survived before, of not being a festival 'virgin'. However in 1995, in place of these previous festival medals the t-shirts that seemed to be most omnipresent were those with Cobain's face peering reluctantly out with the simple caption Kurt Cobain 1967–1994. The two events that I found myself unable to access due to sheer weight of numbers and limited tent-space were the stampedes for both Hole and the Foo Fighters. Cobain's grip on young white middle class British youth was reinforced. It was as if everyone wanted a part of him.

5 Kearney (1998: 158) shows that riot grrrl reclaims words like 'cunt', whore' and 'slut' as positive self-imagery and rejects societal notions of thinness as desirable/ feminine. This coincides with the band name 'Cornershop', used in a similar way, and the Voodoo Queens' philosophy – see the chapter on Asian youth.

6 See 'Pop Goes the Future in a Blur of a Sound' by Pat Kane (*Guardian*, 17 August 1996); 'Which Side Are You On?' by Robert Sandall (*Sunday Times*, 20 August 1995);

'La nouvelle bataille de la pop passione la Grande-Bretagne' (*Le Monde*, 28 October 1995).

7 Cf. the way places including leafy Northwich in Cheshire (home-town of the Charlatans) despite its location several miles south of the city on the approach to Birmingham, were counted as Manchester during the early 1990s 'Madchester' boom.

8 *Daily Telegraph* 'Juice' magazine, Autumn 1997.

9 Figures from 'Who Calls the Tune?', *Observer*, 25 February 1996. Interestingly a survey by the consultancy Media Research Publicity (reported in *The Times*, 16 August 1997) found a decreasing popularity of established acts. Between 1994 and 1996 artists with careers lasting five years or more were responsible for 29 per cent of Britain's best-selling albums compared with 59 per cent in the previous three years.

10 In an interview in centre-right current affairs weekly the *Spectator* (12 December 1996), the Spice Girls came out for Prime Minister John Major's Conservative Party. The band later claimed that they were misquoted but the article itself illustrates pop's placement on a cultural pedestal from quarters once thought to be outside its domain. Also see the *Economist*, 12–18 April 1997, where it was claimed 'The Spice Girls ... have caught the eye of the sort of people whose main contact with pop music is asking for Walkmans to be turned down.'

11 Personal interview, 11 August 1998, published as 'Talking 'Bout my Generation', *Big Issue*, 4 January 1999.

12 Personal interview, 11 August 1998, published as 'Talking 'Bout my Generation', *Big Issue*, 4 January 1999.

13 'For my generation the union jack was associated with the extreme right. I think there's a nationalism in Britpop that wouldn't have been tolerated in the seventies. The way we liked our union jacks was turned upside down, ripped up and stuck together with safety pins! Now it's seen as this iconoclastic, pop-art imagery. There's something rotten in the state of Britpop – and its called nationalism' (Edwyn Collins on Noel Gallagher's union jack guitar, *Melody Maker*, 27 April 1996).

14 This was the term applied to a raft of beat-generation bands, including Manfred Mann, the Animals and of course the Beatles. See http://britishinvasion.eb.com/index2.html

15 This is a description that the band have used themselves; the other two components were *Parklife* and *The Great Escape*, preceded by the more Americanised grunge-like sound of the eponymous *Blur* (1997).

16 'Racism, sexism, masculine aggression and greedy self-aggrandisement pervade pop values and practices, just as they dominate other spheres.'

17 Cf. the female instrumentalists of Elastica and Pulp.

18 See also articles by Pat Kane (*Guardian*, 17 August 1995), Blake (1998), Huq (1996) and Gilbert (1998).

19 Interview conducted by myself at The Vibe Bar, London E1, 1 October 1998.

20 Personal interview at *Festival des Artefacts*, Strasbourg, France, 5 September 1997.

21 Christopher (1999) has the Spice Girls on his cover, Oakland (1998) includes an obscured shot of what looks like a Britpop singer (either Damon Albarn of Blur or Pulp's Jarvis Cocker) while Storry and Childs (1997) have an even blurrier image of a singer and microphone. Of the three Storry and Childs and Christopher both include an entry on Britpop in the index. Oakland has the least pop content.

22 It was claimed 'the red cross flag has been embraced by fans of every class, creed and colour' in the article 'By George' by Jonathan Glancey (*Guardian* G2, 20 June 2002).

23 The article 'There's Always England' by Conservative minister John Redwood (*Guardian* 20 March 1996) saw in the music an extollation of Tory British values. Labour Britpop uses include Tony Blair's 1996 conference speech, which ripped

off the Britpop 'Three Lions' chorus 'Football's coming home' to claim 'Eighteen years of hurt, never stopped us dreaming. Labour's coming home.' In office Blair was photographed with Noel Gallagher at 10 Downing Street, as described above, and appointed Creation Records supremo Alan McGee to his 'Creative Task Force'.

24 'Children to be taught "the value of Britishness" ', *Daily Mail*, 18 July 1995.

25 Blair is on record as stating 'we believe in, and actually welcome a multi-racial and multi-cultural society; that it's a good thing, that it's not something to be frightened of' at a speech at a community meeting in Southwark, quoted in the *Independent on Sunday*, 29 March 1998.

26 Perhaps inspired by the observation of in-house Conservative daily the *Daily Telegraph* (9 October 1997) that 'Chicken tikka masala is more British than morris dancing', or possibly just a coincidence.

27 Savage (1996: 414) writes: 'Scanned closer Britpop reveals itself as an outer-suburban, middle-class fantasy of central London streetlife, with excessively metropolitan models.' In other words then, the swinging London revolving around the axis of Britpop/indie mecca Camden Town, is a particular representation of the capital as it is perceived by suburbanites.

28 Speaking at Sources of Radicalism debate, Green Room theatre, Manchester, 7 February 2001.

29 The Prodigy earned the epithet 'the best live band in Britain' from the *Guardian* (12 October 1996). Dance acts now have their own rock festival-style gatherings, e.g. Creamfields, Tribal Gathering, etc.

30 This category does seem to have been growing in use, e.g. the high profile annual Music Of Black Origin (MOBO) awards, the publicity for which claims that most chart music owes its existence to black music (cf. Gilroy 1993a). The *Guardian's* Caroline Sullivan (9 October 1998) has claimed: 'The suffix "origin" is clever, allowing the inclusion of nominees who wouldn't qualify under a stricter interpretation.'

31 Singh has stated 'Our audience has never really been Asian and we've never really wanted it to be Asian. I mean when we started off in northern clubs. ... If it wasn't the Asians that wanted to kill us, it was the whites. There was always a fight and if it wasn't with any of the audience it was a fight with ourselves' (interview conducted by myself, Stoke Newington, London N16, 28 March 2002). See Huq (2003) for further discussion of this.

8 Conclusion: Rethinking youth and pop beyond subculture

1 'Rock of Ages', interview with Simon Frith by David Walker, *Times Higher Education Supplement*, 1 December 1995.

2 The link was made between the two in the *Independent's* obituary of Shakur (17 October 1996), which began: 'Middle America only began to understand the depression and frustration of the grunge generation when Kurt Cobain killed himself in 1994. The death of rapper Tupac Shakur on Friday from gunshot wounds ... is assuming a similar importance for gangsta and hip-hop fans the world over.' Johnstone (1999: 387) says that Shakur, shot dead in 1986, was 'beatified into Martyrdom' in the process. Between 1996 and 2002 seven albums of his work were posthumously released as well as the 2002 film *Biggie and Tupac*. Similarly, various collections of offcuts of Nirvana material have reached the market since Cobain's death.

3 Interview conducted with Peter Hook at Salford Quays, 7 July 2000.

4 Interview conducted at the Western, Manchester M16, 5 July 2002.

5 *The Wire*, 1994.

6 The number one UK chart-placing of Gareth Gates and the Kumars in April 2003 with the charity fundraising hit 'Spirit in the Sky' showcased an unusual combination comprising a manufactured television talent show winner combining forces with stars of an Asian-themed BBC sitcom.

7 Gilbert (1997: 19), who comes down heavily on the side of dance, attacks the need for pop to take representational form, commenting 'Britpop is nothing more and nothing less than the organised cultural reaction to all that is threatening about rave.' Blake (1998: 150) writes of jungle: 'It is one of the profound failures of New Labour that its symbolic representations of "Cool Britannia" have tended to stress the more nostalgic, monocultural Britpop at the expense of ... genuinely new forms.'

8 See 'Listen with Mother (and Everyone Else on the Train)', *Observer*, 25 July 1999.

9 At 'In Conversation' event with Nitin Sawhney, Bridgewater Hall, Manchester, 21 May 2002.

10 It was announced in 2003 that Britain was to have a new weekly chart by the Official UK Charts Company (OCC), based solely on music downloaded from the internet (*Guardian*, 13 May 2003). The growth in forms of accessing music has meant falling UK sales. In 1984 it took on average 107,700 single sales to have a number one hit. In 1993 this figure was 68,000 and by 2003 this had plummeted to just 25,000. In December 2003 the format of the long-running BBC weekly television show *Top of the Pops* was revised for the first time in its forty year history to depart from its traditional top forty singles chart formula and instead also feature album charts and forthcoming releases.

11 An article by Giles Foden 'Just How Good Is He?' argued 'Never mind the misogyny and homophobia, Eminem is a brilliant poet. ... [T]he controversial rapper ... belongs in the pantheon of literary greats' (*Guardian*, 6 February 2001). The respected poet Seamus Heaney made similar claims in 2003 (*Observer Music Monthly*, December).

12 Other celebrations included the 1997 'Destroy' exhibition of punk artwork at the establishment/high art Royal Festival Hall and the 'Punk: Before and After' season at the National Film Theatre in 1994.

BIBLIOGRAPHY

Abercrombie, N., Hill, S. and Turner, B. (1984) *The Penguin Dictionary of Sociology*. London: Penguin.

Abrams, M. (1959) *The Teenage Consumer*. London: Press Exchange.

—— (1990) 'On Popular Music', in Frith, S. and Goodwin, A. (eds) *On Record: Rock, Pop and the Written Word*. London: Routledge, pp. 43–57.

Adorno, T. (1991 [1941]) 'On Popular Music', in *The Culture Industry*. London: Routledge.

Adorno, T. and Horkheimer, M. (1979) *Dialectic of Enlightenment*. London: Verso.

Airès, P. (1962) *Centuries of Childhood*. London: Jonathan Cape.

Alderman, J. (1999) *Sonic Boom: Napster, P2P and the Battle for the Future of Music*. London: Fourth Estate.

—— (2001) *Sonic Boom: Napster, MP3, and the New Pioneers of Music*. London: Fourth Estate.

Alexander, C. (1996) *The Art of Being Black: the Creation of Black British Youth Identities*. Oxford: Oxford University Press.

—— (2000) *The Asian Gang: Ethnicity, Identity, Masculinity*. Oxford: Berg.

Alleyne, M. (2000) 'White Reggae: Cultural Dilution in the Record Industry', *Popular Music and Society*, 22 March 2000, article accessed at http://www.find-articles.com/cf_0/m2822/1_24/73712453/print.jhtml

Althusser, L. (1971) 'Ideology and the State', in *Lenin and Philosophy and Other Stories*. London: New Left Books.

Amit-Talai, V. and Wulff, H. (eds) (1995) *Youth Cultures: a Cross-cultural Perspective*. London: Routledge.

Andes, L. (1998) 'Growing Up Punk: Meaning and Commitment Careers in a Contemporary Youth Subculture', in Epstein, J. (ed.) *Youth Culture: Identity in a Postmodern World*. Oxford and New York: Blackwell, pp. 212–31.

Andreini, L. (1985) *Le Verlan: petit dictionnaire illustré*. Paris: Veyrier.

Anthony, W. (1998) *Class of 88: The True Acid House Experience*. London: Virgin.

Anwar, M. (1976) *Between Two Cultures*. London: Community Relations Council.

—— (1998) *Between Cultures: Continuity and Change in the lives of Young British Asians*. London: Routledge.

Appadurai, A. (1990) 'Disjuncture and Difference in the Global Cultural Economy' in *Theory, Culture and Society* 7: 295–310.

—— (1996) *Modernity at Large: Cultural Dimensions of Globalization*, Minneapolis: University of Minnesota Press.

Ásmundsson, J.K. (2001) 'Keepin' it Real in an "Unreal" World: Authenticity Discourses in Icelandic Hip-hop', unpublished MA dissertation, University of Leicester, MA in Mass Communication.

Aspinall, P. (2000) 'The challenges of measuring the ethno-cultural diversity of Britain in the new millennium' in *Policy and Politics* vol 28(1): 109–18.

Attali, J. (1989) *Noise: the Political Economy of Music*. Manchester: Manchester University Press.

Austin, J. and Willard, N. (1998) *Generations of Youth: Youth Culture and History in Twentieth Century Amreica*. New York and London: New York Press.

Back, L. (1996) *New Ethnicities and Urban Culture: Racisms and Multiculture in Young Lives*. London: UCL Press.

Back, L. and Solomos, J. (1996) *Racism and Society*, Basingstoke: Macmillan.

Badache, R. (1995) 'Le Monde du "NTM"! Le Sens de l'Injure Rituelle' in *Agora: Debats Jeunesse*, 3eme trimestre.

Baker, H. (1993) *Black Studies, Rap and the Academy*. Chicago: Chicago University Press.

Ball, R. (1990) 'Lexical innovation in present-day French: "le Français branché" ' in *French Cultural Studies* 1(1): 21–35.

Banerji, S. and Baumann, G. (1990) 'Bhangra 1984–8: Fusion and Professionalisation in a Genre of South Asian Dance Music', in Oliver, P. (1990) (ed) *Black Music in Britain: Essays on the Afro-Asian Contribution to Popular Music*. Milton Keynes: Oxford University Press, pp. 137–52.

Banks, M., Lovatt, A., O'Connor, J. and Raffo, C. (2000) 'Risk and trust in the cultural industries' in *Geoforum* 31: 453–64.

Bara, G. (1998) *La Techno*. Paris: Librio Musique/Le Flammarion.

Barker, M. and Beezer, A. (eds) (1992) *Reading into Cultural Studies*. London: Routledge.

Barrett, J. (1996) 'World Music, Nation and Postcolonialism' in *Cultural Studies* 10(2): 237–47.

Barthes, R. (1973) *Mythologies*. London: Paladin.

Baudrillard, J. (1981) *Simulacres et Simulations*. Paris: Éditions Gallilée.

—— (1990) *Cool Memories*. London: Verso.

—— (1996) *Cool Memories II*. London: Verso.

Baumann, G. (1996) *Contesting Culture: Discourses of Identity in Multi-ethnic London*. Cambridge: Cambridge University Press.

Bauman, Z (1987) *Legislators And Interpreters: On Modernity, Post-Modernity And Intellectuals* Cambridge: Polity Press.

Bazin, H. (1995) *La Culture Hip-hop*. Paris: Desclee de Brouwer.

Beadle, J. (1993) *Will Pop Eat Itself? Pop Music in the Soundbite Era*. London: Faber and Faber.

Beck, U. (1992) *Risk Society: Towards a New Modernity*. London: Sage.

—— (1994) 'Living in a Post-Traditional Society', in Beck, U., Giddens, A. and Lash, S., *Reflexive Modernization: Politics, Tradition and Aesthetics in the Modern Social Order*. Cambridge: Polity, pp. 1–55.

Beck, U., Giddens, A. and Lash, S. (1994) *Reflexive Modernization: Politics, Tradition and Aesthetics in the Modern Social Order*. Cambridge: Polity.

Becker, H. (1963) *Outsiders: Studies in the Sociology of Deviance*. Chicago: Free Press.

Bennett, A. (1997) 'Village greens and terraced streets: Britpop and representations of "Britishness" in Britpop', *Young: the Nordic Journal of Youth Research* 5(4): 20–33.

—— (1999) 'Subcultures Or Neo-Tribes? Rethinking the Relationship Between Youth, Style and Musical Taste' in *Sociology* 33(3): 599–618.

—— (2000) *Popular Music and Youth Culture: Music, Identity and Place*. Basingstoke: Macmillan.

—— (2001) Cultures of Popular Music, Buckingham, Open University Press.

Bennett, A. and Harris, K. (eds) (2003) *After Subculture*. Basingstoke: Palgrave.

Bennett, P. (1998) 'Britpop and National Identity' in *Journal for the Study of British Cultures* 5(1): 13–25.

Benson, R. (1997) *Nightfever: Club Writing in the Face 1980–1997*. London: Boxtree.

Best, S. (2002) *A Beginner's Guide to Social Theory*. London: Sage.

Best, S. and Kellner, D. (1998) 'Beavis and Butt-Head: No Future For Postmodern Youth', in Epstein, J. (ed.) *Youth Culture: Identity in a Postmodern World*. Oxford and New York: Blackwell, pp. 74–99.

Bey, H. (1991) TAZ, *The Temporary Autonomous Zone, Ontological Anarchy, Poetic Terrorism* Brooklyn, NY: Autonomedia.

Bilton, T., Bonnett, K., Jones, P., Stanworth, M. and Webster, A. (eds) (1987) *Introductory Sociology*. Cambridge: Polity.

Bhaba, H. (ed.) (1990) *Nation and Narration*. London: Routledge.

—— (1994) *The Location of Culture*. London: Routledge.

Bhatti, G. (1999) Asian Children at Home and at School. London: Routledge.

Blake, A. (1992) *The Music Business*. London: Batsford.

—— (1996) 'The Echoing Corridor: Music in the Postmodern East-End', in Butler, T. and Rustin, M. (eds) *Rising in the East: the Regeneration of East London*. London: Lawrence and Wishart, pp. 197–214.

—— (1997a) *The Land Without Music: Music, Culture and Society in Twentieth Century Britain*. Manchester: Manchester University Press.

—— (1997b) 'Listening to Britain: Advertising and Postmodern Culture', in Nava, M., Blake, A., MacRury, I. and Richards, B., *Buy This Book: Advertising and Consumption since the 1950s*. London: Routledge.

—— (1998) 'Retrolution: culture and heritage in a young country', in Coddington, A. and Perryman, M. (eds) *The Moderniser's Dilemma: Radical Politics in the Age of Blair*. London: Lawrence and Wishart, pp. 143–56.

Bloomaert, J. and Verschueren, J. (1998) *Debating Diversity: Analysing the discourse of Tolerance*. London: Routledge.

Bloomfield, T. (1991) 'It's Sooner Than You Think, or Where Are We in the History of Rock Music?' in *New Left Review* no 190 Nov/Dec pp. 59–81.

Bocquet, J.L. and Pierre-Adolphe, P. (1997) *La Rapologie*. Paris: Mille et Une Nuits.

Bourdieu, P. (1979) *La Distinction: critique sociale du Judgement*. Paris: Les Éditions.

—— (1984a) 'La "jeunesse" n'est qu'un mot', in *Questions de Sociologie*. Paris: les éditions de Minuit, pp. 143–54.

—— (1984b) *Distinction: a Social Critique of the Judgement of Taste*. London: Routledge.

—— (1992) *An Invitation to Reflexive Sociology*. Cambridge: Polity.

—— (1993) *La Misère du Monde*. Paris: Seuil.

Bracewell, M. (1997) *Selling England by the Sound: Pop Life in Albion from Wilde to Goldie*. London: HarperCollins.

Brah, A. (1997) *Cartographies of Diaspora: Contesting Identities*. London: Routledge.

Brake, M. (1980) *The Sociology of Youth Culture and Youth Subcultures: Sex and Drugs and Rock'n'roll.* London: Routledge and Kegan Paul.

—— (1985) *Comparative Youth Culture: the Sociology of Youth Culture in America, Britain and Canada.* London: Routledge.

Breen, M. (1995) 'The End of the World as We Know It: Popular Music's Cultural Mobility' in *Cultural Studies* 9(3): 486–504.

Brewster, B. and Broughton, F. for The Ministry of Sound (1998) *The Manual: The who, the where, the why of clubland* by Bill London: Headline

Brooker, W. (1998) *Teach Yourself Cultural Studies.* London: Hodder and Stoughton.

Broughton, F. and Brewster, B., for the Ministry of Sound (1998) *The Manual.* London: Headline.

Broughton, S., Ellingham, M. and Burton, K. (Eds) (1994) World Music: The Rough Guide London: Rough Guides.

Brown, A. (1997) 'Lets all Have a Disco: Football, Popular Music and Democratization?', in Redhead, S., O'Connor, J. and Wynne, D. (eds) *The Clubcultures Reader: Readings in Popular Cultural Studies.* Oxford: Blackwell, pp. 79–101.

Brulard, I. (1997) 'Laïcité and Islam', in Perry, S. (ed.) *Aspects of Contemporary France.* London: Routledge, pp. 191–208.

Buckingham, D. (1993) *Reading Audiences: Young People and the Media*, Manchester: Manchester University Press.

Buckingham, D. and Sefton-Green, J. (1994) *Cultural Studies Goes to School: Reading and Teaching Popular Media.* London: Taylor and Francis.

Burkhalter, T. (2003) 'Straight Outta Algiers', *Arts International* magazine, Spring.

Burnett, R. (1996) *The Global Jukebox: The International Music Industry.* London: Routledge.

Burton, K, and Awan, S. (1994) 'Bhangra Bandwagon', in Broughton, S., Ellingham, M., Muddyman, D. and Trillo, R. (eds) *Rough Guide to World Music.* London: Penguin.

Bussman, J. (1998) *Once in a Lifetime: The Crazy days of Acid House and Afterwards.* London: Virgin.

Butters, S. (1976) 'The Logic of Participant Observation', in Hall, S. and Jefferson, T. (eds) *Resistance through Rituals: Youth Subcultures in Post-war Britain.* London: Hutchinson, pp. 253–73.

Byrom, H. (1998) 'The Future of Clubbing' in *The Independent on Sunday*, Real Life, 30 August 1998, pp. 1–2.

CCCS (1982) *The Empire strikes back: race and racism in 70s Britain*/Centre for Contemporary Cultural Studies. London: Hutchinson

Cachin, O. (1996) *L'Offensive Rap.* Paris: Galliamard.

Cairns, D. (2003) 'Coming Out of Coventry' in *Sunday Times* culture section, 8 January 2003.

Calcutt, A. (1998) *Arrested Development: Pop Culture and the Erosion of Adulthood.* London: Cassell.

Calio, J. (1998) *Le Rap: une réponse des banlieues.* Lyon: Entpe Aléas.

Cannon, S. (1997) 'Paname City Rapping: B-Boys in the *Banlieues* and Beyond', in Hargreaves, A. and McKinney, M. (eds) *Post-Colonial Cultures in France.* London: Routledge, pp. 150–66.

Carr, R. (1996) *The Beatles at the Movies.* London: UFO Music.

Carr, R. and Dellar, F. (1986) *The Hip.* London: Faber and Faber.

Carr, R. and Farren, M. (1994) *Elvis Presley: the Complete Illustrated Record.* London: Plexus.

Carr, R. and Tyler, T. (1978) *The Beatles: an Illustrated Record.* London: Trew Copplestone.

Carrington, B. and Wilson, B. (2001) 'One Continent Under a Groove: Rethinking the Politics of Youth Subcultural Theory', *Soundscapes* essay, November, downloaded from http://www.icce.rug.nl/~soundscapes/VOLUME04/One_continent.html

Cashmore, E. (1984) *No Future:Youth and Society*. Aldershot: Heineman.

—— (1997) *The Black Culture Industry*. London: Routledge.

—— (1982) *Black Youth For Whites*, in Cashmore and Troyna (1982) pp10–14.

Cashmore E. and Troyna B. (1982) (eds) Black Youth in Crisis. London: Allen and Unwin

Cathus, O. (1994) 'La Vibration de la Rue', in Barreyere, J. and Vulbeau, A., *La Jeunesse et la Rue*. Paris: EPI/DDB Éditions.

—— (1998) *L'Âme-Sueur: le funk et les musiques populaires du XXeme Siécle*. Paris: Desclée de Brouwer.

Chambers, I. (1976) 'A strategy for living: black music and white subcultures', in Hall and Jefferson (1976) pp 157–166.

—— (1985) *Urban Rhythms*. London: Macmillan.

—— (1986) *Popular Culture: the Metropolitan Experience*. London: Methuen.

Champion, S. (1990) *And God Created Manchester*. Manchester: Wordsworth.

Chan, S. (1997) 'The Death of Diversity? The NSW Draft Code of Practice For Dance Parties', downloaded from www.cia-com.au/peril/youth/ravecode.pdf

Cheesman, T. (1998) 'Polyglot Pop Politics: Hip-hop in Germany' in *Debatte* 6(2): 191–214.

——(2002) 'Akçam–Zaimoğlu-'Kanak-Attak': Turkish Lives and Letters in German' in German Life and Letters vol LV(2) pp. 180–195.

Chisholm, L. (1990) 'A Sharper Lens or a New Camera? Youth Research, Young People and Social Change in Britain', in Chisholm, L., Büchner, P., Krüger, H. and Brown, P. (eds) *Childhood, Youth and Social Change: a Comparative Perspective*. London: Falmer Press, pp. 33–57.

Christopher, D. (1999) *British Culture: an Introduction*. London: Routledge.

Clarke, G. (1985) 'Defending Ski-Jumpers: a critique of theories of youth subcultures', in Frith, S. and Goodwin, A. (1990) (eds) *On Record: Rock, Pop and the Written Word*. London: Routledge, pp. 81–96.

Clarke, J. (1973) 'The three R's - repression, rescue and rehabilitation: ideologies of control for working class youth', CCCS occasional stencilled paper no 41, University of Birmingham.

—— (1976) 'The Skinheads and the Magical Recovery of Community', in Hall, S. and Jefferson, T. (eds) *Resistance through Rituals:Youth Subcultures in Post-war Britain*. London: Hutchinson, pp. 99–102.

Clarke, J. and Critcher, C. (1985) *The Devil Makes Work: Leisure in Capitalist Britain*. London: Macmillan.

Clarke, J. and Jefferson, T. (1976) 'Working Class Youth Cultures', in Mungham, G. and Pearson, G. (eds) *Working Class Youth Culture*. London: Routledge and Kegan Paul, pp. 138–59.

Clarke, J., Hall, S., Jefferson, T. and Roberts, B. (1976) 'Subcultures, Cultures and Class', in Hall, S. and Jefferson, T. (1996) (eds) *Resistance through Rituals: Youth Subcultures in Post-war Britain*. London: Hutchinson, pp. 9–74.

Cohen, A. (1955) *Delinquent Boys: the Culture of the Gang*. Chicago: Free Press.

Cohen, P. (1972) 'Subcultural Conflict and Working Class Community', in Gelder, K. and Thornton, S. (eds) *The Subcultures Reader*. London: Routledge, pp. 90–9.

Cohen, P. (1997) *Rethinking the Youth Question: Education, Labour and Cultural Studies.* London: Macmillan.

Cohen, P. and Ainley, P. (2000) 'In the Country of the Blind? Youth Studies and Cultural Studies in Britain', in *Journal of Youth Studies* 3(1): 79–95.

Cohen, P. and Bains, H.S., (eds) (1988) *Multi-racist Britain* Basingstoke : Macmillan.

Cohen, S. (ed.) (1971) *Images of Deviance*, Harmondsworth: Pelican.

—— (1972) *Folk Devils and Moral Panic: the Creation of the Mods and Rockers.* London: McGibbon and McCree.

—— (1980) *Folk Devils and Moral Panic: the Creation of the Mods and Rockers.* London: Martin Robertson.

—— (1991) *Rock Culture in Liverpool: Popular Culture in the Making.* Oxford: Clarendon.

—— (1997) 'Men Making a Scene', in Whiteley, S. (ed.) *Sexing the Groove: Popular Music and Gender.* London: Routledge, pp. 17–36.

Collin, M. (1997) *Altered State: The Story of Ecstasy Culture and Acid House.* London: Serpent's Tail.

Colombié, T. (2001) *Technomades: la Piste Electronique.* Paris: Stock.

Connell, J. and Gibson, C. (2003) *Soundtracks: popular music, identity and place.* London: Routldege.

Corrigan, P. (1979) *Schooling the Smash Street Kids.* London: Macmillan.

Corrigan, P. and Frith, S. (1976) 'The Politics of Youth Culture', in Hall *et al.* (1976) pp. 231–241.

Cosgrove, S. (1991) 'Shaking Up the City: Pop Music in a Moment of Change' in *Whose Cities?* Ed. Mark Fisher and Ursula Owen. Harmondsworth: Penguin pp 196–209.

Crisafulli, C. (1996) *Teen Spirit: the Stories Behind Every Nirvana Song.* London: Omnibus Press.

Croft, J (1997) 'Youth Culture and Age' in M Storry and P Childs (eds.) *British Cultural Identities*, London: Routledge.

Cross, B. (1993) *It's Not About A Salary: Rap, Race and Resistance in Los Angeles.* London and New York: Verso.

Daoudi, B. and Milani, H. (1996) *L'aventure du raï.* Paris: Le Flammarion.

Daoudi, B. (2000) *Le Raï*, Paris: Librio Musique/Le Flammarion

Davis, J. (1991) *Youth and the Condition of Britain: Images of Adolescent Conflict.* London: Athlone.

—— (2002) 'I am who I am', interview with Eminem published in the *Guardian* G2, 30 April 2002, pp. 6–7.

Dawson, R. (1997) 'Conclusion: present and future Britain', in Storry, M. and Childs, P. (eds) *British Cultural Identities.* London: Routledge, pp. 315–24.

Deleuze, G. and Guattari, F. (1972) *L'anti-Oedipe: capitalisme et schizonphrenié.* Paris: Les éditions de minuit.

—— (1983) *Anti-Oedipous: capitalism and schizophrenia.* London: Athlone Press.

Denning, M. (1991) 'The End of Mass Culture', in Naremore, J. and Bratlinger, P. (eds) *Modernity and Mass Culture.* Indiana: Indiana University Press.

Dennis, F. (1998) 'Birmingham: blades of Frustration', in Owusu, K. (ed.) (1998) *Black British Culture and Society: a text reader.* London: Routledge pp. 181–94.

Dimitriadis, G. (2001) *Performing Identity/Performing Culture: Hip hop as Text, Pedagogy and Lived Practice.* New York: Peter Lang.

Donnell, A. (2002) *Companion to Contemporary Black British Culture.* London: Routledge.

Downes, D. (1966) *The Delinquent Solution.* London: Routledge Kegan and Paul.

Dudrah, R. (2002) 'Drum'n'dhol: British Bhangra Music and Diasporic South Asian Identity Formation', in *European Journal of Cultural Studies* 5(3): 383–403.

During, S. (1993) *The Cultural Studies Reader*. London: Routledge.

Dwyer, P. and Wyn, J. (2001) *Youth, Education and Risk*. London: Routledge Falmer.

Dyer, R. (1997) *White: Essays on Race and Culture*. London: Routledge.

Eade, J. and Zaman, H. (1993) *Routes and Beyond: Voices from Educationally Successful Bengalis*, Centre From Bangladeshi Research. London: QMW and Roehampton Institute

Eliot, M. (1990) *Rockonomics: the Money Behind the Music*, London: Omnibus.

Epstein, J. (1998) 'Introduction: Generation X, Youth Culture and Identity', in Epstein, J. (ed.) *Youth Culture: Identity in a Postmodern World*. Oxford and New York: Blackwell, pp. 1–23.

FAS (1996) 'Les Jeunes et les Violences Urbain dans les Quartiers Alsaciens'. *Cahier de l'Observatoire Régional de l'intégration et de la ville* 18, Strasbourg: FAS.

Featherstone, M. (1991) *Consumer Culture and Postmodernism*. London: Sage.

—— (1993) 'Global and local cultures', in Bird, J. (ed.) *Mapping the Future: Local Cultures, Global Change*. London: Routledge.

—— (1995) *Undoing Culture*. London: Sage.

Feixa, C. (2001) ' "Tribus urbanas" and "Chavos banda": Youth Microcultures in Catalonia and Mexico', paper presented at Finnish Youth Research Network Multidisciplinary European Winter School, Karjaa, Finland, 5 December 2001.

Feixa, C., Costa, C. and Pallarés, J. (2001) 'From *okupas* to *makineros*: citizenship and youth cultures in Spain', in Furlong, A. and Guidikova, I. (eds) *Transitions in Youth Citizenship in Europe: Culture, Subculture and Identity*. Strasbourg: Council of Europe Publishing, pp. 289–304.

Festin, J.P. (1999) *Le Petit Dico Illustré des Rappeurs*. Geneva: Source.

Fikentscher, K. (2000) *You Better Work: Underground Dance Music in New York City*. Hanover: Weslyan University Press.

Fine, M., Powell, L., Weis, L. and Wong, M. (1997) *Off White*. London and New York: Routledge.

Finn, D. (1987) *Training Without Jobs: New Deals and Broken Promises*. London: Macmillan.

Finnegan, R. (1989) *The Hidden Music Makers: Making Music in an English Town*. Cambridge: Cambridge University Press.

Fisher, M. (1995) 'Indie Revolutionaries' in *New Statesman and Society*, 7 July 1995.

Fiske, J. (1989) *Reading the Popular*. Cambridge, MA and London: Unwin Hyman.

Fock, E. (1999) 'With the Background in the Foreground – Music among young Danes with immigrant backgrounds' in *Young: the Nordic Journal of Youth Research* vol. 7(2).

Fontaine, A. and Fontana, C. (1996) *Raver*. Poche ethno-sociologie series, Paris: Anthropos.

Fornäs, J. and Bolin, G. (1995) *Youth Culture in Late Modernity*. London: Sage.

Fornäs, J., Lindberg, U. and Sernhede, O. (1995) *In Garageland: Rock, Youth and Modernity*. London: Routledge.

Forrest, E. (1993) 'MC Who's PC' in *Sunday Times* culture section, 7 November 1993.

—— (2002) 'Busker in Babylon' in *Guardian* Weekend, 13 April 2002.

Foucault, M. (1978) *Les Mots et Les Choses: une archaeologie des sciences*. Paris: Gallimard.

—— (1980) *Power/Knowledge: Selected Interviews and Other Writings*. New York: Pantheon.

France, A. (2000) 'Towards a Sociological Understanding of Youth and their Risk-taking' in *Journal of Youth Studies* 3(3): 317–32.

Frankenberg, R. (1994) *White Women, Race Matters: the Social Construction of Whiteness*. Minneapolis: University of Minnesota Press.

Friedlander, P. (1996) *Rock and Roll: A Social History*. Boulder: Westview.

Frith, S. (1978) *The Sociology of Rock*. London: Constable.

—— (1983) *Sound Effects: Youth, Leisure and the Politics of Rock'n'Roll*. London: Constable.

—— (1985) 'The Sociology of Youth', in Haralambos M., *Sociology: New Directions*. Ormskirk, Lancashire: Causeway, pp. 303–68.

—— (1989) *Facing the Music: Essays on Pop, Rock and Culture*. London: Mandarin.

—— (1990) 'Frankie Said: But What Did They Mean?', in Tomlinson, A. (ed.) *Consumption, Identity and Style: Marketing, Meanings and the Packaging of Pleasure*. London: Routledge, pp. 172–85.

—— (1992) 'From the Beatles to Bros: Twenty-five Years of British Pop', in Abercrombie, N. and Warde, A., *Social Change in Contemporary Britain*, Cambridge: Polity.

—— (ed.) (1993) *Music and Copyright*. Edinburgh: Edinburgh University Press.

—— (1994) 'Music for Pleasure', in *The Polity Reader in Cultural Theory*. Cambridge: Polity, p. 237.

—— (1996) *Performing Rites: On the Value of Popular Music*. Oxford: Oxford University Press.

Frith, S. and Horne, H. (1987) *Art into Pop*. London: Methuen.

Frith, S. and Goodwin, A. (eds) (1990) *On Record: Rock, Pop and the Written Word*. London: Routledge.

Frith, S., Goodwin, A. and Grossberg, L. (eds) (1993) *Sound and Vision: the Music Video Reader*. London: Routledge.

Furlong, A. and Cartmel, F. (1997) *Young People and Social Change: Individualisation and Risk in Late Modernity*. London: Sage.

Furlong, A. and Guidikova, I. (eds) (2001) *Transitions in Youth Citizenship in Europe: Culture, Subculture and Identity*. Strasbourg: Council of Europe Publishing.

Furnham, A. and Gunter, B. (1989) *The Anatomy of Adolescence: Young People's Social Attitudes in Britain*. London: Routledge.

Furnham, A. and Stacey, B. (1991) *Young People's Understanding of Society*. London: Routledge.

Gabriel, J. (1998) *Whitewash: Racialised Politics and the Media*. London: Routledge.

Gaines, D. (1991) *Teenage Wasteland: Suburbia's Dead End Kids*. Chicago and London: University of Chicago Press.

Garratt, S. (1998) *Adventures in Wonderland: a Decade of Club Culture*. London: Headline.

Gaspard, F. and Khoroskavar, F. (1995) *La Foulard et la République*. Paris: La Découverte.

Geertz, C. (1985) 'Wading In' in *Times Literary Supplement*, 7 June, pp. 623–4.

Gelder, K. and Thornton, S. (eds) (1997) *The Subcultures Reader*. London: Routledge.

Giddens, A. (1990) *The Consequences of Modernity*. Stanford, CA: Stanford University Press.

—— (1994) 'Living in a Post-Traditional Society', in Beck, U., Giddens, A. and Lash, S. *Reflexive Modernization: Politics, Tradition and Aesthetics in the Modern Social Order*. Cambridge: Polity, pp. 56–109.

Gilbert, J. (1997) 'Soundtrack to an Uncivil Society: rave culture, the Criminal Justice Act and the Politics of Modernity', in *New Formations* 31 (Spring/Summer): 5–24.

—— (1998) 'Blurred Vision: pop, populism and politics' in Coddington, A. and Perrryman, M. (1998) (eds) *The Modeniser's Dilemma: Radical Politics in the Age of Blair*. London: Lawrence and Wishart, pp. 75–90.

Gilbert, J. and Pearson, E. (1999) *Discographies: Dance Music, Culture and the Politics of Sound*. London: Routledge.

Gillespie, M. (1995) *Television, Ethnicity and Cultural Change*. London: Routledge.

Gillis, J.R. (1974) *Youth and History*. London: Academic Press.

Gilroy, P. (1982) 'Police and Thieves' in CCCS (1982) pp. 143–176.

—— (1987) *There Ain't No Black in the Union Jack: the Cultural Politics of Nation*. London: Hutchinson.

—— (1993a) *The Black Atlantic: Modernity and Double Consciousness*. London: Verso.

—— (1993b) *Small Acts: Thoughts on the Politics of Black Cultures*. London: Serpent's Tail.

—— (1993c) 'Between Afro-centrism and Euro-centrism: youth culture and the problem of hybridity' in *Young: the Nordic Journal of Youth Research* 1(2).

Giroux, H. (1996) *Fugitive Cultures: Race, Violence and Youth*. New York: Routledge.

—— (1997) *Channel Surfing: Race and the Destruction of Today's Youth*. Basingstoke: Macmillan.

Gladwell, W. (1997) 'The Coolhunt', article from the *New Yorker*, 17 March 1997, at http://www.gladwell.com/1997/1997_03_17_a_cool.htm

Glover, D. and Pickering, M. (1988) 'Youth in Postwar British Fiction: the Fifties and Sixties' in *Youth and Policy* 23: 23–34.

Goffman, E. (1956) *The Presentation of Self in Everyday Life*. New York: Overlook Press

—— (1963) *Behaviour in Public Places: Notes on the Social Organisation of Gatherings*. New York: Free Press.

Goldthorpe, J.H., Lookwood, D., Bechohofer, D. and Platt, J. (1968) *The Affluent Worker in the Class Structure: Political Attitudes and Behaviour*. Cambridge: Cambridge University Press.

Goode, E. and Ben-Yehuda, N. (1994) *Moral Panics: the Social Construction of Deviance*. Oxford: Blackwell.

Goodey, J. (2001) 'The Criminalization of British Asian Youth: Research from Bradford and Sheffield' in *Journal of Youth Studies* 4(4): 429–50.

Goodwin, A. (1987) 'Sample and Hold: Pop music in the Age of Digital Reproduction', in Frith and Goodwin (1987) pp. 258–273.

Goodwin, A. (1991) 'Popular Music and Postmodern Theory' in *Cultural Studies* 5(2).

Goodwin, A. (1993) *Dancing in the Distraction Factory: Music Television and Popular Culture*. London: Routledge.

Gordon, M. (1947) 'The Concept of the Sub-culture and its Application', in Gelder, K. and Thornton, S. (eds) *The Subcultures Reader*. London: Routledge, pp. 40–3.

Gottlieb, J. and Wald, J. (1994) 'Smells Like Teen Spirit: Riot Grrrls, Revolution and Women in Independent Rock', in Ross, A. and Rose, C., *Microphone Fiends: Youth Music and Youth Culture*. New York and London: Routledge, pp. 250–74.

Gramsci, A. (1971) *Selections from the Prison Notebooks*, edited and translated by Quentin Hoare. London: Lawrence and Wishart.

Gray, A. and McGuigan, J. (1993) *Studying Culture*. London: Edward Arnold.

Greer, G. (1971) *The Female Eunuch*. London: Paladin.

Grenfell, M. and James, A. (1998) *Bourdieu and Education: Practical Themes*. London: Falmer Press.

Griffin, C. (1995) *Representations of Youth: the Study of Adolescence in Britain and America*. Cambridge: Polity.

Grossberg, L. (1986) 'Is There Rock After Punk?', in Frith, S. and Goodwin, A. (eds) *On Record: Rock, Pop and the Written Word*. London: Routledge, pp. 111–23.

—— (1994a) 'Is Anybody Listening? Does Anybody Care? On the state of rock', in Ross, A. and Rose, C. (1994) pp. 41–58. *Microphone Fiends: Youth Music and Youth Culture*. New York and London: Routledge, pp. 41–58.

—— (1994b) *We Gotta Get Out of This Place: Popular Conservatism and Postmodern Culture*. New York and London: Routledge.

Gudmundsson, G. (1999) 'To Find Your Voice in a Foreign Language – Authenticity and Reflexivity in the Anglocentric World of Rock' in *Young: the Nordic Journal of Youth Research* 7(2): 43–61.

Guidikova, I. and Siurala, L. (2001) 'Introduction: a Weird, Wired Winsome Generation – Across Contemporary Discourses on Subculture and Citizenship', in Furlong, A. and Guidikova, I. (eds) *Transitions in Youth Citizenship in Europe: Culture, Subculture and Identity*. Strasbourg: Council of Europe Publishing, pp. 5–16.

Habermas, J (1981) The Theory of Communicative Action, London: Beacon Press.

Hackett, C. (1997) 'Young People and Political Participation', in Roche, J. and Tucker, S. (1997), *Youth in Society*. London: Sage, pp. 81–8.

Hall, C. (2002) *White, Male and Middle Class*. London: Routledge.

Hall, S. (1988) 'New Ethnicities', in Mercer, K. (ed.) *Black Film, British Cinema*. London: ICA, pp. 27–31.

—— (1990) 'Cultural Identity and Diaspora', in Rutherford, J., (1990) *Identity, Community, Culture*. London: Lawrence and Wishart, pp. 222–37.

—— (1991) 'Old and New Ethnicities', in King, A. (ed.) *Culture, Globalisation and the World System: Contemporary Conditions*. Basingstoke: Macmillan, pp. 41–68.

Hall, S. and Jefferson, T. (eds) (1976) *Resistance through Rituals: Youth Subcultures in Post-war Britain*. London: Hutchinson.

Hall, S., Clarke, J., Critcher, C., Jefferson, T. and Roberts, B. (1978) *Policing the Crisis: Mugging, the State and Law and Order*. London: Macmillan.

Hardy, P. and Laing, D. (1995) *The Faber Companion to 20th Century Popular Music*. London: Faber and Faber.

Hargreaves, A. and McKinney, M. (eds) (1997) *Post-Colonial Cultures in France*. London: Routledge.

Harker D (1980) *One For the Money: Politics and Popular Song*, London: Hutchinson.

Harris, D. (1992) *From Class Struggle to the Politics of Pleasure: the Effects of Gramscianism on Cultural Studies*. London: Routledge.

Harris, J. (2003) *The Last Party: Britpop, Blair and the Demise of English Rock*. London: Fourth Estate.

Harris, R. (1996) 'Opening. Absences and Omissions: Aspects of the Treatment of 'Race', Culture and Ethnicity in British Cultural Studies', in Owusu (2000) pp. 395–404.

Harrison, M. (1998) *High Society: the real voices of Club Culture*. London: Piatkus.

Haslam, D. (1999) *Manchester, England: the Story of Pop Cult City*. London: Fourth Estate.

Heath, S. and Kenyon, L. (2001) 'Single Young Professionals and Shared Household Living' in *Journal of Youth Studies* 4(1): 83–100.

Hebdige, D. (1979) *Subculture: the Meaning of Style*. London: Routledge.

—— (1988) *Hiding in the Light: On Images and Things*. London: Routledge.

Heidensohn, F. (1985) *Women and Crime*. London: Macmillan.

Hemment, D. (1998) 'Dangerous Dancing and Disco Riots: the Northern Warehouse Parties', in McKay, G., *DIY Culture: Party and Protest in Nineties Britain*. London: Verso, pp. 208–27.

Hendry, L. *et al.* (1993) *Young People's Leisure and Lifestyles*. London: Routledge.

Herman, A., Swiss, T. and Sloop, J. (1998) 'Mapping the Beat: Spaces of Noise and Places of Music', introduction to Swiss, T., Sloop, T. and Herman, A., *Mapping the Beat: Popular Music and Contemporary Theory*. Oxford: Blackwell, pp. 3–29.

Hesmondhalgh, D. (1997) 'The Cultural Politics of Dance Music' in *Soundings: a Journal of Politics and Culture* 6: 167–78.

Hetherington, K. (1998) 'Vanloads of Uproarious Harmony: New Age Travellers and the Utopics of the Countryside' in Skelton, T. and Valentine, G. *Cool Places: Geographies of Youth Cultures*. London: Routledge. pp. 328–342.

Hewitt, R. (1986) *White Talk Black Talk: Inter-racial Friendship and Communication Amongst Adults*. Cambridge: Cambridge University Press.

Hewitt, R. (1990) 'Youth, Race and Language in Contemporary Britain: Deconstructing Ethnicity', in Chisholm, L., Büchner, P., Krüger, H. and Brown, P. (1990) (eds) *Childhood, Youth and Social Change: a comparative perspective*. London: Falmer Press. (1990), pp. 185–196.

Hill, M. (ed.) (1997) *Whiteness: A Critical Reader*. New York: New York University Press.

Hoggart, R. (1958) *The Uses of Literacy: Aspects of Working Class Culture*. Harmondsworth: Penguin.

Hollands, R. (1990) *The Long Transition: Class, Culture and Youth Training*. London: Macmillan.

Hooks, b. (1992) 'Representations of Whiteness in the Black Imagination', in *Black Looks: Race and Representation*. Boston: South End Press, pp. 165–78.

—— (1994) *Outlaw Culture: Resisting Representations*. New York and London: Routledge.

Hope, J. and Sparks, R. (2000) *Crime, Risk and Insecurity*. London: Routledge.

Housee, S. and Dar, M. (1996) 'Re-Mixing Identities: "Off" the Turn-Table', in Hutnyk *et al.* (1996) pp. 81–104.

Hughes, R. (1993) *Culture of Complaint: The Fraying of America*, Oxford: Oxford University Press.

Huq, R. (1996) 'Asian Kool? Bhangra and Beyond', in Sharma S., Sharma, A. and Hutnyk, J. (eds) *Dis-Orienting Rhythms: the Politics of the New Asian Dance Music*. London: Zed Books, pp. 61–80.

—— (1997) 'Paradigm Lost? Youth and Pop in the 90s' in *Soundings: a Journal of Politics and Culture* 6: 180–7.

—— (1998a) 'Currying Favour? Race and Diaspora in New Britain' in Perryman, M. and Coddington, A. (eds) *The Moderniser's Dilemma: Radical Politics in the Age of Blair*. London: Lawrence and Wishart, pp. 59–74.

—— (1998b) 'Paradigm Lost? Rethinking the Relationship between Youth and Pop', in Rutherford, J. (ed.) *Young Britain: Politics, Pleasures and Predicaments*. London: Lawrence and Wishart.

—— (1999a) 'The Right to Rave: Opposition the Criminal Justice and Public Order Act 1994', in Jordan, T. (ed.) *Storming the Millennium: the New Politics of Change*. London: Lawrence and Wishart, pp. 15–33.

—— (1999b) 'Living in France: the Parallel Universe of Hexagonal Pop', in Blake, A. (ed.) *Living Through Pop*. London: Routledge, pp. 131–45.

—— (2001a) 'Rap à la Française: Hip-hop as Youth Culture in Contemporary Postcolonial France', in Furlong, A. and Guidikova, I. (eds) *Transitions in Youth Citizenship in Europe: Culture, Subculture and Identity*. Strasbourg: Council of Europe Publishing, pp. 41–60.

—— (2001b) 'The French Connection: Francophone Hip-hop as an Institution in Contemporary Postcolonial France' in *Taboo: the Journal of Culture and Education*, Fall–Winter 2001, pp. 65–79.

—— (2002) 'Rave New World' in *Entertainment Law* 1(3), pp. 117–124.

—— (2003) 'From the Margins to the Mainstream? Representations and Realities of British Asian Youth in Music' in *Young: the Nordic Journal of Youth Research* 11(1): 29–48.

Hutnyk, J. (1996) 'Repetitive Beatings or Criminal Justice?', in Sharma S., Sharma, A. and Hutnyk, J. (eds) *Dis-Orienting Rhythms: the Politics of the New Asian Dance Music*. London: Zed Books, pp. 156–89.

—— (2000) *Critique of Exotica: Music, Politics and the Culture Industry*. London: Pluto.

Inglis, F. (1993) *Cultural Studies*. Oxford: Blackwell.

James, M. (1997) *State of Bass: Jungle the Story So Far*. London: Boxtree.

Jameson, F. (1991) '*Postmodernism or the cultural logic of late capitalism*' London: Verso.

Jenkins, R. (1997) *Rethinking Ethnicity: Arguments and Explorations*. London: Sage.

Johnson, P. (1996) *Straight Outta Bristol: Massive Attack, Portishead, Tricky and the Roots of Trip Hop*. London: Spectre.

Johnson, R. (1994) 'Cultural Studies: Tradition or Process?' in *Curriculum Studies* 2(3).

Johnstone, N. (1999) *Melody Maker History of 20th Century Popular Music*. London: Bloomsbury.

Jones, G. and Wallace, C. (1992) *Youth, Family and Citizenship*. Oxford: Oxford University Press.

Jones, S. (1988) *Black Culture, White Youth: From JA to UK*. London: Macmillan.

Jordan, T. (1995) 'Collective Bodies: raving and the politics of Gilles Deleuze and Felix Guattari', in *The Body and Society* 1(1) pp 125-144.

Jordan, T. and Lent, A. (1998) *Storming the Millennium: the New Politics of Change*. London: Lawrence and Wishart.

Junankar, P. N. (ed.) (1987) *From School to Unemployment? The Labour Market for Young People*. London: Macmillan.

Kalra, V. (2000) *From textile mills to taxi ranks: experiences of migration, labour and social change*. Aldershot: Ashgate.

Kane, P. (1995) 'Pop Goes the Future in a Blur of a Sound', *Guardian*, 17 August 1995.

Kaplan, E.A. (1987) *Rocking Around the Clock: Music Television, Postmodernism and Consumer Culture*. London: Routledge.

Kaufman, N. and Bertaud, E. (2001) *Musique! Pour s'y retrouver dans les courants musicaux*. Paris: Manitoba.

Kaur, R. and Kalra, V. (1996) 'New Paths for South Asian Identity and Musical Creativity', in Sharma S., Sharma, A. and Hutnyk, J. (eds) *Dis-Orienting Rhythms: the Politics of the New Asian Dance Music*. London: Zed Books, pp. 217–31.

Kearney, M. (1997) 'The Missing Links: Riot Grrrl – Feminism – Lesbian Culture', in Whiteley, S. (ed.) *Sexing the Groove: Popular Music and Gender*. London: Routledge, pp. 207–29.

—— (1998) ' "Don't need You": rethinking identity politics and separatism from a Grrrl persepective', in Epstein, J. (1998) (ed.) *Youth Culture: Identity in a Postmodern World*. Main and Oxford: Blackwell, pp 148–186.

Kellner, D. (1995) *Media Culture: Cultural Studies, Identity and Politics*. London: Routledge.

Kershaw, A. (1989) 'Vinyl Frontier' in *Time Out*, 18–25 October.

Kosamin, B. and DeLange, D. (1980) 'Conflicting Urban Ideologies: London's New Towns and the Metropolitan Performance of London's Jews', *London Journal* 6(2): 162.

Krims, A. (2000) *Rap Music and the Poetics of Identity*. Cambridge: Cambridge University Press.

Laing, D. (1985) *One Chord Wonders: Power and Meaning in Punk Rock*. Milton Keynes: Open University Press.

——— (1990) 'Making Popular Music: the Consumer as Producer', in Tomlinson, A. (ed.) *Consumption, Identity and Style: Marketing, Meanings and the Packaging of Pleasure*. London: Routledge, pp. 186–94.

Langlois, T. (1992) 'Can you feel it? DJs and House Culture in the UK' in *Popular Music* 11(12).

Lapassade, G. (1990) *Le Rap ou La Fureur de Dire*. Paris: Loris Talmart.

Lash, S. (1994) 'Reflexivity and its Doubles: Structure, Aesthetics, Community', in Beck, U., Giddens, A. and Lash, S., *Reflexive Modernization: Politics, Tradition and Aesthetics in the Modern Social Order*. Cambridge: Polity, pp. 110–73.

Lave, J. and Wenger, E. (1990) *Situated Learning: Legitimate Peripheral Participation*. Cambridge: Cambridge University Press.

Lawrence, E. (1982) 'Just Plain Common Sense: The "Roots" of Racism,' *The Empire Strikes Back*, Centre for Contemporary Cultural Studies, London: Hutchinson.

Lawrence, E. (1983) 'In the abundance of water the fool is thirsty: sociology and black "pathology",' in CCCS (1992), pp 95–142.

Leech, K. (1973) *Youthquake: the Growth of a Counterculture through Two Decades*. London: Sheldon Press.

Leenhardt, J. (1989) 'The Role of the Intellectuals in France', in Appigannesi, L. (ed.) *Postmodernism: ICA Documents 5*. London: Free Association Books.

Leonard, M. (1997) ' "Rebel Girl, You are Queen of My World": Feminism, "subculture" and grrl power', in Whiteley, S. (ed.) *Sexing the Groove: Popular Music and Gender*. London: Routledge, pp. 230–55.

——— (1998) 'Paper Planes: Travelling the New Grrrl Geographies', in Skelton, T. and Valentine, G., *Cool Places: Geographies of Youth Cultures*. London: Routledge, pp. 101–18.

Lévi-Strauss, C. (1955) *Tristes Tropiques*. Paris: Plon.

——— (1964) *Le Cru et Le Cuit*. Paris: Plon.

Lipsitz, G. (1994) *Dangerous Crossroads: Popular Music, Postmodernism and the Dangers of Place*. London: Verso.

——— (1998) 'The Hip-hop Hearings: Censorship, Social Memory, and Intergenerational Tensions among African Americans', in Austin, J. and Willard, M., *Generations of Youth*. New York: New York University Press, pp. 395–411.

Llewellyn, M. (2000) 'Popular Music in the Welsh Language and the Affirmation of Youth Identities' in *Popular Music* 19(3).

Longhurst, B. (1994) *Popular Music and Society*. Cambridge: Polity.

Lovatt, A. (1996) 'The Ecstasy of Urban Regeneration: Regulation of the Night-time Economy in the Transition to a Post-Fordist City', in O'Connor, J. and Wynne, D., *From the Margins to the Centre: Cultural Production and Consumption in the Post Industrial City*. Aldershot: Avebury/Arena, pp. 141–68.

Lowe, R. and Shaw, W. (1993) *Travellers: Voices from the New Age Nomads*. London: Fourth Estate.

Lupton, D. (1999) *Risk: Key Ideas*. London: Routledge.

MacInnes, C. (1967) 'Old Youth and Young' in *Encounter*, September.

——— (1986) *The McInnes Omnibus: Mr Love and Justice* [1957], *Absolute Beginners* [1959], *City of Spades* [1960]. London: Allison and Busby.

McKay, G. (1996) *Senseless Acts of Beauty: Cultures of Resistance Since the Sixties*. London: Verso.

——— (1998) *DIY Culture: Party and Protest in Nineties Britain*. London: Verso.

McRobbie, A. (1980) 'Settling Accounts with Subcultures' in *Screen Education* 34: 37–50.

—— (1984) Dance and social fantasy in *Gender and generation*, ed. McRobbie, A. and Nava, M. London: Macmillan. Pp 130–161.

—— (1991) *Feminism and Youth Culture: From Jackie to Just Seventeen*. London: Macmillan.

—— (1993) 'Shut up and Dance: Youth Culture and Changing Modes of Femininity' in *Young: the Nordic Journal of Youth Research* 1(2).

—— (1994a) *Postmodernism and Popular Culture*. London: Routledge.

—— (1994b) 'Folk Devils Fight Back' in *New Left Review* 203: 107–16.

—— (1997) '*More!* New Sexualities in girls' and women's magazines' in McRobbie, A. (ed.) *Back to Reality? Social Experience and Cultural Studies*. Manchester: Manchester University Press, pp. 190–209.

—— (1999) *In the Culture Society: Art, Fashion and Popular Music*. London: Routledge.

McRobbie, A. and Garber, J. (1976) 'Girls and Subcultures: an Exploration', in Hall, S. and Jefferson, T. (eds) *Resistance through Rituals: Youth Subcultures in Post-war Britain*. London: Hutchinson, pp. 209–22.

Maffesoli, M. (1988) *Les Temps des Tribus: le declin de l'invididualisme dans les societes de masse*. Paris: Meridiens Klincksieck.

—— (1996a) *The Time of the Tribes: the Decline of Individualism in Mass Society*, translated by Don Smith. London: Sage.

—— (1996b) 'Du Tribalisme' in *Le Temps des Clans* (1996) Marseille: editions du Cheve.

Maira, S. (2002) *Desis in the House: Indian American Youth Culture in New York City*. Philadelphia: Temple University Press.

Malbon, B. (1998) 'The Club: Clubbing: Consumption, Identity and the Spatial Practices of Every-Night Life', in Skelton, T. and Valentine, G. (1998) pp. 266–286.

—— (1999) *Clubbing: dancing, ecstasy and vitality*. London: Routledge.

Malik (2002) Keeping It Real: Why White Kids Wanna Play Black, cover feature of Guardian Guide.

Marsh, P. Rosser, E. and Hare, R. (1978) *The Rules of Disorder*. London: Routledge.

Marshall, G. (1998) *A Dictionary of Sociology*. Oxford: Oxford University Press.

Martin, G. (2002) 'Conceptualizing Cultural Politics in Subcultural and Social Movement Studies' in *Social Movement Studies: Journal of Social, Cultural and Political Protest* 1(1): 73–88.

Mayol, P. (1997) *Les Enfants de la liberté: études sur l'autonomie sociale et la cultures des jeunes*. Paris: L'Harmattan.

Matza, D. (1969) *Becoming Delinquent*. Englewood Cliffs: Prentice Hall.

Matza, D. and Sykes, G. (1961) 'Juvenile Deliquency and Subterranean Values', in *American Sociological Review* 26.

Mazouzi, B. (1990) La Musique Algerienne et la question raï, Paris: Richard-Masse.

Melechi A. (1993) 'The Ecstasy of Disappearance', in Redhead, S. (ed.) *Rave Off: Politics and Deviance in Contemporary Youth Culture*. Aldershot: Avebury / Arena, pp. 183–9.

Melly, G. (1970) *Revolt into Style: the Pop Arts in the 50s and 60s*. Oxford: Oxford University Press.

Ménard, F. (2000) 'Public Policy and Urban Cultures in France', in Blowen, S., Demoissier, M. and Picard, J. (eds) *Recollections of France: Memories, Identities and Heritage in Contemporary France*. Oxford: Berghahn Books, pp. 209–25.

Mercer, K. (1994) *Welcome to the Jungle: New Positions in Black Cultural Studies*. London: Routledge.

Merle, P. (1999) *Le Dico du Français Branché*. Paris: Seuil.

Merton, R. (1938) 'Social Structure and Anomie' in *American Sociological Review* 3.

Miles, S. (1998) *Consumerism – as a Way of Life*. London: Sage.

Mitchell, T. (1996) *Popular Music and Local Identity: Rock, Pop and Rap in Europe and Oceania*. London: Leicester University Press.

——— (ed.) (2001) *Global Noise: Rap and Hip-hop outside the USA*. Connecticut: Wesleyan University Press.

Modood, T. (1992) *Not Easy Being British: Colour, Culture and Citizenship*. London: Runnymede Trust/Trentham Books.

Modood T., Virdee, S. and Bershon, S. (1994) *Changing Ethnic Identities*. London: PSI.

Modood, T. Berthoud, R., Lakey, J., Nazroo, J., Smith, P., Virdee, S. and Beishon, S. *et al* (1997) *Britain's Ethnic Minorities: Diversity and Disadvantage* (London: Policy Studies Institute).

Moore, D. (1994) *The Lads in Action: Social Process in an Urban Youth Subculture*. Aldershot: Arena.

——— (2001) 'Beyond "Subculture" in the Ethnography of Illicit Drug Use', paper delivered at *Youth Cultures and Subcultures: Functions and Patterns of Drinking and Drug Use* conference, Stockholm University, 27 April 2001.

Moore, M. (2002) *Stupid White Men*. London: HarperCollins.

Moore, N. (1995) 'Multimedia: the New European Challenge' in Policy Studies, 16 (2).

Moore, R. (1998) ' "And Tomorrow Is Just Another Crazy Scam": Postmodernity, Youth, and the Downward Mobility of the Middle Class', in Austin, J. and Willard, M., *Generations of Youth*. New York: New York University Press, pp. 253–71.

Morgan, A. (1994) 'Thursday Night Fever: Algeria's Happiest Hour', in Broughton, S., Ellingham, M., Muddyman, D. and Trillo, R. (eds) *Rough Guide to World Music*. London: Penguin, pp. 127–134.

Morley, K. and Robins, D. (1996) *Spaces of Identity: Global Media, Electronic Landscapes and Cultural Borders*. London: Routledge.

Morrison, T. (1993) *Playing in the Dark: Whiteness and the Literary Imagination*. New York: Vintage.

Muggleton, D. (1997) 'The Post-subculturalist', in Redhead, S., O'Connor, J. and Wynne, D. (eds) *The Clubcultures Reader: Readings in Popular Cultural Studies*. Oxford: Blackwell, pp. 185–203.

——— (2000) *Inside Subculture: The Post Modern Meaning of Style*. Oxford: Berg.

Muggleton, D. and Weinzierl, R. (eds) (2003) *The Post-Subcultures Reader*. Oxford: Berg.

Muncie, J. (1984) *The Trouble With Kids Today: Youth and Crime in Post-war Britain*. London: Heinemann.

Mungham, G. and Pearson, G. (eds) (1976) *Working Class Youth Culture*. London: Routledge and Kegan Paul.

Munns, J. and Rajan, G. (1995) *A Cultural Studies Reader: History, Theory, Practice*. Harlow: Longman.

Murphy, P. (1984) *Hooligans Abroad: the Behaviour and Control of the English Fans*. London: Routledge.

——— (1990) *Football on Trial: Spectator Violence and Development in the Football World*. London: Routledge.

Murphy, P., Williams, J. and Dunning, E. (1988) *The Roots of Football Hooliganism: an Historical and Sociological Study*. London: Routledge.

Musgrove, F. (1974) *Ecstasy and Holiness: Counterculture and the Open Society*. London: Methuen.

Nava, M. (1984) 'Youth Service Provision, Social Order and the Question of Girls', in McRobbie, A. and Nava, M., *Gender and Generation*. London: Macmillan, pp. 1–30.

—— (1992) *Changing Cultures*. London: Sage.

Nayak, A. (2003) *Race, Place and Globalization*. Oxford: Berg.

Neal, M. (1999) *What the Music Said: Black Popular Music and Black Public Culture*. London and New York: Routledge.

Negus, K. (1993) *Producing Pop: Culture and Conflict in the Popular Music Industry*. London: Routledge.

—— (1997) *Popular Music in Theory: an Introduction*. Cambridge: Polity.

Negus, N. (1999) *Music Genres and Corporate Cultures*. London: Routledge.

Newits, A. and Wray, M. (1997) *White Trash*. London and New York: Routledge.

Nielsen, H. (1993) 'Youth Culture and the Completion of Cultural Modernisation' in *Young: the Nordic Journal of Youth Studies* 1(3): 16–26.

Oakland, J. (1998) *British Civilization: an Introduction*. London: Routledge.

O'Connor, J. and Wynne, D. (1996) *From the Margins to the Centre: Cultural Production and Consumption in the Post Industrial City*. Aldershot: Avebury/Arena.

Oliver, P. (ed.) (1990) *Black Music in Britain: Essays on the Afro-Asian Contribution to Popular Music*. Milton Keynes: Oxford University Press.

OMB (Office of Management and Budget) (1998) *Revisions to the Standards for the Classification of Federal Data on Race and Ethnicity (Federal Register Notice)*, Washington, DC: Office of Management and Budget.

Osborne, J. (1957) *Look Back in Anger*. London: Eyre and Spottiswoode.

Osgerby, B. (1997) *Youth in Britian since 1945*. Oxford: Blackwell.

Owen, F. (1986) 'Last Night a DJ Saved my life' in *Melody Maker*, 17 August 1986, reprinted in Johnstone, N., *Melody Maker History of 20th Century Popular Music*. London: Bloomsbury, pp. 288–9.

Owusu, K. (ed.) (1999) *Black British Culture and Society: a Text Reader*. London: Routledge.

Paphides, P. (2002) 'Crew's Control' in *Guardian* Guide, 5–11 October, pp. 4–6.

Parekh, B. (2000) *The Future of Multi-ethnic Britain: Report of the Commission on the Future of Multi-Ethnic Britain*. London: Profile Books.

Parker, H., Aldridge, J. and Measham, F. (1998) *Illegal Leisure: the Normalization of Adolescent Recreational Drug Use*. London: Routledge.

Pathi, D. (1996) "Punjabi Goes Pop!" in *The Face* 71 (March) pp 58-63.

Peach, C. (1996) 'Black Carribeans: Class, Gender and Geography', in Peach, C. (ed.) *Ethnicity in the 1991 Census, vol. 2: the Ethnic Minority Populations of Great Britain*. London: HMSO, pp. 25–43.

Pearson, G. (1976) ' "Paki -Bashing" in a North-east Lancashire Cotton Town: a Case Study in its History', in Mungham, G. and Pearson, G. (eds) *Working Class Youth Culture*. London: Routledge and Kegan Paul, pp. 48–81.

—— (1983) *Hooligan: a History of Respectable Fears*. London: Macmillan.

Pearson, G. and Twohig, J. (1976) 'Ethnography through the Looking Glass: the Case of Howard Becker', in Hall, S. and Jefferson, T. (eds) *Resistance through Rituals: Youth Subcultures in Post-war Britain*. London: Hutchinson, pp. 119–26.

Perrier, J.C. (2000) *Le Rap Français*. Paris: L'Harmattan.

Perron, E. (2001) 'Rave: d'une nuit d'été' in *Télérama*, 1 August 2001, pp. 8–13.

Pfiel, F. (1995) *White Guys: Studies in Postmodern Domination and Difference*. London: Routldege.

Pickering, M. (1997) *History, Experience, and Cultural Studies*. New York: St Martin's Press.

Pierre-Adolphe, P. (1995) *Le dico de la banlieue*. Boulogne: La Sirène.

Pilkington, H. (2001) 'Strategies for Glocal Living: a 'Peripheral' View on Post-subcultural Youth Formations', paper presented at at *Post Subcultural Studies? New Post-Political Formations and their Political Impact* conference, Vienna, Austria, 12 May 2001.

Pini, M. (1997) 'Women and the Early British Rave-Scene' in McRobbie (ed.) *Back to Reality? The Social Experience of Cultural Studies*. Manchester: Manchester University Press, pp. 153–69.

—— (2001) *Club Cultures and Female Subjectivity: the Move From House to Home*, Basingstoke: Palgrave/Macmillan.

Polhemus, T. (1994) *Streetstyle*. London: Thames and Hudson.

—— (1997) 'In the Supermarket of Style', in Redhead, S, O'Connor, J. and Wynne, D. (eds) *The Clubcultures Reader: Readings in Popular Cultural Studies*. Oxford: Blackwell, pp. 148–51.

Postman, N. (1994) *The Disappearance of Childhood*. New York: Vintage.

Potter, R. (1998) Not the Same: 'Race, Repetition, and Difference in Hip-Hop and Dance Music', in *Mapping the Beat: Popular Music and Contemporary Theory,* ed. Thomas Swiss, John Sloop, and Andrew Herman (1997) Oxford and New York: Basil Blackwell, pp 31–46.

Poulet, G. (1993) 'Popular Music', in Cook, M. (ed.) *French Culture since 1945*. Harlow: Longman, pp. 192–214.

Press, J. (1995) 'The Killing of Crusty', in Savage, J. and Kureishi, H., *The Faber Book of Pop*. London: Faber and Faber, pp. 797–806.

Prévos, A. (1997) 'The Origins and Evolution of French Rap Music and Hip Hop Culture in the 1980s and 1990s', in McKay, G., *Yankee Go Home (And Take Me With U)*. Sheffield: Sheffield Academic Press, pp. 146–60.

—— (2001) 'Rap music and hip-hop culture in the 1980s and 1990s: Post colonial popular music in France in Reynolds, S. and Oldfield, B. (1990) 'Acid Reign', in Reynolds, S. (1990) *Blissed Out: the raptures of rock*. London: Serpent's Tail. pp. 14–179.

PSI (1993) 'Cultural Trends 5(19) Museums and Galleries; Records, Tapes, CDs and the Recording Industry'. London: PSI.

Punter, D. (1988) *Introduction to Contemporary Cultural Studies*. Harlow, Essex: Longman.

Punter, D. (1997) 'Fictional Maps of Britain', in Bassnett, S. (1997) *Studying British Cultures: an introduction*. London: Routledge, pp 65–82.

Rampton, B. (1995) *Crossing: Language and Ethnicity Among Adolescents*. London: Longman.

Redhead, S. (1987) *Sing When You're Winning: the last football book*. London and New Hampshire: Pluto Press.

—— (1990) *The End of the Century Party: Youth and Pop towards 2000*. Manchester: Manchester University Press.

—— (ed.) (1993a) *Rave Off: Politics and Deviance in Contemporary Youth Culture*. Aldershot: Avebury/Arena.

—— (1993b) *The Passion and the Fashion: Football Fandom in the New Europe*. Aldershot: Ashgate/Arena.

—— (1995) *Unpopular Cultures: the Birth of Law and Popular Culture*. Manchester: Manchester University Press.

—— (1997a) *From Subculture to Clubcultures*. Oxford: Blackwell.

—— (1997b) *Post Fandom and the Millennial Blues: the Transformation of Soccer Culture*. London: Routledge.

—— (1999) *Repetitive Beat Generation*. Edinburgh: Canongate/Rebel Inc.

Redhead, S., O'Connor, J. and Wynne, D. (eds) (1997) *The Clubcultures Reader: Readings in Popular Cultural Studies*. Oxford: Blackwell.

Reimer, B. (1995) 'Youth and Modern Lifestyles', in Fornäs, J. and Bolin, G., *Youth Culture in Late Modernity*. London: Sage, pp. 120–44.

Rex, J. (1982) 'Three Stages of Immigrant Housing and Community in Birmingham, England', in Solomos, J, (ed.), *Migrant Workers in Metropolitan Cities*, European Science Foundation, Strasbourg, pp.101–117.

Reynolds, S. (1990) *Blissed Out: the Raptures of Rock*. London: Serpent's Tail.

—— (1997) 'Rave Culture: Living Dream or Living Death?' in Redhead, S., O'Connor, J. and Wynne, D. (eds) *The Clubcultures Reader: Readings in Popular Cultural Studies*. Oxford: Blackwell, pp. 102–11.

—— (1998a) *Energy Flash: a Journey through Rave Music and Dance Culture*. London: Picador.

—— (1998b) *Generation Ecstasy: Into the World of Rave and Techno Culture*. New York: Little Brown and Company.

Reynolds, S. and Oakenfold, P. (1990) 'Acid Reign', in Reynolds, S., *Blissed Out: the Raptures of Rock*. London: Serpent's Tail, pp. 14–179.

Reynolds, S. and Press, J. (1995) *The Sex Revolts*. London: Serpent's Tail.

Reynolds, S. and Stubbs, D. (1990) 'Acid Over', in Reynolds, S., *Blissed Out: the Raptures of Rock*. London: Serpent's Tail, pp. 167–71.

Richard, B. and Kruger, H. (1998) 'Raver's Paradise?', in Skelton, T. and Valentine, G., *Cool Places: Geographies of Youth Cultures*. London: Routledge, pp. 161–74.

Richards, C. (2003) *Teen Spirits: music and identity in media education*. London: Routledege.

Rietveld, H. (1993) 'Living the Dream', in Redhead, S., *Rave Off: Politics and Deviance in Contemporary Youth Culture*. Aldershot: Avebury / Arena, pp. 41–78.

—— (1997) 'The House Sound of Chicago', in Redhead, S., O'Connor, J. and Wynne, D. (eds) *The Clubcultures Reader: Readings in Popular Cultural Studies*. Oxford: Blackwell, pp. 124–136.

—— (1998a) 'Repetetive Beats: free parties and the contemporary DiY dance culture in Britain', in McKay, G., *DIY Culture: Party and Protest in Nineties Britain*. London: Verso, pp. 243–67.

—— (1998b) *This is Our House*. Aldershot: Avebury / Arena.

Rimmer, D. (1985) *Like Punk Never Happened*. London: Faber and Faber.

Ritzer, G. (1993) *The McDonaldization of Society: An Investigation into the Changing Character of Contemporary Social Life*. California: Pine Forge Press.

Robb, J. (1999) *The Nineties*. London: Random House.

Roberts, B. (1976) 'Naturalistic Research into Subcultures and Deviance: An account of sociological tendency' in Hall and jefferson (1976) pp. 243–252.

Roberts, K. (1984) *School-leavers and their Prospects: Youth in the Labour Market in the 1990s*. Oxford: Oxford University Press.

—— (1999) *Leisure in Contemporary Society*. Wallingford, Oxon: CABI.

Robins, D. and Cohen, P. (1978) *Knuckle Sandwich: Growing Up in the Working Class City*. Harmondsworth: Penguin.

Robins, K. and Morely, D. (1996) 'Al Man Ci, Yabanci' in *Cultural Studies*: 248–54.

Robinson, V. (1990) 'Boom and gloom: the success and failure of South Asians in Britain', in ed Clarke, C., Peach, C. and Vertore, S. (eds) (1990) *South Asians Overseas: Migration and Ethnicity*. Cambridge: CUP

Roche, J. and Tucker, S. (1997) *Youth in Society*. London: Sage.

Roediger, D. (1991) *The Wages of Whiteness: Race and the Making of the American Working Class*. London: Verso.

—— (1994) *Towards the Abolition of Whiteness*. London: Verso.

—— (1998) 'What to Make of Wiggers: a Work in Progress', in Austin and Willard, pp. 358–66.

Rojek, C. (1995) *Decentring Leisure: Rethinking Leisure Theory*. London: Sage.

Rose, T. (1994) *Black Noise: Rap Music and Black Culture in Contemporary America*. Hanover: Weslyan University Press.

Rousseau, JJ (1755) *A Discourse on Political Economy* in Rousseau, JJ tranls Cranston, M. (1987) *The Social Contract and Discourses*, London: Penguin classics.

Rowntree, J. and Rowntree, M. (1968) *The Political Economy of Youth*. Toronto: the Radical Education Project.

Russell, K. (1993) 'Lysergia Suburbia', in Redhead, S., *Rave Off: Politics and Deviance in Contemporary Youth Culture*. Aldershot: Avebury / Arena, pp. 91–174.

Sabin, R. (1998) *Punk Rock: So What? The Cultural Legacy of Punk*. London: Routledge.

Said, E. (1978) *Orientalism: Western Conceptions of the Orient*. London: Routledge.

—— (1993) *Culture and Imperialism*. London: Chatto and Windus.

Sanjek, R. and Sanjek, D. (1991) *American Popular Music Business in the 20th Century*. New York and Oxford: Oxford University Press.

Santiago-Lucerna, J. (1998) ' "Frances Farmer will have her Revenge on Seattle": Pancapitalism and Alternative Rock', in Epstein, J. (ed.) *Youth Culture: Identity in a Postmodern World*. Oxford and New York: Blackwell, pp. 189–94.

Saunders, N. (1995) *Ecstasy and the Dance Culture*. London: self-published.

Saussure, F. (1996 [1915]) *Cours de Linguistique Général*. Paris: Payot.

Savage, J. (1990) 'Tainted Love: the Influence of Male Homosexuality and Sexual Difference on Pop Music and Culture since the War', in Tomlinson, A. (ed.) *Consumption, Identity and Style: Marketing, Meanings and the Packaging of Pleasure*. London: Routledge, pp. 153–70.

—— (1991) *England's Dreaming: the Sex Pistols and Punk Rock*. London: Faber and Faber.

—— (ed.) (1992) *The Haçienda Must be Built!* Manchester: International Music Publications.

—— (1996) *Time Travel: Pop, Media and Sexuality 1976–96*. London: Chatto and Windus.

Savage, J. and Kureshi, H. (1995) *The Faber Book of Pop*. London: Faber and Faber.

Sberna, B. (2002) *Une Sociologie du rap à Marseilles identité marginale et immigrée*. Paris: L'Harmattan.

Schade-Poulsen, M. (1995) 'The Power of Love: Raï Music and Youth in Algeria', in Amit-Talai, V. and Wulff, H. (1995) (eds) *Youth Cultures: A Cross-cultural Perspective*. London: Routledge, pp. 81–113.

Schaffer, R.M. (1977) *The Turning of the World*. New York: Albert E. Knopf.

Schehr, S. (1995) 'L'errance comme bulletin de vote' in *Future Anterieur* 25.

Schwarz, B. (1996) 'Black Metropolis, White England', in *Modern Times: reflections of a century of English modernity* Nava, M. and O'Shea, A. (1996) (eds) London: Routledge, pp 176–207.

Sedgwick, P. and Edgar, A. (1999) *Key Concepts in Social Theory*. London: Routledge.

Seshardi-Crooks, K. (2000) *Desiring Whiteness*. London and New York: Routledge.

Shepherd, J. (1994) 'The Analysis of Popular Music' in *The Polity Reader in Cultural Theory*. Cambridge: Polity, pp. 231–41.

Sharma, S., Sharma, A. and Hutnyk, J. (eds) (1996) *Disorienting Rhythms: the Politics of the New Asian Dance Music*. London: Zed Books.

Shiner, M. and Newburn, T. (1999) 'Taking Tea With Noel: Drugs Discourse for the 1990s', in South, N. (ed.) *Drugs: Cultures, Controls and Everyday Life*. London: Sage.

Shuker, R. (1994) *Understanding Popular Music*. London: Routledge.

—— (1998) *Key Concepts in Popular Music*. London: Routledge.

Shuker, R. (2001) Understanding Popular Music. London: Routledege.

Shusterman, R. (1992a) *L'art à l'état vif*. Paris: Minuit.

—— (1992b) *Pragmatist Aesthetics: Living Beauty, Rethinking Art*. Oxford: Blackwell.

Skelton, T. and Valentine, G. (eds) (1997) *Cool Places: Geographies of Youth Cultures*. London: Routledge.

Soysal, L. (1998) 'Diversity of Experience, Experience of Diversity: Turkish Migrant Youth Culture in Berlin', in *Cultural Dynamics* 13(1): 5–28.

—— (2001) 'Hip-hop, Globalization and Migrant Youth Culture', paper presented at 'Beyond Hip-Hop: Youth Cultures and Globalization' ESRC Interdisciplinary Youth Studies seminar, Sheffield University, 26 November 2001.

Spivak, G. (1988) *In OtherWords*. London: Routledge.

Springhall, J. (1998) *Youth, Popular Culture and Moral Panics: Penny Gaffs to Gangsta-Rap 1830–1996*. London: Macmillan.

Stahl. G. (1999) 'Still "Winning Space?": Updating Subcultural Theory' in *Invisible Culture: an Electronic Journal for Visual Studies*, downloaded at http://www.rochester.edu/in_visible_culture/issue2/stahl.htm

Stanley, C. (1997) 'Urban Narratives of Dissent in the Wild Zone', in Redhead, S., O'Connor, J. and Wynne, D. (eds) *The Clubcultures Reader: Readings in Popular Cultural Studies*. Oxford: Blackwell, pp. 36–54.

Stokes, M. (1994) *Ethnicity, Identity and Music: the Musical Construction of Place*. Oxford: Berg.

Stone, C.J. (1996) *Fierce Dancing: Adventures in the Underground*. London: Faber.

Storry, M. and Childs, P. (eds) (1997) *British Cultural Identities*. London: Routledge.

Strinati, D. (1995) *An Introduction to the Theories of Popular Culture*. London: Routledge.

Sugarman, B. (1973) *The School and Moral Development*, London: Croom Helm.

Sweeting, A. (2000) 'The Chart busters' in *Guardian* review section, 4 April 2000.

Swiss, T., Sloop, T. and Herman, A. (1998) *Mapping the Beat: Popular Music and Contemporary Theory*. Oxford: Blackwell.

Taylor, I. (1971) 'Soccer Consciousness and Soccer Hooliganism', in Cohen, S, (ed) *Images of Deviance*. Harmondsworth: Penguin. pp. 134–164.

Taylor, T. (1997) *Global Pop: World Music, World Markets*. London and New York: Routledge.

Tennaille, F. (2002) Le Raï: De la bâtardise à la reconnaissance internationale. Paris : Actes Sud.

Thoday, P. (1995) *Le Franglais*. London: Althone.

Thompson, B. (1998) *Seven Years of Plenty: a Handbook of Irrefutable Pop Greatness 1991–1998*. London: Phoenix.

Thompson, K. (1998) *Moral Panics*. London: Routledge.

Thornton, S. (1995) *Clubcultures: Music, Media and Subcultural Capital*. Cambridge: Polity.

Timelords, The (1988) *The Manual: How to Have a Number One the Easy Way*. London: Curfew Press.

Tomlinson, L. (1998) ' "This Ain't No Disco": Or Is It? Youth Culture and the Rave Phenomenon', in Epstein, J. (ed.) *Youth Culture: Identity in a Postmodern World*. Oxford and New York: Blackwell, pp. 195–211.

Toop, D. (1991) *Rap Attack 2: African Rap To Global Hip Hop*, London: Serpent's Tail.

Toop, D. (1995) *Ocean of Sound: Aether talk, Ambient Sound and Imaginary Worlds*. London: Serpent's Tail.

—— (1999) *Exotica: Fabricated soundscapes in a real world*. London: Serpent's Tail.

Toynbee, J. (1993) 'Policing Bohemia, Pinning Up Grunge: the Music Press and Generic Change in British Pop and Rock' in *Popular Music* 12(3): 189–200.

Tunstall, J. (1977) *The Media are American*. New York: Columbia University Press.

Turner, B. (1996) *British Cultural Studies*. London: Routledge.

Van Der Lee (1998) 'Sitars and bossas: World Music Influences' in *Popular Music* 17(1): 45–70.

Van Loon, J. (2002) *Risk and Technological Culture: Towards a Socoiology of Virulence*. London: Routledge.

Verdelhan-Bourgade, M. (1990) 'Communiquer en Français contemporain: Quelque part ça m'interpelle, phénomènes syntaxiques en Français branché' in *La Linguistique* 26(1).

Vestel, V. (1999) 'Breakdance, Red Eyed Penguins, Vikings, Grunge and Straight Rock 'n'roll: the Construction of Place in Musical Discourse in Rudenga, East Side Oslo' in *Young: the Nordic Journal of Youth Research* 7(2): 4–24.

Vulbeau, A. (1992) *Du Tag Au Tag*. Paris: Descleé du Brouwer.

Wallace, C. (1987) *For Richer, for Poorer: Growing Up In and Out of Employment*. London: Tavistock.

Waller, S. and Barton, L. (eds) (1986) *Youth, Unemployment and Schooling*. Milton Keynes: Open University Press.

Walser, R. (1993) *Running With The Devil: Power, Gender and Madness in Heavy Metal Music*. Connecticut: Wesleyan University Press.

Ware, V. (1992) *Beyond the Pale: White Women, Racism and History*. London: Verso.

Warne, C. (1997) 'The Impact of World Music in France', in Hargreaves, A. and McKinney, M. (1997) (eds) *Post Colonial Cultures in France*. London: Routledge, pp. 133–49.

—— (2000) 'The Mean(ing of the) Streets: Reading Urban Cultures in Contemporary France', in Blowen, S., Demoissier, M. and Picard, J. (eds) *Recollections of France: Memories, Identities and Hertiage in Contemporary France*. Oxford: Berghan Books, pp. 226–45.

Watson, J. (ed.) (1977) *Between Two Cultures: Migrants and Minorities in Britain*. Oxford: Blackwell.

Watson, B. (1999) 'Decoding Society Versus the Popsicle Academy: On the Value of Being Unpopular' in Blake, Andrew, ed. 1999. *Living Through Pop*. New York: Routlege pp. 79-97.

Weaver, J. and Daspit, T. (2001) 'Rap (in) the academy: Academic Work, Education, and Cultural Studies' in *Taboo: the Journal of Culture and Education*, Fall/Winter, pp. 103–31.

Weaver, J., Dimitriadis, G. and Daspit, T. (2001) 'Hip Hop pedagogies and Youth Cultures: Rhythmic Blends of Globalization and the Lost Third Ear of the Academy' in *Taboo: the Journal of Culture and Education*, Fall/Winter, pp. 7–13.

Weinstein, D. (1991). *Heavy metal: A cultural sociology*. New York: Macmillan.

—— (1995) 'Alternative Youth: the Ironies of Recapturing Youth Culture' in *Young: the Nordic Journal of Youth Research* 3(1) pp. 61–71.

Whiteley, S. (ed.) (1997) *Sexing the Groove: Popular Music and Gender*. London: Routledge.

Whyte, W. (1955) *Street Corner Society*. Chicago: Chicago University Press.

Wicke, P. (1987) *Rock Music: Cultures, Aesthetics and Sociology*. Cambridge: Cambridge University Press.

Widdicombe, S. and Woofit, R. (1995) *The Language of Youth Subculture*. Hemel Hempstead: Harvester Wheatsheaf.

Wilkinson, I. (2001) *Anxiety in a 'Risk' Society*. London: Routledge.

Wilkinson, R. (2001) 'Crouching Tiger, Hidden Depths?' in *Q*, July, pp. 96–9.

Williams, R. (1976) *Keywords: a Vocabulary of Culture and Society*. London: Fontana.

—— (1993 [1958]) 'Culture is ordinary', in Gray, A. and McGuigan, J., *Studying Culture*. London: Edward Arnold, pp. 5–14.

Willis, P. (1977) *Learning to Labour: How Working Class Kids get Working Class Jobs*. Farnborough: Saxon House.

—— (1978) *Profane Culture*. London: Routledge.

—— (1990) *Common Culture: Symbolic Work at Play in the Everyday Lives of Young People*. Milton Keynes: Open University Press.

—— (1998) 'Notes on Common Culture: Towards a Grounded Aesthetics', in *European Journal of Cultural Studies* 1(2): 163–76.

Wilson, J. (2002) 'What You Need to Be a DJ' in *NME*, 14 December 2002, p. 45.

Wright, B.S. (2000) 'Dub Poet Lekka Mi: an Exploration of Performance Poetry, Power and Identity Politics in Black Britain', in Owusu (2000), pp. 271–88.

Wright, S. (2000) ' "A Love Born of Hate": Autonomist Rap in Italy' in *Theory, Culture and Society* 17(3): 117–35.

Wulff, H. (1995a) 'Inter-racial Friendship: Consuming Youth Styles, Ethnicity and Teenage Feminity in South London', in Amit-Talai, V. and Wulff, H. (eds) *Youth Cultures: a Cross-cultural Perspective*. London: Routledge, pp. 63–80.

—— (1995b) 'Introducing Youth Culture in its Own Right: the state of the art and new possibilities', in Amit-Talai, V. and Wulff, H. (eds) *Youth Cultures: a Cross-cultural Perspective*. London: Routledge, pp. 1–18.

Wyn, J. and White, R. (1996) *Rethinking Youth*. London: Sage.

York, P. (1980 [1977]) 'The Post-Punk Mortem', in *Style Wars*. London: Sidgwick and Jackson, pp. 129–44.

Young, R. (1990) *White Mythologies*. London and New York: Routledge.

Younge, G. (1994) column in *Guardian* Impact Magazine.

INDEX